Sow One Thought

Sow One Thought

HELPING YOU REACH YOUR DESTINY
ONE THOUGHT AT A TIME

Ted Beam

ISBN-13: 9781530685226
ISBN-10: 1530685222

Preface

§

THE BOOK YOU HOLD IN your hand is a collection of stories and points of information from the Bible and theology that have affected me—some more than others, but every one of them has impacted my life. None are fictional. Every story is about a real person, and I have changed only some of the names. Most of the persons whose stories I have included are friends, family members, or members of churches where I have served as pastor.

The title of this book comes from one idea I learned as a young man. The idea is anonymous but was made famous by Samuel Smiles, a British author and reformer who lived from December 23, 1812, to April 16, 1904.

Sow a thought, and you reap an act.
Sow an act, and you reap a habit.
Sow a habit, and you reap a character.
Sow a character, and you reap a destiny.

Often we find ourselves in situations wondering how we arrived. I have learned that every situation in which I find myself is the result of a collection of decisions made by me or other people or by a combination of my choices and choices made by others. When I discovered that amazing and powerful fact, my life pivoted from selfishness, loneliness, and self-destruction to a life of joy, peace, and hope.

At a very early age, I discovered I wanted to connect with God, the living God, but I did not know how. I lived several years without asking anyone for help. At nineteen years of age, I became desperate to know the living God. I took a Bible my home church gave me upon my graduation from high school and began to read it. I read that Bible entirely about four times over a three-week period. During those days I met the living Christ. Jesus is my Savior and Lord. As the song says, "Jesus is all the world to me, my life, my joy, my all. He is my strength from day to day. Without Him I would fall. Following Him I know I'm right. He watches o'er me day and night. Following Him both day and night. He's my friend." These lyrics are from "Jesus Is All The World to Me" by Will Thompson, 1904.

Since that time I have discovered the combination of reading my Bible, prayer, reading biographies, and asking people to tell me their individual stories of coming to know Jesus Christ as Savior and Lord. This fourfold combination has resulted in me knowing God and knowing Him well.

My parents, Cletus and Shirley Beam, were extraordinary in helping me learn. My father-in-law and mother-in-law, Larry and Linda Williamson, have added to my growth in many ways.

In addition to my parents and my in-laws several people have had a significant impact on my life. I am going to risk listing them here; Anna Jean Bush, Bob Link, Matt Link, Tom Brown, Steve Gill, Bill Lyle, David Whitaker, Eric Francis, Ben Russo, Al Coppedge, Larry Cochran, Lawson Stone, Eugene Carpenter, David Thompson, Bob Mulholland, Harold Burgess, David Bauer, John Oswalt, Dennis Kinlaw, my sisters Deb and Barb, Ellsworth Kalas, Paul Kiser, Dave Thompson, David Seamands, Stan Beck, Jim Kingry, Wayne Watts, Everett Rogers, Phil Bertram, and Reggie McGraw. Many friends, fellow pastors, and church members have invested in my life in various ways. Obviously, I am indebted to a multitude of people.

I first noticed my wife, Debbie, when we were in the fifth grade. She was cute and I looked across the room at her a lot. In sixth grade I learned she was very smart. Later I learned how she could make my heart pound by holding my hand as we skated around a roller rink. As seniors in high school, we began spending a lot of time together. She was my date for the senior prom. Together we have lived a most amazing life. We have four miracle children—Ariel, Alexander, Alissa, and Amelia. Every day my life is blessed because of Debbie and our children. God has been so good to me, and I am grateful. Debbie is my sunrise and my sunset. She is my dream come true.

Over the years, I have prayed a few things almost every day. While in my first year as a believer I noticed Paul's statement "Earnestly desire spiritual gifts, but especially that you may prophesy" (1 Corinthians 14:1). So I began to pray for this specific gift. I have also prayed that God would open my mind to understand the scriptures just like Jesus did for the disciples after the resurrection (Luke 24:45). Also the priest Ezra is described as having, "Set his heart to study the law of the Lord, to practice it, and to teach His statutes and ordinances" (Ezra 7:10). That three-point description of Ezra has guided my daily prayer for most of my life. As I sit down each day to open my Bible and listen to God, I pray, "Father, I am setting my heart to study Your word, to practice it, and to teach it to your people. Please pour out Your Spirit on me, empowering me to succeed in those three areas. Please open my mind to understand the scriptures. I want to know You and know You well. Please help me teach Your word with clarity, conviction, courage, and compassion." I prayed that prayer in some way each time I sat down to type this manuscript.

During my career as a pastor, many people have responded to the stories I tell or the Bible teaching I provide by saying, "You should write a book." These stories and Bible lessons have shaped my life and have shaped my destiny one thought at a time. My prayer is that they will help you come to know God even better, Father, Son, and Holy Spirit. Since they helped me, maybe they will help you also to practice your faith more successfully. I offer them to you with gratitude, with joy, and with hope.

JANUARY 1

Today, we begin a new year, with endless possibilities and staggering potential: 365 days, 8,760 hours, 525,600 minutes. Wow! Over half a million minutes to invest or waste, to help someone or hurt someone, to do evil or to do good.

God has built into this world some object lessons to teach us about our potential. Look at any ordinary apple. The apple's outside skin can be a variety of colors—green, red, or yellow. But once you sink your teeth into the fruit, all apples have wonderful tastes and textures. All provide nourishment-giving energy. Human beings have different skin colors, but all races have persons who are compassionate, courageous, and ready to make contributions to the world.

How many seeds lie within an apple? There might be as few as three or as many as ten. But how many potential apples lie within each seed? Hundreds? Thousands? Potentially even millions. So what about the potential God has built into you? Are you developing it for the benefit of your community? How about investing some of those half—million minutes to benefit others?

§

JANUARY 2

About 2,500 years ago, Jeremiah wrote a book about depression and despair. Instead of speaking from theory, he wrote from his own experience. Knowing depression intimately, he opened his eyes each morning to face the day with despair suffocating his soul, but that suffocation did not last.

In the middle of that book, he took his eyes off of himself, looked squarely into the face of God, and wrote, "The Lord's lovingkindnesses indeed never cease. For His compassions never fail. They are new every morning; Great is Your faithfulness" (Lam. 3:22—23).

"His mercies begin afresh each day." Each day brings twenty—four hours, 1,440 minutes, 86,400 seconds, with each one directly from the hand of God. Each day God causes the sun to rise, promising us another opportunity, a brand-new 86,400 seconds to use as we choose. We can look at our predicaments and become discouraged, or we can invest those thousands of seconds into helping someone else who is hurting or discouraged. Take action. Look for a person who needs help, and then give him or her a gift: your attention and time.

JANUARY 3

At the age of ten, Ted received a telescope for Christmas. He looked at the stars and the moon, wondering about the greatness of God. He saw his first solar eclipse—the moon crossing in front of the sun, bringing darkness in the middle of the day. Gazing at the asteroid field that lies between Mars and Jupiter, his young head would spin with the grandeur of the universe and of creation.

The next Christmas Ted received a microscope. He looked at the fine details of a fly's wing and the intricacies of a blade of grass. Amazement gripped him as he studied the antennae of an ant. The world had come alive to him, or maybe he had become alive to the world.

As children we stand amazed among God's creation. As adults the busyness of life can steal time away from enjoying the wonder and greatness of the very world in which God has placed us, trading the joyous energy that follows discovery for a busy schedule. However, life does not have to lose out to busyness. We can invest those moments in gazing and discovery. We can even grab such a moment today.

§

JANUARY 4

Let me share with you two things I have learned. First, a tree twelve inches in diameter will pull fifty-five gallons of water from the earth each day. The roots reach deep and spread out, and against all gravity that tree pulls water out of the ground, up its trunk, and through the branches, to finally arrive at each leaf. Each leaf drinks its part of those fifty-five gallons.

Second, by staying green, each leaf combines sunshine with the carbon dioxide from the air, transforming these into oxygen. Green plants need carbon dioxide to live. Giraffes, peacocks, gerbils, and all other animals, including human beings, need oxygen to live. This is a fascinating interdependent process.

So the next time it rains, whisper a prayer to God, thanking Him for it. He has designed the earth with this interdependence. The rain keeps the leaves green. The leaves take in carbon dioxide and put out oxygen. The animals and humans breathe in that fresh oxygen and put out carbon dioxide. This is a wonder of creation.

JANUARY 5

Adversity builds character. Adversity also reveals character. When we have difficulties, pains, or disappointments, how we handle those hard times, how we react, reveals what our characters have become.

Some teenagers took a four—day backpacking trip through Red River Gorge in Kentucky. John, a tall, lanky seventeen—year—old from Frankfort, tripped over roots, and even slipped on some mossy stones, and fell into a stream. Everyone expected him to complain or criticize. He certainly seemed like that kind of person.

On their third day, John reported he had started to complain, but through that adversity he had realized he had become a whiner, a complainer. So he prayed God would change him from the inside out. He prayed God would set his mind to discover all the positive things about the hike. He identified over thirty—five positive things he had experienced in just the first two days. So on day three, he turned away from being a complainer. God had changed him from the inside out. God had answered his prayer.

§

JANUARY 6

Proverbs 3:5—6 reads, "Trust in the Lord with all your heart, and do not lean on your own understanding. In all your ways acknowledge Him, and He will make your paths straight." Often we ask, "Why?" We see things we cannot explain. God doesn't expect us to understand everything, but He does hope we will trust Him.

We might not understand why people abuse children or why children die of various diseases. We might not understand why a good friend is killed in a car crash. We might not understand why our sons or daughters become addicted to drugs. And we might not understand why hurricanes, floods, tsunamis, and tornadoes kill so many people. We might not understand, but God hopes we will trust Him.

You see God does understand when diseases kill our children and when our family members are harming themselves with drugs. He does understand why car crashes kill good people. He does understand. That is exactly why God hopes we will trust Him.

JANUARY 7

John bought a five—dollar string of blue beads at a pawnshop in China and gave them to his wife for their anniversary. Years later when the clasp on the necklace needed repairing John took it to Tiffany's in New York where Mr. Tiffany offered him $50,000 for the necklace. Shocked, John pocketed the beads and quickly left.

Later John traveled to Chicago to Spaulding's jewelry store wanting some answers. The jeweler there offered him $75,000. Instead of leaving John asked him to explain. He wanted to know why jewelers would pay so much for junk jewelry.

Spaulding's jeweler explained there was an inscription on each blue bead identifying it as part of the string of blue pearls Napoleon had engraved as a love gift to Josephine. The five—dollar string of beads John had purchased in a pawnshop turned out to be a priceless part of history.

Many times when we look in the mirror, we see five—dollar junk jewelry, but when God looks at us, He sees His image stamped on our souls, a priceless part of His creation. We are created in the image of God. Did you know God thinks you are a priceless treasure of His creation?

§

JANUARY 8

If you haven't seen the movie *End of the Spear*, you will likely benefit from watching this reenactment of the true story of five missionaries killed in the Amazon Jungle in 1956. The Waodani tribesmen who later turned their lives to Jesus Christ speared to death Nate Saint, Pete Fleming, Roger Youderian, Ed McCulley, and Jim Elliot.

Nate Saint, a missionary jungle pilot made the initial contact with the tribe. Nate's son, Steve, who is also a missionary jungle pilot served as one of the technical advisors. The other technical advisors were the elderly tribesmen who had speared Nate Saint fifty years earlier. They stood side by side with Steve. Today Steve and the tribesmen consider each other to be family.

People who love Jesus forgive others when an offense is made. You see, when you genuinely forgive someone, you are experiencing the supernatural power of God. Instead of hanging onto how much you have been harmed, reach for the supernatural power of God. Who do you need to forgive today?

JANUARY 9

Often we do not think very highly of ourselves. This can result from any variety of things: relationships, lack of accomplishments, upbringing, or even our performance at work. But do we know how God feels about us?

In Matthew 13:44, Jesus tells a parable comparing the Kingdom of Heaven to a treasure hidden in the field. He says when a man found the treasure, he went and sold everything he had, took the proceeds, and purchased the field. Many people tell me this is the very thing I have to do when I turn my life over to Jesus Christ; however, I do not have enough wealth to buy the Kingdom of Heaven. As a matter of fact, only Jesus has enough, and He did so by shedding His blood for you and for me. His blood was the price He paid when He purchased us from sin and death.

If Jesus is the one who purchases the Kingdom of Heaven, then what or who is the treasure? The Kingdom of Heaven Jesus calls a treasure is made up of you and me. You are the treasure Jesus purchased with His blood. He calls you the treasure. Did you know that's exactly what God thinks? You are His treasure.

§

JANUARY 10

When you speak with another person, do you listen, or are you merely waiting for your turn to speak? In Stephen Covey's book *The Seven Habits of Highly Effective People*, he states that people who are highly effective in their lives and at work seek first to understand and then to be understood.

Within the design of creation, God gave us each two eyes, two ears, and one mouth. According to many leaders in a variety of fields that design reveals to us how much we need to observe and how much we need to speak. By watching and listening four times as much as we speak we increase the probability that we will understand others; however, while others speak, we usually do not listen. We gather our thoughts for our next comment.

Instead of focusing on our own thoughts, why not try to engage in conversations according to God's design? Listening well involves watching facial expressions and body language as well as hearing words and tone. Listening requires concentration. Why not watch and listen to another person seeking first to understand? This can strengthen every relationship you have.

JANUARY 11

Is there one thing that, if you did it every day and did it well, would greatly benefit your personal life and professional life? Many people might say the answer is praying everyday. Others might say it's reading their Bible. Still others might mention exercise. Some might think that if they are getting enough rest. And some might even say it's a combination of all these.

King Solomon is considered the wisest person who ever lived. Politicians, educators, attorneys, and others have quoted him many times throughout history. His insights and wisdom expressed three thousand years ago have even been used in law schools to train future attorneys and judges. Ecclesiastes 10:10 offers his guidance for our daily priorities, "If the axe is dull and he does not sharpen its edge, then he must exert more strength. Wisdom has the advantage of giving success."

By "sharpening your saw" every day you can accomplish your work more effectively with less effort. Sharpening yourself is the most strategic tactic to achieve success. Prioritize your time daily so you sharpen yourself.

§

JANUARY 12

Have you ever watched large birds soar through the sky? Maybe you have seen eagles, red-tailed hawks, or buzzards that seem to lift effortlessly from the bounds of gravity. They all stretch out their wings and just seem to float. They all rely on three things.

First they rely on God's design, which gives them the ability to soar. God created them with hollow bones almost as light as their feathers. With those light bones and those abundant feathers, they ride the wind currents just as God designed them to do.

Second, they rely on the God—designed law of aerodynamics to soar above the surface of the earth. Gravity has little effect on them while they obey the transcendent law of aerodynamics.

Third, they rely on the wind currents to carry them north, south, east, west or wherever they gracefully turn their heads. Isaiah 40:31 tells us if we wait for the Lord, we also will live beyond our natural abilities and will tap into the supernatural abilities provided by God Himself. Read it. See what you think.

JANUARY 13

Years ago the ancient Inca Empire worshiped the sun which they personified into a god. Then one day their king noticed that the sun followed the same path each and every day. He also noticed that a cloud could cover the sun for hours at a time.

The Inca king concluded in his own heart that if the sun were a god, it would not follow the same path each day nor would a cloud ever have the ability to close it off. So, he inferred there had to be a God who placed the cloud in the sky and who placed the sun on its course. From that point the king decided to worship that God. He recorded this discovery in the royal archives but did not choose to share it with his people.

When the Apostle Paul wrote his letter to the church in Rome, he included in chapter one, "since the creation of the world, God's invisible attributes, His eternal power and divine nature, have been clearly seen, being understood through what has been made, so that they are without excuse" (Rom. 1:20). The ancient Inca king found God by looking at the world. Have you found God?

§

JANUARY 14

About 2500 years ago, the prophet Jeremiah began to think about God and about the people of God. He noticed that the people consistently rebelled against God and rebelled against His will for their lives. Jeremiah noticed that God tried to win them back every time. Sometimes they returned. Other times they continued to rebel.

Jeremiah mentioned that God has revealed His plan and dream for His people. If you have a moment today, read Jeremiah 29:11, "I know the plans that I have for you," declares the Lord, "plans for blessing and not for calamity, plans to give you a future and a hope." God never gives up on us. Never.

God gives hope. God gives a future. Instead of punishing us for our mistakes or for our sins, He chooses to be merciful and gracious. He chooses to win us back with His love and His promises for our future. When you mess up, take courage. God will not throw you away. He plans to restore you and He plans to give you hope for a brighter future.

JANUARY 15

Years ago Queen Victoria took a carriage ride through the countryside. As she admired the orchards stretching across the green land a potential assassin, with knife in hand, charged the carriage with full intention of killing the queen. The queen's guards stopped the attacker and later, back at the palace, brought her before the queen.

The attacker asked the queen for mercy. At that point the queen demanded the woman provide proof that she deserved mercy. The would—be assassin responded, "If I deserve mercy, then it would not be mercy. It would be my due. I am asking for mercy." Queen Victoria extended mercy that day and history reports the woman became a great supporter of the queen.

Now, make no mistake. We do not deserve anything but judgment from God, but God loves us with an incredible love and instead of judgment, offers us mercy. Have you accepted His mercy yet? Why not accept it today? Why not pray right now, "God, I accept Your mercy offered to me in Jesus Christ. Teach me. I will trust You and I will obey Your guidance."

§

JANUARY 16

How are you with a little Bible trivia? Who was the first person mentioned in the Bible as being filled with the Holy Spirit? Maybe it was a hero of the faith. Maybe it was a great leader. Have you looked? It was not Adam, Abraham, or Moses. It was not the prophets or even the king.

You will find this person mentioned in Exodus 31. Bezalel was a tailor, an architect, a stonemason, and the craftsman responsible for designing and building the Tabernacle. His anointing from the Holy Spirit was specifically to prepare the place of worship so the people of God could go there to worship God.

Often we think those responsible for teaching and preaching are the ones filled with the Spirit. The Bible records that the first one filled with the Holy Spirit was responsible for preparing the place for worship.

One person works laying bricks to get a paycheck. Another person works to provide for his family and to help his children reach their dreams. Another person works with his attention focused toward God because he knows he is building a place of worship where people will come face to face with the living God.

JANUARY 17

Have you ever been angry with God? I have. Often. I get angry when I stand at the casket of a young person or when I read about a drunk driver harming another person. I get angry because these things should not occur.

Our community has many people working desperately to eliminate illegal drug use. We want our young people to grow up healthy instead of hooked. It simply is not right to sit back and do nothing.

We have many children growing up in poverty. We have families being ripped apart by divorce, domestic violence, and other expressions of selfishness. God expects us to "do justice" as recorded in Micah 6:8.

Read the Apostle Paul's command found in Ephesians 4:26: "Be angry, but do not sin." Anger motivated a woman to start Mothers Against Drunk Driving and motivated a man to start a TV program that helps catch child killers. One man started Teen Challenge. Anger has motivated many people to serve as mentors in schools and with Big Brothers Big Sisters. How are you expressing the immense energy generated through your anger?

§

JANUARY 18

Have you ever felt discouraged by your pastor and those boring sermons? Do you wish the sermons would feed your soul more? Well, let's try an experiment for three months by doing three things.

First, take notes on the sermons just as if you were going to repeat them. This will help you pay attention and not daydream during the messages. Then go back over those notes at two different times during the week. Try to remember what your pastor was trying to get you to understand.

Second, pray each day for your pastor's sermon preparation. God sent your pastor and your pastor needs to speak more than opinions. Your pastor needs to speak the word of God. He and your pastor both know this.

Third, once each week contact your pastor asking for more explanation on a point from that week's sermon. This will encourage your pastor who will then invest more intentional effort in preparing the messages. When you combine your prayers, your pastor's efforts to communicate, and your efforts to understand you will gain much more from those sermons.

JANUARY 19

About 500 years ago, Martin Luther pointed out that God pours out his love on everyone. Luther called it Common Grace. He pointed to Jesus's statement in the Sermon on the Mount: "God causes the sun to rise on the evil and the good and He sends rain on the just and the unjust" (Matt. 5:45). He also showed how Psalm 139:14—"I am fearfully and wonderfully made"—pointed to this common grace of God offered to each person.

In other words, God gives you life. He gives you air to breathe and He gives the sun to warm your day and light your way. He gives you the abilities you have. God gives grace to you by just giving you life and sustaining you in your life.

So what is the difference? The answer is simple. The difference is how you and I respond to God's grace. Do we reject Him altogether? Do we pick and choose what we want and what we don't want? Do we say yes to Him for a while until following Jesus becomes difficult or inconvenient? Or do we say yes to His grace and tell Him we are grateful for all He has done for us? How do you respond to God?

§

JANUARY 20

The Bible talks about attitude quite often. The Bible points out that we choose whether to be negative or positive. We choose whether to believe in God or not to believe. We choose to trust Him or not to trust Him. Your attitude is either your greatest asset or your greatest liability.

We often point to circumstances and take the position of a victim. We sell off our power ignoring that our attitude and free will hold our greatest power.

The Bible teaches we "can do all things through Christ who strengthens" us (Phil. 4:13 author's translation). Do you cultivate your relationship with Jesus Christ? Do you live out that fact in your life, or do you claim the difficult things cannot be done?

Have you ever watched the blind golfers who shoot in the nineties? Do you remember the 1940s Olympic champion swimmer who had only one leg? Do you know much about Helen Keller who could not see, hear, or speak but became one of the most respected persons of the twentieth century because of her incredible positive attitude and faith in God? Does your attitude need a tune-up today?

JANUARY 21

Have you conquered your hurts, habits, or hang-ups? Like most of us, do you still have struggles you would like to conquer? There are answers. There is victory. God is still in the victory giving business.

For anyone struggling with alcohol, drugs, or any other hurt, habit, or hang-up that sabotages health and relationships, the Apostle Paul wrote, "Now the Lord is the Spirit. And where the Spirit of the Lord is, there is freedom" (2 Cor. 3:17). In John 8:36 Jesus said, "If the Son has set you free, you are free indeed."

When the Bible lists the fruit of the Spirit in Galatians 5:22—23, "self—control" is the last one listed. Do you struggle with self—control? Do you find yourself losing a particular battle more often than you win? Call on Jesus. He overcame sin on the cross and overcame death with His resurrection. He can empower you to win your internal battle. He can set you free from your hurt, habit, or hang—up. Sir Edmund Hillary, the first person to reach the top of Mt. Everest said it like this: "It's not the mountain that we conquer but ourselves."

§

JANUARY 22

An anonymous adage states, "When wealth is lost, nothing is lost; when health is lost, something is lost; when character is lost, all is lost." Integrity matters. Character stands supreme. General Norman Schwarzkopf told his soldiers, "Leadership is a potent combination of strategy and character. But if you must be without one, be without the strategy." Character ensures reliability.

Do you remember Job? Do you remember what Satan accused God of doing to Job? Satan accused God of buying Job's loyalty. Read the first two chapters of Job in your Bible. You will see that Job's character could not be bought with blessings and he could not be discouraged to the point of turning away from God compromising his integrity by suffering tragedies. Job's integrity was authentic.

No one stood beside Job when the news came about his children being killed in the storm or about his farms and livestock being destroyed by robbers. His wife advised him to curse God. Job refused to compromise his character. We need champions like that today. We hear a lot about trusting God, but can God trust you? Do you have the character that makes you reliable no matter what?

JANUARY 23

Instead of telling God how big your problem is, why not tell your problem how big your God is? When diagnosed with cancer, Suzie kept repeating to herself and anyone around her that God was bigger than her cancer. Halfway through her scheduled chemotherapy tests revealed she had no cancer. We all have problems and some problems are bigger than others.

When the Aramean army circled around Elisha the prophet, his attendant became afraid (2 Kings 6:8—23). He even cried out to Elisha about the hundreds of chariots and horses gathering for war. Elisha knew that God stood near. Elisha prayed God would open the eyes of the young man so he could see what Elisha knew to be true.

In answer to that prayer, God did open the eyes of the attendant and he saw hundreds of flaming chariots all over the hillsides ready to battle the Aramean army. With this insight the attendant saw what Elisha already knew. God is bigger than the problem he faced. Even today God is bigger than any problem we might face and He still stands ready to empower us through to victory.

§

JANUARY 24

The Bible tells us that after the flood, Noah sent out a dove, which returned with an olive twig in its beak (Gen. 8:11). The Bible records how God sent ravens to bring food to Elijah as he recovered from exhaustion by the river (1 Kings 17:6). The prophet Isaiah tells us if we wait on God, He will empower us in a way similar to how He empowers the great birds to float on the breezes (Isa.40:31).

While Corrie ten Boom was a prisoner at Ravensbrück, a Nazi concentration camp during World War II, she was often forced to stand in the hot sun. She tells how God sent a bird to fly overhead and sing beautifully. While Bruce Olsen was chained to a tree, imprisoned in the Andes Mountains by terrorists in 1988, he tells how God sent a Myrla bird at night to chirp out a familiar song. Birds do not sing at night in the jungle. Nevertheless, this bird came to him and chirped out the native hymn "God Walks the Trail with Us." God uses His creation to encourage His people.

Does the wonder of birds in flight or the beauty of their songs bring encouragement from God to you? He sends them to remind you of His care.

JANUARY 25

The Bible records for us that the Apostle Peter walked on water (Matt. 14:22—33). We are told that in the middle of the night, as lightning lit up the sky, the disciples saw Jesus walking on the water and thought they were seeing a ghost. He identified himself and told them not to fear. As a test of that identity, Peter responded, "If it really is you, Jesus, let me walk on the water to you." Jesus invited him to step out of the boat. Out of all twelve disciples, Peter was the only one to climb out of the boat.

So often we remember only the end of the story. Peter took his eyes off of Jesus, saw the storm, and sank into the waves. Please remember one important fact recorded in the story: Peter did walk on the water. For at least two or three steps, or maybe even several steps Peter did the impossible. For just a few seconds, he did what the entire world believes cannot be done. Nevertheless, Peter did it. He walked on the water.

How did he do it? He did it because for just a few seconds he believed Jesus beyond his common sense. He believed Jesus and overcame the impossible. What impossible thing in your life might you overcome if you would just believe Jesus?

§

JANUARY 26

"Sow a thought and you reap an act. Sow an act, and you reap a habit. Sow a habit, and you reap a character. Sow a character and you reap a destiny." With this you can safely conclude that what you think about or dwell on does in fact shape your character and guide your decision making which shapes your future.

For all of time, leaders know one thing: character stands supreme. We cannot control which thoughts enter our minds, but science has clearly proven we can control which thoughts remain in our minds, which thoughts get our continued attention. The Apostle Paul understood this when he wrote to the Philippians (4:8), "Whatever is true, whatever is honorable, whatever is right, whatever is pure, whatever is lovely, whatever is of good repute, if there is any excellence and anything worthy of praise, dwell on these things."

Do you keep your mind on things that are true and right and honorable? Do you focus your attention on what is lovely and good? Exercise your free will and focus your thoughts on what is true, honorable, and right. It might not be easy at first, but you can do it. God will help you if you ask Him for His help.

JANUARY 27

Love is more than emotion. Love is a commitment to give the very best to another person. Have you ever sat down and planned how to express your love for someone? Normally we do this on birthdays, on anniversaries, and at Christmas—only on special occasions.

The Apostle Paul wrote that love is a proactive, strategic expression more than an emotion. In the love chapter, 1 Corinthians 13, the Apostle Paul tells us what love is and what love is not. He says, "Love looks for ways to be constructive" (1 Cor. 13:4, PHILLIPS). Paul points out strategic forethought guides love.

Love is a proactive, planned out, strategic expression of our affection for another person. Love is so much more than just an emotion. What would happen in your marriage if you expressed your love strategically in this way? Love is when you plan to rearrange your schedule and your life in such a way that another person can receive the best in this life. Do not wait on some emotion. Instead, love in this way. Strategically look for ways to be constructive.

§

JANUARY 28

When God created the world, He told Adam to cultivate and care for the Garden of Eden (Gen. 2:15). God brought the animals to Adam so Adam could name them (Gen. 2:18—23). The ancient people believed that by naming something or someone, you were taking responsibility for its well being.

Even though Adam named Eve committing himself to her well being, God did not tell him what to do with her. Have you ever wondered why she came with no instructions?

God had already given Adam standing orders. He was to cultivate and care for her. Instead of blaming her for his problems, instead of manipulating or overpowering her, instead of bossing her around, yelling at her, slapping her down, or any other expression of his own insecurities, Adam was to cultivate and care for Eve. Read it yourself. That was part of God's plan for marriage.

God designed marriage for us husbands to cultivate and care for our wives so they grow and thrive. He never intended us husbands to harm our wives. So men, call out to God to help you be the husband He created you to be.

JANUARY 29

In his book *The Five Love Languages*, Gary Chapman claims we express and receive love in different ways, especially in our marriages. He gives five general differences: quality time, gifts, physical touch, deeds of service, and words of affirmation.

God did not create us as interchangeable; He created opposites, male and female (Gen. 1:27). Since opposites attract, the normal husband and wife will express love and receive love differently. Both the husband and the wife will have to make changes in how they express love, affection, and commitment to one another if they want to have a wonderful marriage.

My wife is the leading expert on what makes her feel loved and valued. So if I am to learn how to value her effectively, I must learn from her. Ask the question "What can I do to make you feel like I love you and value you?" Then listen. Don't try to defend yourself. Don't try to convince your spouse that your way is best. Ask how it works for her or him. Then choose to express your love in the way your spouse prefers. Your marriage will feel like it was made in heaven.

§

JANUARY 30

Dwight L. Moody invested his life in building the kingdom of God here on earth. His father died when he was four years old. His mother then reared Dwight and his eight brothers and sisters who were all under the age of thirteen. She never encouraged young Dwight to get an education and she never encouraged him to read the Bible.

At seventeen years of age, he left home to become a traveling shoe salesman. After his conversion to Jesus Christ he became an evangelist and one of the champions of the Christian faith in the nineteenth century. He started the Moody Bible Institute, which has sent thousands of missionaries and ministers into the world to proclaim the Gospel.

One man asked Moody if God ever gets tired of us coming to Him with all of our problems. He responded, "The only way to trouble God is not to come to Him at all." The Apostle Paul wrote, "In everything by prayer and supplication with thanksgiving, let your requests be made known to God" (Phil. 4:6). Speak to Him. He's as near as your next breath.

January 31

Casper was a hero of the faith. An elderly man by the time World War II began, he distinguished himself as a watchmaker in Holland. After the Nazis invaded Poland and were working their way across Europe, Christians in Holland began to help Jews escape.

One day a Jewish sympathizer brought a Jewish baby to Casper's home. Casper's pastor happened to be visiting and refused to take the baby to his home in the country citing that in so doing he would put his entire family in danger. At that statement the elderly Casper took the baby into his arms, looked into the baby's eyes, and stated to the pastor, "You say we could lose our lives for this baby. I would consider that the greatest honor that could come to my family."

And so Casper embraced the less than popular promise written by the Apostle Paul: "All who desire to live godly in Christ Jesus will be persecuted" (2 Tim. 3:12). He led his family to hide Jews in their home helping them escape from the Nazis. Casper died in a Nazi concentration camp, but his story of love has been told all over the world by his daughter, Corrie ten Boom in her book *The Hiding Place*.

FEBRUARY 1

The Bible states, "As far as the east is from the west, so far has God removed our sins from us" (Ps. 103:12). Why doesn't it say, "As far as the north is from the south"? Is it because the ancient people thought the world was flat? Actually, some of them questioned that idea. Was it because Israel was afraid to go north because all their enemies came from the north? More possibly, when God, the Holy Spirit inspired that idea, He knew there is a specific distance from north to south. You can measure it.

In contrast, you cannot measure from east to west. If you get on a plane and travel north, at some point you can no longer travel north, but that is not the case east to west. You could continue going east or west continually.

God wanted to communicate to us that there is no end to His mercy. There is no limit to His grace. No matter what we have done, He stands ready to forgive. Do you need to turn back to God? Do you need His endless mercy?

§

FEBRUARY 2

Have you heard this joke? For God so loved the world He did not send a committee. Have you noticed He normally uses an individual to accomplish His purposes? God has great confidence in the ability of one person, side by side with Him, to accomplish anything.

God asked Noah to build the ark one hundred years before He sent the rain (Gen. 6:13—22). Noah must have felt foolish at times. God sent Moses to the Egyptian Pharaoh to demand the release of the Hebrew nation (Exod. 3:7—22). Moses must have felt pretty alone at times. God sent David to fight Goliath (1 Sam. 17:20—58). God called on Daniel to pray and Daniel was thrown to the lions as a result (Dan. 6:1—28). God chose Joshua to lead the nation to take Jericho and other cities (Josh. 6:1—27).

Repeatedly God sends one person to make a difference in a family or even in an entire community. Regularly God puts his hand on the shoulder of one person and says something like, "I have shown you what is wrong, now go make it right." What one thing is God calling you to make right in your family or in your community?

FEBRUARY 3

There was a time when silver had little value (1 Kings 10:21). It has value now. And so does gold. If you have been paying attention to the gold market, you have probably noticed that in the last couple of generations, gold and silver have consistently climbed in value. As a matter of fact, outside of jewels, gold and silver are probably the two things in the world with the most lasting value.

Do you find it interesting when you read in the Bible, in Peter's first letter that he wrote "you were not redeemed with perishable things like gold or silver" but with the imperishable blood of Jesus (1 Pet. 1:18—19)? Did you catch that? The Bible says you are of so much value gold and silver cannot give you eternal salvation. Only the blood of the Son of God has the eternal value high enough to redeem you. Did you know you are of such high value that not even gold or silver can buy you back, so to speak? Gold and silver cannot do it. Only the blood of Jesus has that much value.

§

FEBRUARY 4

In order to convict a person of a crime, often we use an eyewitness. When we look at this procedure of the legal system and we think about Jesus, we must ask: why do so few people believe He was resurrected from the dead?

Read the last couple of chapters of each Gospel—Matthew, Mark, Luke, and John—along with Acts 9 and 1 Corinthians 15. You will discover a rather long list of eyewitnesses to the resurrection of Jesus including the eleven disciples; some women; a pair walking along to a town called Emmaus; and the premier persecutor of Christians at that time, a fellow named Saul of Tarsus. At another time Jesus appeared to over five hundred people (1 Cor. 15:5—8).

These accounts have nineteen eyewitnesses—nineteen people identified by name who saw the resurrected Jesus. Would anyone in the court system today be released if nineteen persons stood to testify as eyewitnesses? One eyewitness transferred allegiance from persecuting Christians to serving with Christians when he saw the resurrected Jesus. We no longer call him Saul of Tarsus but the Apostle Paul.

FEBRUARY 5

Have you ever considered your potential? Years ago an article in *Readers Digest* told about a man who had climbed the eight highest mountain peaks in the world, flown across North America in a hot air balloon, sailed around the world in a sailboat, hiked the two-thousand mile Appalachian Trail, scuba dived off the coast of every continent, earned his pilot's license, and more finishing with this statement: "And having passed my twentieth birthday, I want to attend college to see what I can learn there."

Potential. We hear about it, read about it, and try to understand it. Only God knows our potential. You know that and I know that. So how does God equip us to reach our potential?

When writing to the Church in Rome, the Apostle Paul mentioned that the same Spirit who raised Jesus from the dead is alive in you if you are a Christian (Rom. 8:11). Wow. The Spirit who empowered Jesus to overcome death itself now resides within each Christian with the assignment from God: Empower them and equip them to reach their potential. Embrace His presence and power.

§

FEBRUARY 6

The Bible records for us in Matthew 9 that Jesus told a paralyzed man to get up and walk. In Mark 3 He told a man with a withered hand to stretch it out. In Matthew 14 He told Peter to walk on water.

The Bible also records for us that the paralyzed man got up, his legs were strengthened, and he went home. We read that the second man did stretch out his hand, and it was restored to normal. And we are told that for several steps, Peter did in fact walk on water.

On these three occasions and even more, Jesus told various persons to do things that were impossible, absolutely impossible. Nevertheless, He told them, and they did them.

What is this impossible thing in your life? Is it a marriage that's breaking up? Is it your child on drugs? Is it that you have cancer or some other disease? Is it impatience that keeps rearing its ugly head in the form of tantrums? What is the impossible thing in your life where you need Jesus to work a miracle? If He tells you to do the impossible, will you do it?

February 7

As a pastor I have asked people, "How do you imagine God feels about you?" They report words like *disappointed* and *angry* or they might reply, "He loves me because of Jesus."

One verse that clarifies God's feeling about you in the Bible is Zephaniah 3:17: "The Lord, your God is with you. He is mighty to save. He will exult over you with joy, He will be quiet in his love, He will rejoice over you with singing" (Zeph. 3:17 author's translation). God rejoices over you.

The prophets of old knew God well. Zephaniah told the people God takes great joy in them. As a matter of fact, Zephaniah reported that God would rejoice with shouts of joy and with singing over His people.

Zephaniah reports God is a victorious warrior and rejoices over His people. Did you know you give God that much joy? Did you know God rejoices over you? Do you feel like that is the way God feels about you? You might not feel like that today, or you might not feel like that any day, but Zephaniah wrote down for us that God rejoices over us with shouts of joy and with singing. God takes great joy in you. Ask Him to let you hear Him sing.

§

February 8

Do you remember the old Bible story about the Garden of Eden and the tree of the knowledge of good and evil recorded in Genesis 2:9? Eating fruit from that tree has caused a lot of problems in our world, then and now.

Do you remember where God planted that tree? Was it out along the edge of the garden? Did He plant it among the sweet limes or in the midst of the pineapples? No, the Bible records for us that the tree stood right in the middle of the garden. Why did God plant that tree there? Many people believe it would have been better to plant it way out on the edge.

For Adam and Eve, the central issue remained whether or not they would obey God. Obedience to God is the most important test in life, the central focus of the entire world. The tree of the knowledge of good and evil stood in the middle of the garden, giving shade from the warm sunshine, providing a place for birds to weave their nests, and as a constant reminder that God expects us to obey. The central goal and purpose of life is to obey God.

FEBRUARY 9

Have you ever heard the definition of insanity as doing the same thing repeatedly, but expecting different results? Life proves this to us. Life also shows us if we do something different, we will get different results.

When we look at the Bible story of the nation of Israel crossing the Jordan River, notice that God mentions to them that they are getting ready to do a new thing. The Bible records this for us in Joshua 3:4. Read it sometime. God tells the nation that as they cross the Jordan, they need to keep their eyes focused on Him, because they never passed that way before.

God plans to take them where they have never been and give them what they have never received. With this sort of promise some people fear the future while others embrace the faithfulness and goodness of God.

Does God want to do something new in your life? Does He want to take you somewhere you have never been? Will you fear and resist, or will you trust and embrace? Follow His lead. Keep your eyes focused on Him.

§

FEBRUARY 10

In Gary Chapman's book *The Five Love Languages*, he explains that God designed husbands and wives differently. God made them male and female (Gen. 1:27) and since opposites attract, it is a guarantee you and your spouse express love and commitment to one another in different ways—probably ways that are actually foreign to each other. You might tell your husband you love him, but he might think talk is cheap. He might show you his love by buying you gifts or by doing kind acts for you. He might enjoy a back rub as he goes to sleep or you might enjoy a foot massage after a long day of walking and standing.

Gary Chapman identifies five main ways to express your love and commitment to each other: physical touch, like a hug or a pat on the back as you walk by; gifts, like flowers or cards; quality time, like a walk in the evening or sitting around the table talking about the day; words of affirmation, like, "I appreciate you" or "You really helped me today;" and deeds of service, like doing the dishes or the laundry. Try expressing your love differently each day.

FEBRUARY 11

In Africa, when they talk about forgiveness, they use the phrase, "to take the rope off," meaning to take a rope off of someone's neck, to set him or her free from slavery, from bondage. To take the rope off is the imagery, the word picture used to communicate forgiveness.

You might remember the Bible story about Jacob and Esau (Gen. 27:1—28:9). Jacob deceived his father disguising himself to look, smell, and feel like his brother, Esau. His father, Isaac gave Jacob the family blessing instead of giving it to Esau. When Esau discovered what had happened, he vowed to kill his brother.

Later the elderly father told Esau, "You will be a slave to your brother until the day when you become restless, and when you become restless, you will break his yoke from your neck" (Gen. 27:40). The father recognized his son's anger, resentment, bitterness, and unforgiveness were nothing more than a form of slavery. Esau needed to forgive. The same thing is true today. Do you need to forgive someone today and break his or her yoke from your neck?

§

FEBRUARY 12

At one point in the classic story *Rikki—Tikki—Tavi*, a cobra decides to kill a family. She curls around the family commode and waits for an unsuspecting person to come near.

God gives a similar picture personifying sin to Cain, recorded in Genesis 4:6—7. We read that Cain and Abel brought offerings to God. Abel brought a lamb and was accepted by God. Cain brought an offering of grain from the harvest and was not accepted. His offering was not acceptable because God had already set the precedent. In the previous chapter when Adam and Eve sinned, they tried to cover their sin with fig leaves but God used animal skins (Gen. 3:21).

For redemption, forgiveness, or salvation to occur God chooses to have something die as a substitute life for life. Blood has to be shed. And it is God who makes the sacrifice. This is identical to Jesus' death on Calvary. He was the substitute life for life for us. His blood had to flow to bring our redemption. And He was the "Lamb of God who takes away the sin of the world" according to John 1:29.

God told Cain that sin was crouching at the door waiting for him, but he had to overcome it. God gave a picture of sin as a predator stalking its prey. This is the very nature of sin. As a predator it tries to get us to offend God, to harm ourselves, or to harm others. Just like the cobra coiled around the commode, sin must be overcome. God calls us to resist or to overcome the predatory nature of sin. With His empowering grace to help us, we can.

FEBRUARY 13

The Bible talks about faith, trust in God, and entrusting ourselves into God's hands. The Bible says faith can move mountains, that faith in God has marked the prophets, the apostles, the church fathers, the reformers, and the great missionaries throughout the centuries. You can read in Hebrews 11 many examples of how faith in God helped people overcome incredible obstacles, accomplish great feats, and stay true to God.

In the Andes Mountains, the Motilone tribe received a missionary in the 1960s. As Bruce Olson made friends with them, he learned they did not have a word that meant faith, so he ran into some difficulty telling them about this facet of walking with God.

Over the early years of living with the Motilone, Bruce noticed the pits of quicksand and their own term for *solid ground*. So instead of making up a word, he told them following God is like walking on solid ground. That's a good expression even for us. Many people refer to faith as a blind leap, but biblically defined faith is walking on the solid ground of God.

§

FEBRUARY 14

St. Valentine's Day originated with a Roman priest when Emperor Claudius II persecuted the church by prohibiting the marriage of young people because he believed unmarried soldiers fought better than married soldiers. Rome was a very permissive society. Having many wives was more popular than having only one wife. Yet some people remained attracted to the Christian faith. The church taught (and still teaches) that marriage is sacred between one man and one woman. Valentine encouraged people to marry within the Christian Church and performed ceremonies secretly.

The authorities imprisoned Valentine, tortured him, and executed him in AD 269 because of his efforts to promote Christian marriage. There is a story about Valentine praying for the blind daughter of Asterias, a man who served on the jury at Valentine's trial. God restored her sight, and Asterias became a Christian. Before his own execution, Valentine wrote a letter to the daughter encouraging her in the Christian faith and signed it "from your Valentine." Christian marriage takes a lifetime commitment and courage to stand together through every difficulty.

FEBRUARY 15

Ephesians 5:25—33 says men are to love their wives, and wives are to respect their husbands. That can be hard to do when you have stress at work, money is tight, and you are trying to raise your children. Sometimes you argue just because of the strain of life.

Recently John had just finished paying the household bills. Well, actually he had finished with the money, but there were still bills left. When his wife asked if they had any money left, he simply and quietly said no. She raised her voice and told him how their teenage daughter wanted to go to the movies with some friends. She then lectured their daughter, telling her that money doesn't grow on trees, and they just didn't have enough money to go to the movies right then.

Interrupting his wife, John blurted out, "I know one thing. I wouldn't want to be financially strapped with anyone but you."

His wife giggled and replied, "I wouldn't want to go broke with anyone but you."

They both laughed, and instead of complaining and arguing they expressed their love for and commitment to one another.

§

FEBRUARY 16

The great football coach of the Green Bay Packers, Vince Lombardi is often quoted as saying, "Winning isn't the main thing; it's the only thing." Lombardi remains a legend among coaches and the entire sporting world, and rightly so.

Lombardi inspired many young men to win; however, the one thing that motivated Vince Lombardi more than any other facet of his life was the fact that he attended Mass every morning. David Maraniss shares in the biography *When Pride Still Mattered* that no matter where the Packers were, Lombardi attended Mass in the morning. Every day he attended to his faith in God.

Lombardi drove his teams hard expecting the absolute best from them, and he drove himself even harder. This drive and this level of expectation can be explained by one thing: his incredible faith in and dependence upon God. He embodied Acts 2:42: "They devoted themselves to the apostles' teaching, to fellowship, to the breaking of bread, and to prayer." Every day of the year Lombardi attended a worship service, he received Holy Communion, he heard the word of God, and he prayed. Maybe this daily empowerment explains Lombardi's unusual success.

FEBRUARY 17

The Apostle Paul tells us in Ephesians 6:10—17 that we do not wrestle with flesh and blood but against spiritual forces of wickedness. This is true. Other people are not the enemy.

I wish every church could learn this. Often we find members of the church arguing and separating from one another. Often we find members of the church and their pastors at odds. The entire time Satan just giggles as he skips and dances through Hell. He knows the spiritual life is similar to a war and he uses the same battle tactics that are used in war.

By getting church members to argue among themselves, Satan employs the tactic of "divide and conquer" or "creating diversions" all to keep the church distracted with secondary issues. While we argue over our hurt feelings, our neighbors and coworkers are living without Jesus on their way to Hell.

Satan knows eternal destinies are at stake, so he creates diversions or divides us from one another weakening us. We lose our victory. Let us truly believe the Bible and realize we do not battle against flesh and blood.

§

FEBRUARY 18

Are you willing to ask yourself some tough questions? Investing time in thinking is not a luxury but an absolute necessity. Self-examination is vital to long-term success. Without taking the time to think, we can get sidetracked by the busyness of life. Without taking the time to think, the routines of our schedules can cause us to forget dreams or goals we might have.

Without taking the time to think, we could easily make decisions based on the need of the moment and mess up some long range plans. We could lose perspective and respond with the emotions of the moment. Instead of having our dreams determine how we invest our time, we let the busyness of the day determine if we will make progress toward our dreams.

The Apostle Paul tells us in Ephesians 4:2—24 and Romans 12:2 that we must be renewed in our minds. He tells us the key to our attitude and our behavior lies within how we think. In Philippians 4:8 he tells us what to think about. All of this indicates that we control our minds. So make the time to think and do not allow the routine of life to derail you from your dreams.

FEBRUARY 19

Have you ever taken a close look at Joseph, the eleventh son of Jacob whose life story is recorded for us in Genesis 37—50? He had a dream once that convinced him God's hand was upon him. He told his brothers about it. He even told his parents about the dream. He knew God's hand was on him and he wanted his family to know.

They did not understand and they responded with envy, jealousy, and even hatred. Nevertheless, Joseph knew God's hand was on him.

God's hand is on you also. Psalm 139:14 tells us God wove you together in your mother's womb. You are fearfully and wonderfully made. The prophet Jeremiah tells us God knew us before we were born (Jer. 1:5) and that He has great plans for us (Jer. 29:11—14)—plans to give us hope and a future.

Because Joseph knew God's hand was on him, he was able to stay strong when his brothers attacked him. Because God's hand is also on you, you can stay strong when people insult you, mistreat you, and harm you. You can stay strong.

§

FEBRUARY 20

In Genesis 37—50 we can read about a man named Joseph who was mistreated by his family, lied about at work, and framed for a crime of which he was innocent. He had a lot of troubles, but through it all he stayed faithful to God.

His story begins in Genesis 37 and covers fourteen chapters. Only two chapters are given to telling us about the creation of the world. Personally, I would like to know more about the beginning of the world. Could ostriches fly? Did dinosaurs have hair? Which came first, the chicken or the egg?

Instead, in God's economy He supplied us with only two chapters on the creation and fourteen chapters on Joseph. Maybe God said, "Creation? Yeah, I did it. But let me tell you about one faithful man."

God used seven times as much material to present the details of how Joseph stayed faithful to Him in spite of great adversity—seven times as much material to tell us that if He can empower Joseph to stay faithful, He will also empower us to stay faithful in spite of any adversity. If you will cooperate with God as Joseph did, God will empower you as He empowered Joseph.

FEBRUARY 21

The Apostle Paul tells us that creation, when studied closely will reveal God and His character (Romans 1:18—20). Any Christian can feel right at home with science because science simply reveals the specific design of God's hand.

Have you ever watched a flock of Canada geese fly in *V* formation across the sky? The formation allows the geese that are following to get a lift from the wing downbeats of the geese in front of them. The lead goose never honks. The followers honk encouragement urging the leader forward. By flying in formation, the geese can fly seventy percent farther than if they flew side by side.

When a goose becomes injured or fatigued to the point where it needs to stop, another goose will stop and stay with it so that no goose is ever alone. They coordinate life so none are ever alone.

This wonder of God's creation can help us learn the importance of teamwork, of the principle of life being interdependent upon one another. We learn the importance of staying together, encouraging one another, and accepting our relationships with each other. God can show us a lot about life if we will only give Him the time and attention.

§

FEBRUARY 22

Jesus tells us, "Unless a kernel of wheat falls into the ground and dies, it remains alone. But if it dies, it produces much fruit" (John 12:24). With this statement Jesus presents the principle that life cannot be reproduced by power. Life can reproduce only through self—sacrifice.

Jesus indicates that not even God can bring change through power. God can bring lasting substantial change only through self—sacrifice.

God destroyed the world in Noah's day through the flood, a demonstration of power that brought no change. Since Jesus gave himself sacrificially on the cross, the world has never been the same.

Why do we believe we can save someone through power? Why do we think we can bring any substantial change by getting in positions of power? Jesus demonstrates that only through giving sacrificial love will anyone be saved. The same is true for you and me. Only when we demonstrate sacrificial love for someone will that person recognize the love of Jesus in us.

FEBRUARY 23

Many years ago the London Missionary Society sent Dr. Harley and his pregnant wife into the jungles of Liberia. Dr. Harley had a theology degree and a medical degree and with these he began his mission in the jungles of Liberia.

Years later, still with no converts, his young son contracted a deadly tropical disease, slipped into a coma, and died within a day. Dr. Harley took his son and walked through the village joined by one Liberian man who helped him dig a shallow grave.

When the first shovel of dirt hit the boy, Dr. Harley collapsed crying out to God, "Why have you taken my son, my only son?"

The Liberian man grabbed Dr. Harley by the hair, lifted his dirty tear—soaked face and laughed. The Liberian man then ran back to the village screaming, "Come and see. The white man cries just like we cry." God did not cause the boy's death but He did "cause all things to work together for good to those who love God" (Rom. 8:28).

The next week as Dr. Harley and his wife came together to worship Jesus the entire tribe joined them for the first time in all the years they had been there. God never allows pain to go unused toward the benefit of others. Allow Him to use your pain to benefit another person.

§

FEBRUARY 24

Have you experienced the power of focus in your life? Tino Wallenda, the great high—wire walker of the Wallenda family tells about lessons he has learned about life and faith in his book, *Walking the Straight and Narrow: Lessons from the High Wire.*

Tino explains that every walker of the high—wire keeps his eyes focused on a spot at the end of the wire, a spot that does not move. He says that is important for perspective and balance so he does not waver to the right or left. He explains that even the slightest glance to the side actually causes a slight shift that could cause him to lose his balance and fall, costing him his life. So regardless of anything going on around him, he keeps his eyes and attention focused on that point just at the end of the wire.

Tino reminds us of the passage in Hebrews 12:2 that reads, "Let us fix our eyes on Jesus, the author and finisher of our faith who for the joy set before Him endured the cross." He tells us that fixing our eyes on Jesus, not looking to the right or left will prevent the shift in balance that could result in a fall into sin.

February 25

Have you ever thanked God for the difficulties or adversities you face? That sounds kind of ridiculous at first, I know, but think about it for a moment. The experts tell us adversity can build character within us. So, is it possible God allows difficulties to come our way so we can become stronger persons even if we don't enjoy the situations or even understand them?

The Nazis arrested Betsy ten Boom and her sister Corrie in Holland for helping Jews escape during World War II. Along with the women in the concentration camp at Ravensbrück, fleas lived in the barracks. Betsy remembered a Bible verse: "In everything by prayer and supplication with thanksgiving let your requests be made known to God" (Phil. 4:6). So she suggested she and her sister thank God for the fleas. Corrie refused to do so stating she could never thank God for sleeping with a bunch of fleas.

Not too many days later, Corrie realized the guards stayed away from the barracks because of the fleas. Consequently the ladies had more freedom to read their only Bible and discuss their love of Jesus. Corrie thanked God for the fleas.

§

February 26

Tekie and his family came from Ethiopia to the United States to study at one of our many seminaries. He was quiet and his broken English made it hard to understand him but his faith in Jesus shone through like a sunbeam on a cloudy day.

Tekie had brought his family here in a mad rush when Ethiopia was overtaken by a communist regime. He knew the new government would give orders to have him arrested because he was a Christian pastor. He would either have to leave or be imprisoned. He knew imprisonment also meant death.

Tekie gathered his wife and children and left overnight. He learned English as quickly as he could. Then one day the student body at the seminary received word from the dean that Tekie's brother and sister had been arrested. Since they were leaders in the church also, they had been rounded up. Tekie's brother had been beaten to death by prison guards and his sister had disappeared after her arrest.

Being a Christian is not very popular, especially in other countries. Persecution, imprisonment, and death happen daily. The Christians in other countries need our prayers to stay faithful in the midst of such hostilities.

February 27

One morning John went to start his car and discovered the battery was dead. He quickly jumped into his wife's car and its battery also was dead. So he walked a couple of blocks to find his elderly friend, Ed who John knew would help him.

Ed was trimming the hedges that day, singing gospel hymns above the hum of the trimmer. When John explained his difficulty Ed replied, "Praise the dear Father lad. Isn't God good?"

John just stood there looking at Ed, and then he said, "Ed, you'll have to help me here. I don't see how this is a good time to praise God."

Ed pointed one finger to the heavens and blared, "A God—made horse would never let you down like a man—made car will. Dear lad, understand this important lesson. People will disappoint you and let you down. God will not. He is faithful, reliable, and trustworthy. He will never let you down."

As John and Ed drove back to John's trailer in Ed's truck John remembered that Jesus had not entrusted Himself to people for He knew what was in all people (John 2:24—25).

Often we love God and trust people only to be disappointed when people let us down. Instead it seems as though God is calling us to love people and trust Him. John has remembered the lesson about the faithfulness of God.

§

February 28

In the very first chapter of the Bible we read that God created human beings in His image (Gen. 1:26—27). This involves many facets, one of which is the ability to think ahead to plan activities, think through various results, and then act in a way that will give the best probability for the most desired result.

No animal has the ability to think ahead about different outcomes. A tiger cannot think, *if I drive eighty—five miles per hour across town, will I crash? Will I get caught? Well then, maybe I had better not drive that way.* A monkey cannot reason within her own mind, *If I go home and complain about my day and take out my frustrations on my husband, then maybe he will spend even more time in the garage working on the car.*

We humans have the ability to think about what is happening in our lives. We can evaluate previous events, consider future options, and then think about the possible results of each option. We can then form conclusions that lead us to rational decisions about how we will act, all because God created us in His image.

FEBRUARY 29

The Apostle John recorded for us that "God is light and in Him is no darkness at all" (1 John 1:5). Because God created the world, He is able to produce a huge collection of object lessons to teach us about Himself. Even a brief study of light can reveal to us something significant about God.

When we look at sunlight, we see the collection of all light wavelengths together. Using a prism we can split this collection of light into the spectrum or a rainbow. All colors of the rainbow originate from the three primary colors: red, blue, and yellow. These three primary colors exist distinctly as seen through the prism yet simultaneously they exist in the sunlight.

We have a parallel experience with God. There is one God who exists. When we read the pages of the Bible we can see the three persons—the Father, Son, and Holy Spirit. These three exist distinctly as seen through the pages of the Bible yet simultaneously they exist as one God.

As the prism splits sunlight into three primary colors, so the Bible reveals three Persons who make up the one true, living God.

MARCH 1

Almost seven hundred years before Jesus walked the earth, the prophet Isaiah wrote, "Come now, and let us reason together, says the Lord, "Though your sins are as scarlet, they will be as white as snow; though they are red like crimson, they will be like wool. If you consent and obey, you will eat the best of the land; but if you refuse and rebel, you will be devoured by the sword" (Isa. 1:18—20). Isaiah served God as a prophet for many years.

Isaiah tells us God's design has us working cooperatively with God so He can forgive our sins. God invites us to work it out together. Because He holds us in such high esteem, He will not forgive us of our sins if we do not agree to that offer of forgiveness. He will not force us. He respects us.

Isaiah urges us to receive God's forgiveness and cleansing. He urges us to obey God. He says if we refuse and rebel against God then we will perish, but if we obey and allow Him to work His grace within us, we will experience the best God has to offer. God's part is to forgive and cleanse. Our part is to consent and obey.

§

MARCH 2

Have you ever heard the heavenly choir break out in song? There is a heavenly choir. It has basses that can be mistaken for thunder and tenors envied by even the great Pavarotti. It has altos that sound like Niagara Falls and sopranos that can split the universe wide open. Its main recital occurred one night on a hillside near Bethlehem, where they sang, "Glory to God in the highest, and on earth peace, good will toward everyone" (Luke 2:14 author's paraphrase).

Not only do they perform great concerts, but they also break out in command performances all over the world. Have you ever invited them to sing? Jesus said the heavenly choir would break out in multipart harmony rejoicing in heaven whenever someone turned from his or her sins and turned to Him (Luke 15:6—7, 9—10, 23—24, 32).

Yes, we have all sinned. Yes, we all need God's grace. But if you have not turned to Jesus, what about reading Luke, chapter 15 today? If you turn your life to Jesus today, the heavenly choir will celebrate that decision with great and joyful singing.

MARCH 3

In our society we place such a high priority on sports, on playing, and on leisure, we have made it hard to grow up. We overspend. We see this selfish indulgence in our rising divorce rate and in our increasingly unhealthy society.

The Apostle Paul tells us in the love chapter, 1 Corinthians 13:11 that when he was a child he thought like a child, spoke like a child, and made decisions like a child, but when he became a man he put away childish things. He recognized he was no longer a child. So he deliberately stopped thinking like a child. He stopped speaking and making decisions like a child. He chose to think, speak, and make his decisions like a grown up, mature man.

More than merely setting something off to the side, Paul uses a very strong word here: *katargeo*, which means a thoughtful, deliberate, purposeful putting aside or putting away. Paul set aside the childish demands for self-indulgence, for happiness, and for entertainment. He put away the childish ideas about love and nurturing relationships. He put away the childish ideas about life and love. He made a conscious choice to grow up, to mature, to become a man.

MARCH 4

The Apostle Paul wrote The Love Chapter, 1 Corinthians 13 for the Christians who lived in the ancient Greek city of Corinth, to explain to them what love is and what love is not. Even though they were Christians, they did not have built—in moral compasses pointing them toward true and honest love.

Paul realized they were Christians. They had been born again. The Holy Spirit had gifted them in many ways. Yet they still did not automatically understand or demonstrate love in their relationships. Even though they had given themselves to Christ, their love was still based on conditions and circumstances. They loved in selfish ways, rooted in what they each gained from the relationship. They loved only if they would be loved in return or like predators consuming the other instead of living for the other's benefit.

After Paul discussed marriage in this letter and after he wrote about the church, he then turned his attention to love. He obviously believed they needed to bring real love into their marriages and into their church. Do we need to bring real love into our marriages and into our churches today?

MARCH 5

In the love chapter of the Bible, 1 Corinthians 13, the Apostle Paul tells us what love is and what love is not. He does not leave love to our individual subjective imaginations. Nor does he believe that just because we are Christians we will intuitively know the difference.

Paul makes the comment that "love does not seek its own way" (1 Cor. 13:5). Now that is a big statement. Read it for yourself. Let those few words sink into your heart.

If you were to follow these few words, would it change your marriage? Would it change the way you rear your children? Would it change the way you act at work? Love does not seek its own way.

We are taught in our society that we have to be assertive in order to get ahead. We are taught that we have to stand up for ourselves and fight for what we believe is right. These ideas are not at odds with one another.

Simply and honestly ask God to help you in your marriage for one week to express your love so that you are not seeking your own way. And if that week turns out well, then keep on trusting God for the next week, and so on. Try it for yourself to see if God's word will improve your life.

§

MARCH 6

The Apostle Paul tells us in 1 Corinthians 13 that love does not keep an account of a wrong suffered (1 Cor. 13:5). Wow. What would happen to your marriage if you no longer kept track of all the times your spouse offended you?

When you get into an argument with your husband or your wife, does one of you pull out that list and go over it again? Do you list all the times you have been offended, taken for granted, insulted by the other's sarcasm, kept waiting for an apology that never came? Do you remind your spouse that he or she did this to you years ago as well as every year since then? Do you remind him or her that every time you two are in such a situation, he or she takes you for granted?

The Apostle Paul says love does not keep an account of wrongs suffered. If you love someone, you will not keep a running tally in your head or on paper about the offenses he or she has caused. I realize Paul was not married and probably did not experience the daily annoyances we experience in marriage. I also realize the Bible tries to tell us love does not keep track of a wrong suffered. Ask God to help you let it go. He will help you.

MARCH 7

With today's technological advances, I often wonder if God understands our technology. For example, does God understand the intricacies of modern radar? Before you say, "Why sure, God knows everything" think it through and come up with proof for your opinion.

The Bible records for us in Genesis 1, the very first chapter that God created the world. He spoke and light began to shine, plants sprang forth from the soil, animals began to walk the earth, fish began to swim, the sun began to shine, and birds began to soar. He spoke and humans began to breathe, walk, explore, and eat the fruit.

So have you figured out the answer to the question, "Does God understand the intricacies of modern radar?" He spoke and the bats began to fly. By sending out high—pitched sounds that bounce off of objects and catching those reverberations with their ears, bats use a radar—type system called echolocation. Though bats are practically blind, they fly at night by using echolocation, avoiding tree limbs, locating their prey, and getting back and forth to their nesting places.

§

MARCH 8

According to Jeremiah 29:11, God has some plans for us. He plans to give us prosperity, hope, and a future. How are the schools doing in your community? Are they meeting even the minimum requirements? Do children excel?

Is it God's will for our children to meet less than the minimum standards? Is less than the minimum what God means when He says He wants to give us hope and a future? Most children are left on their own. You could be their hope.

As a member of your community, it is your responsibility and privilege to carve out two to three hours each week to offer yourself as a mentor or a volunteer in the schools. You could help an elementary student learn to read. You could listen to a seventh grader without a friend or hope. You could help in the office.

Go to the school in person. Tell them you want to volunteer. Fill out the paperwork and do the background check. Make yourself available to help the children growing up in your community. If you are willing, the school will guide you.

God has plans for our future, but He can accomplish those plans only through you training up the rising generation. Instead of being interested in our ability He is interested in our availability.

March 9

Often Christians do not recognize the opportunities for ministry even though God has placed many opportunities in our own communities. There is always a child in a nearby school who needs a friend, a mentor, or someone who will just offer some time and attention.

From Jeremiah 29:11, you can infer at least some of God's dreams for your community. You could begin by praying for the superintendent of the school system, the principals of each school, the teachers and aides, the cafeteria and office workers, and the custodian. Every one of these adults interacts with many children daily.

Pray for the adults in the schools to have the courage to model honest and responsible lives for the children. Pray that they will have the patience they need daily. Pray for their families asking God to bless them with healthy family relationships that cross over into the classroom so the students can learn to develop healthy relationships.

Pray for the students because many are reared by grandparents, aunts, cousins, or by another adult other than his or her own mother or father. Many students go home each day not knowing where they will sleep and if they will eat an evening meal. Consequently many students have trouble learning because they do not have stable home lives. God needs you to pray for the children in your community.

§

March 10

The Apostle Paul used a very strong word, *katargeo* when he wrote that he put away childish things (1 Cor. 13:11). This word cannot be translated easily because the nuance involves contemplation, evaluation, and strategic action.

You cannot put away childish things in an emotional moment. You cannot put away childish things in a moment of frustration with repeated circumstances brought on by impulsive behavior. You can only put away childish things by determined, deliberate, decisive redirecting the way you view yourself and your stage in life. Paul gave three specific areas: how he thought, how he reasoned, and how he spoke.

Have you looked at the way you speak to other people? Do you still use sarcasm as humor? Do you degrade someone or insult someone as a means of being funny? Do you tear someone down just to get a laugh? Before you say, "Now wait a minute, it's all in fun" think it through. Children speak this way. Adolescents insult their friends just to get cheap laughs. Mature adults are different. They find humor in ways other than degrading other people.

MARCH 11

The Apostle Paul talks about putting away childish things in 1 Corinthians 13:11, within the love chapter. He says that he used to speak as a child, but since he has become a man he has put away childish things.

How do you speak to your children? When you are angry, do you speak to them with profanity or in degrading ways? Do you use your anger as an excuse to speak in a way that is normally unacceptable? Do you model for your children that anger is a great excuse to lose control?

What if you speak to your children the same way when you are angry as when you are not? What if you model for them that even when angry, you are an adult exercising self-control? What if you set an example that even when angry, you are not some two—year—old throwing a tantrum?

What if you model this self—control for your children so that as they grow up, they know they are to put away childish things as well? Instead of offering excuses, they will more likely follow your example.

§

MARCH 12

The Apostle Paul chose to grow up when it came to what he believed about love. He used to think childish things about love. But when he became a man, he purposefully put away those childish ideas.

On his first wedding anniversary, David was so happy. His wife prepared a delicious dinner, set a beautiful table, and prepared for a romantic evening, but then he noticed a tear in her eye as she said, "Honey, aren't you glad we don't have to live that year over again?" Devastated, David realized his wife had not been happy with him. She had even had moments when she had regretted marrying him.

So he set his heart to make her happy. When she was happy, he found greater joy and fulfillment than when pursuing his own happiness. Maybe Paul knew something when he wrote "love does not seek its own way" (1 Cor. 13:5).

Have you realized yet that working for the happiness of your spouse holds greater satisfaction than your own happiness? Instead of seeking your own happiness, why not set your heart today to put away childish ideas about love and grow up in love?

MARCH 13

You might be getting ready for work or taking a break at work. Maybe you have finished your work for the day. In Deuteronomy 8:18, Moses tells us God gave each of us the ability to earn a wage, to work.

With this belief established in his own mind, the Apostle Paul tells us in Colossians 3:23 to do our work as unto the Lord and not unto men, to work honestly, efficiently, and productively so our coworkers recognize a difference in us.

A common practice is to clock in and then enjoy a cup of coffee before starting work. This is just a leisurely way of stealing. By doing this you are taking money you have not earned. Whether you work retail, in a factory, or at a service job, avoid stealing from your boss in every way. Work honestly.

Recognize that God has given you the ability to work, to think, to earn a wage. Work heartily. Your work is an expression of your faith; an expression of your gratitude to God. Instead of complaining or arguing, embrace the fact that God has gifted you with abilities so you can take care of your family. Work honestly, with gusto, as your daily expression of gratitude to God for giving you the ability to work.

§

MARCH 14

You might remember that Jesus found himself in the mud crying out to God for help on the night he was betrayed and arrested (Mark 14:32—42; Luke 22:39—46). Some scholars tell us he experienced an acute case of depression.

Have you experienced depression? Do you ever feel like just giving up? Do you ever feel like not getting out of bed in the morning? Do you ever feel like you are drowning because of all the stress and strain in your life? Do you ever feel like you are in Hell and cannot find the door to get out? You are not alone. Jesus has walked those trails and He really does understand.

Contact churches in your community. One of them will have a depression support group that can help you in numerous ways. The church of Jesus Christ cares deeply for you. He has people who will be your friends and will offer you acceptance, support, and love. You will find the encouragement and strength to get through your day. You will find ways to connect with God. Just as God sent an angel to strengthen Jesus during His dark hours (Luke 22:43), God will also send grace and mercy to help you during your difficult hours.

MARCH 15

The Bible records for us in Exodus 20:12, "Honor your father and mother that your days may be prolonged in the land." About 1,400 years later in his letter to the Ephesians (Eph. 6:1—3), the Apostle Paul points out that this is the first commandment with a promise. Of all things to carry with it a promise, you might find this one from God to be very interesting.

So what is it about this whole thing of honoring my father and mother? Some people reply, "Are you kidding? After what my old man did to me? He does not deserve it" or "You have no clue what my mom did. How can I honor her after the way she treated me?" Some say, "Preacher, you wouldn't say that if you had grown up in my home; we had it hard."

Frankly, I have heard it all before. Difficult? Possibly. Simple? Absolutely. Will you honor your father and mother? God did not say to honor them conditioned on if they deserve it. He did not say to honor them if they have earned it according to your standards. He simply commanded, "Honor your father and mother." Treat them with respect and dignity and you will find yourself pleasing God.

§

MARCH 16

In the longest chapter of the Bible we have a man who thinks, considers options, and acts decisively. Psalm 119:59 states this: "I considered my ways and turned my feet to your testimonies."

He considered his ways. He thought it through. He looked over his life and did not like what he saw. Maybe he cut short his integrity when no one was looking. Maybe he acted against his values when he was alone. Maybe he made compromises in his honesty or lack thereof. Maybe he lacked compassion for his neighbors in need. Maybe he lacked the courage to make the hard decisions at work losing effective workers because he did not want to dismiss the ineffective workers for fear they would no longer like him. Maybe he lacked the self—control he needed to stop the destructive habit that had harmed him for years.

All we do know is he sat down and deliberately took a ruthlessly honest look at his life and then turned it over to God. Have you ever taken a ruthlessly honest look at your life? Is it time for you to turn your life over to God? Ask Jesus Christ to help you. He will, guaranteed.

MARCH 17

One of the more beloved passages in the Bible is Psalm 23. We do not know when, but we do know David wrote it. He makes it clear in the opening verse that because the Lord is his Shepherd all of David's needs are met. God Himself fulfills all of David's needs, physical, emotional, and spiritual.

The physical needs for food and water, for clothing and shelter, for warmth and protection—David claims God covers every detail. What about the emotional needs for love, security, and purpose? God covers them all as well.

As David sat out under the stars, keeping watch over the family's flock of sheep, he discovered that God loves unconditionally. He learned that God brings security. He found out a relationship with God supplies anyone's purpose in life. David discovered that God is the fulfillment for every single need. This is why David wrote, "He restores my soul."

David knew what it's like to have stress and strain in life. He knew what it's like to have loss and sorrow. But David also had come to know that God was his entire fulfillment. Have you discovered this yet?

§

MARCH 18

The Bible makes an incredible promise about steadfastness at the end of Psalm 15, "He who does these things will never be shaken." What things? Is it actually possible to practice a list of things that will result in never being shaken? Now that is an incredible statement to make.

Many people would argue that just on principle. Never be shaken? After beginning as a shepherd and spending decades as a warrior, David finished his life as the king of Israel. He starts Psalm 15 with the questions, "Lord, who may abide in Your tent? Who may dwell on Your holy hill?" He then gives an answer involving a list of several items.

First on David's list are integrity and righteousness. David then explains the importance of how we treat our friends and our neighbors. He points out the key factors for honesty and fair play in business, especially banking. He even speaks about impartial justice in the court of law. He talks about how we speak to one another, whether we are encouraging and honest or discouraging and dishonest. It's only five verses long, ending with that incredible promise "He who does these things will never be shaken." I want to encourage you today, go for the promise.

March 19

Salvation is a multi—faceted relationship with God. The Bible reveals to us that God is a righteous Judge, a sovereign King, a loving Father, a compassionate Shepherd, a purifying Priest, a transcendent Creator, an atoning Savior, and even a jealous Lover as well as several other roles and attributes.

If we take all of God's roles and their corresponding attributes and look at the various facets of salvation we can gain a more complete and accurate view of the relationship God offers to us. How much richer our understanding becomes when we recognize just one of these role and attribute combinations, that a compassionate shepherd is the one who carries the rod and the staff that bring us comfort.

Psalm 23 reveals that within the role of shepherd, we find the discipline of God. The rod David speaks of in this psalm was a club used to beat off predators and to discipline wandering sheep to bring them back into the fold. Maybe it brings you the comfort David wrote about to know it is a compassionate Shepherd who attends to your discipline.

March 20

Within salvation, one of the issues the Bible addresses is our emotional or psychological need to be free from guilt. We need forgiveness or pardon. This does not mean we are not guilty but simply that there has been forgiveness and we are free from prosecution or punishment as a result of our guilt.

A study done in the 1980s revealed that three out of four patients in psychiatric facilities across America could go home immediately if they believed they were forgiven. Guilt and shame had crippled their souls to the point of needing hospitalization, therapy, and even medication in some instances.

God understands this emotional need within us. He understands we need forgiveness. So what is His solution? His solution is to provide forgiveness immediately following our confessions of our sins. Just like a king or a president pardons a criminal, God offers pardon to us. 1 John 1:9 reveals that "if we confess our sins, He is faithful and just to forgive us our sins, and to cleanse us from all unrighteousness." God offers forgiveness. He offers cleansing. He is a righteous judge who reads off our pardon having written it in the blood of Jesus.

March 21

The Bible reveals to us in John 3:16 that God is a loving Father. You probably know this; the most quoted verse in history is "for God so loved the world that He gave His only begotten Son, that whosoever believes in Him shall not perish but have eternal life."

Have you ever noticed what is not written in that verse? It does not say God felt sorry for us. It does not say God looked down from heaven, saw the mess we were in, and pitied us. He does not feel pity. He does not feel sorry for us. He feels love for us. That's what the Bible clearly says. John 3:16 records that God our Heavenly Father looked at our sinful and lost state and loved us. A judge feels no love for a lawbreaker. In the court system, we have criminals against the law of the land. Prosecution is to be conducted without prejudice, without passion, and with complete indifference.

Different from an unfeeling judge, our Heavenly Father feels incredible love for His children. The Bible reveals that one of the facets of our salvation is that God is a loving Father. He loves us.

§

March 22

In the Apostle Paul's first letter to the Corinthians, Paul tells us that love builds up (1 Cor. 13:4—7). Paul wrote that love is strategic. Love is proactive. Love is prior planning. With that idea, tell me men, how would your marriages be different if you changed from reacting to proactively setting strategies for showing your love to your wives? What if you calmly, strategically set plans to show your love to your wives and then followed them to completion? And did it repeatedly?

No one builds a home without drawing up plans. No general goes into battle without a strategy. No coach leads his team into competition without a game plan. They determine the best ways to accomplish their objective of victory. And then they begin. So what do you have to do over the next year to help your wife to feel secure, to feel loved, to find joy when she spends time with you? What do you need to do to express your love to her daily? Why not do what the Bible says to do? A match made in heaven is still built on earth. Build, men. Build.

MARCH 23

In chapter 13 of 1 Corinthians, the Apostle Paul tells us love builds up (1 Cor. 13:4—7). Love is strategic, proactive; it is thinking ahead and then implementing a love plan. Love is not just reacting to what others do to us but thinking ahead and putting loving expressions into action.

Tell me, ladies, what would happen in your marriages if you determined today that you were going to stop waiting on your husbands to figure it out? What would you have to do over the next twelve months to get your marriages closer to how you want them to be? Are you willing to go past reacting to proactive planning?

What are the weekly steps to take? Would you add the romance back into your marriage? Would you make a commitment to no longer allow self-pity into your life? Would you stop being moody? Would you stop complaining about all the areas of your husband's life that leave you wishing for more? Would you stay focused on loving him instead of waiting on him to love you? For what would you ask his forgiveness? Why not make this year the year to build that marriage made in heaven?

MARCH 24

Sherry's new baby began to scoot around in her crib. She would raise her rear end into the air and then straighten her legs pushing herself across the surface of the bed. She could push forward, but she could not back up. She had not yet learned those skills.

One day Sherry noticed that the baby had wedged herself into the corner and was having trouble breathing. Immediately Sherry lectured her, "You got yourself into that mess. You can get yourself out of that mess." Right? No. Instead Sherry immediately reached down, scooped the baby into her arms, and examined her. Once she determined her baby was breathing okay, she relaxed again.

According to Ephesians 2:1—5, God knows we got ourselves into a big mess: "And you were dead in your trespasses and sins, in which you formerly walked according to the course of this world, according to the prince of the power of the air, of the spirit that is now working in the sons of disobedience. Among them we too all formerly lived in the lusts of our flesh, indulging the desires of the flesh and of the mind, and were by nature children of wrath, even as the rest. But God, being rich in mercy, because of His great love with which He loved us, even when we were dead in our transgressions, made us alive together with Christ (by grace you have been saved)."

Because He is a loving Father, God sent Jesus to rescue us from this mess called sin. Even more than asking for forgiveness, have you asked Jesus to deliver you from the power of sin? Because of His incredible love for you, He will rescue you from your mess, guaranteed.

MARCH 25

Paul's letter to the Galatians gives the blueprint for how to become a fulfilled, complete person. According to some of the newer translations of the Bible, in Galatians 2:20 Paul makes reference to himself seven times. Paul explains that he lives his life in a way that puts the attention on Jesus. He lives so people see Jesus in him.

Within the first two chapters of the Bible, Genesis 1—2, the number seven is presented as a symbol for completion: there are seven days of creation, seven times God calls His creation "good." From these examples and a few others we infer that seven is the number of completion. When we apply that idea to this verse in Galatians, we find that the Bible reveals for us how to become a fulfilled, satisfied, and complete person.

The only way is to live a life that gives attention to Jesus—a life lived completely to the glory of God. Being complete does not depend upon riches, education, or accomplishments. Instead a complete person is one who lives to the glory of Jesus who loves us and who has given Himself for us. Christ living in us is fulfillment. He is our completion. Be a complete person. Live to the glory of Jesus Christ.

MARCH 26

When Ted began his senior year of high school football he lined up for calisthenics in a patch of many four—leaf clovers. He picked some and placed them in various parts of his uniform hoping they would bring him good luck.

During the second day of practice, he sat among the four—leaf clovers and a thought came into his mind: *How can anything dead be good luck?* So he decided right then that he would stop picking the four—leaf clovers.

About a year later he gave his life to Jesus Christ. He asked God to forgive him for his sins and he asked Jesus to come into his heart as his Lord and Savior. During those early months of being a Christian he realized something. Mohammed is in his grave, as are Confucius, Buddha, and all the other founders of the world's religions. Jesus is not dead. He's alive.

It's been many years since those days on the football field. If you were to look on Ted's desk today you would see a framed four—leaf clover with a note including part of the statement from the angel recorded in Matthew 28:6: "Nothing dead is good luck. Jesus is alive. He is risen."

MARCH 27

The Bible records for us in Genesis 24 the story of Eliezer, Abraham's chief servant converting to a belief in the Lord. Five times he prayed. The first four times he addressed the Lord with the identifier "God of my master, Abraham" but in the fifth prayer he left off the identifying statement leading us to the conclusion that he had taken the Lord as his God as well.

Abraham sent the servant on a mission to get a wife for his son, Isaac. The pressure to succeed increased greatly as Eliezer began to think about it. He knew when his master Abraham died, Isaac would inherit him as a servant. He envisioned an evening in the kitchen, with Isaac glaring at him and growling, "She burned dinner again. She keeps saying *no* to me in our bedroom. She sits around all day instead of helping with the chores. You picked her for my wife." That is a high level of pressure at work.

So the servant thought, *I need help.* And he called on the Lord, the God of Abraham and the Lord guided him to the right woman. By the end of the story, Eliezer had taken the Lord as his God as well. Read it today and see how Eliezer becomes convinced that the Lord is the God for him.

§

MARCH 28

The Bible records for us in Genesis 24 the story of Eliezer, Abraham's chief servant coming to a belief in the Lord as his God. We are not told which god Eliezer had previously served. We are told only that he did convert to serve the Lord.

Abraham sent Eliezer on a mission to get a wife for his son, Isaac. We know from previous stories in Genesis that Abraham had as many as three hundred eighteen hired hands helping him with his livestock (Genesis 14:14). That was a pretty big operation and Eliezer was the ranch boss so to speak.

We know he succeeded on his assigned mission to get a bride for Isaac. Probably more than one factor contributed to his decision to convert to serve the Lord as his god, but one in particular was the daily influence of Abraham. Eliezer worked side by side with Abraham. He watched Abraham daily. He heard what Abraham said daily.

We know our co—workers can have daily influences on us and we on them. Do we act and speak in ways that influence our coworkers toward the Lord? Do they trust God more fully because of what they see and hear from us?

MARCH 29

The Bible records for us in Genesis 24 the story of Abraham's chief servant, Eliezer converting to a belief in the Lord, the God of Abraham. One of the convincing reasons is that the Lord answered Eliezer's prayer for guidance. He prayed in detail and God answered in detail.

Abraham sent Eliezer on a mission to get a wife for his son, Isaac. The task seemed so huge, but Eliezer took the risk. He decided to pray to the God of Abraham for help. His prayer involved details about watering his ten camels.

In the ancient world, everybody believed in some god or even many gods. Eliezer realized Abraham's God might be on Abraham's side. So he prayed. Abraham's God answered the servant's prayer. He answered it in such a precise and convincing way that the servant decided he also could trust this God with his life. Paul's letter to the Romans (Rom. 2:4) tells us it is the kindness of God that leads us to change our allegiance to Him.

Eliezer bowed low and prayed to the Lord, who was no longer only the God of Abraham but had also become his own God. God's kindness won Eliezer.

MARCH 30

The Bible records for us in Genesis 24 the story of Abraham sending his chief servant, Eliezer to get a wife for his son, Isaac. Eliezer took along ten camels. He must have felt the difficulty of choosing a wife for his employer's son, so he deliberately prayed to "the Lord, the God of my master, Abraham" that the woman the Lord chose to become Isaac's wife would offer to water his camels for him.

Most young men are interested in one thing: is she pretty? Eliezer understood that physical beauty fades, but internal beauty of character emerges like the dawn and shines brighter and brighter throughout a woman's life. So Eliezer prayed for a woman who was kind, hospitable, and generous knowing these traits would please Isaac for years and years.

A female camel can drink twenty gallons of water at a time, and a male can drink thirty gallons. A woman named Rebecca offered to water those ten camels and dropped her bucket into the well many times to get those two hundred to three hundred gallons. The servant knew character shines more than beauty and will please a husband for a lifetime. Are you developing the inner beauty of your character?

MARCH 31

Do hard times make your faith shine even brighter? In the book of Ruth, chapter 1, Ruth turned to the Lord as a result of what she personally witnessed in the life of her mother—in—law.

Naomi and her husband moved to a land called Moab. Over the next ten years, their two sons both married. Naomi's husband died, and then both her sons died, leaving her with two grieving daughters—in—law. Orpa went home. But Ruth swore an oath, an allegiance to Naomi.

Ruth told Naomi that wherever Naomi went, she would go. Naomi's people would be her people. Naomi's God would be her God. Ruth turned away from Chemosh the Moabite god and turned to the Lord because of the incredible faith she saw within Naomi especially when Naomi lost her husband and both sons. Naomi was bitter. Naomi grieved. But Naomi did not turn away from the Lord.

Ruth wanted a faithful god who carries someone through great heartache. Ruth knew any god could buy followers with blessings and with prosperity, but she needed a god who was so distinct in his character, so faithful to his follow-ers, that their allegiance to him only deepened in difficulties and trials.

April 1

You have probably heard about Moses and the Ten Commandments. But do you know about the day when Moses sat down with his father-in-law, Jethro and told him what the Lord had done for Israel in bringing them out of Egyptian slavery? Jethro's subsequent conversion is recorded for us in Exodus 18:1—12.

Moses told Jethro about the ten plagues on Egypt, each one a mockery of one of Egypt's gods. He spoke about the Lord conquering Hapi, the god of the Nile by turning the Nile to blood for seven days. He told about the three days of darkness proving the Lord's superiority over Amun—Ra, the sun god who was probably the national god for Egypt. The Bible records for us that Jethro recognized that "the Lord is greater than all the gods." Jethro turned from following Baal and Asherah, the gods of Midian and turned to the Lord, worshiped the Lord and made vows of loyalty to Him.

Jethro had been a priest of the gods of Midian and he knew about the more than thirty gods Egypt worshiped. Even today the Lord is greater than Allah, the god of Islam. He is greater than Vishnu, Shiva, or Krishna or any other Hindu god. He is greater than Buddha, Confucius, Thor, Neptune, Zeus, Mercury, or any other god. The Lord, He is God.

APRIL 2

John wrote a letter to a friend revealing the emptiness of his soul. He explained how he preached sermons and visited the sick. He attended church, sang the songs, and led the prayers. He listened to the praise band and the soloists. He enjoyed the children. But he wrote to his friend about the emptiness of his soul.

John said he was empty because he realized he was not desperate for God's presence. God did not show up in the church service. The other people sang, prayed, listened to John preach, and then went home. God has promised to manifest Himself where His people have gathered together. He has promised more than just a warm feeling of happiness. He has promised healings, salvations, marriages repaired, and lost children brought home. John was starting again to hunger for God's presence.

John confessed he relied on his knowledge, the praise team's skill, the choir's preparation, and the great programming and curriculum for the various ministries. Even though all these things were great blessings from God, John wanted a desperation for God like he used to have. He used to pray Psalm 42:1: "as the deer pants and thirsts for water, so my soul longs for You, O God."

Do you feel the same longing for the manifest presence of God? Do you yearn to see God show up as you and others worship Him? Grow restless and call out to Him.

April 3

You might have heard about Jonah and the whale, but do you remember the sailors? Do you remember what they did that day both before and after the great fish swallowed Jonah?

The sailors grew frightened because the storm grew more ferocious and more deadly. They called on their gods and not one god answered. The captain woke up Jonah who told the captain and the sailors that he served the Lord who had created the sea and the dry land.

At that point the sailors knew they had the culprit who had offended his god and that the Lord was the God with whom they now had to do business. When Jonah told them to throw him into the sea, instead they rowed faster. After a few minutes of futile rowing, they recognized the Lord was intensifying the storm. He wanted Jonah. So the sailors threw Jonah into the sea as he had told them to do. Then the Bible records the sea grew calm and the sailors realized the Lord was the one true God. Turning away from their gods whom they had earlier called on for help they offered sacrifices to the Lord and made vows of allegiance to Him. They converted from their gods to serve the Lord.

APRIL 4

Anna Jean has lived for Jesus Christ. She brought her children to church. While singing in the choir she would look up and her face would shine with the presence of God. With a smile and a tear rolling down her cheek she focused her attention on Jesus. Just like the Apostle Paul she would whisper, "For me to live is Christ" (Phil. 1:21).

She would take her laundry to the Laundromat and tell others about Jesus. No one listened, but she refused to give up. On Sundays she hugged all the children telling them how much she loved them. She saw little results.

One day one young man returned to that church for the Christmas break from college. He had not told anyone, including Anna Jean about his prayer: "Lord Jesus, if You can give me what Anna Jean and Bob have, I want it, amen." He had prayed a simple authentic prayer of love, perseverance, and passion. He approached Anna Jean to get her usual hug and as she closed her arms around him she began to cry as she whispered, "You did it! You did it! You took my Jesus! You did it!" He never did discover how she knew.

Years later he returned to that church for a visit. He had attended seminary and served as a pastor for a church in another state. He told her stories of leading people to Jesus, baptizing children, and even training pastors in other countries. He had great joy telling her that the seeds of love she had sown in his little heart had grown and her Jesus was being shared all over the world.

If you are like Anna Jean, don't get discouraged; stay faithful. God will honor your faithfulness, and someday you will see the fruit of your labor.

April 5

Have you ever noticed that God used business owners to do much of His work? Many times we assume God used priests or scribes. When we look at the Bible identifying the vocations of God's servants, God simply did not use priests and scribes consistently. He called on business owners.

Abraham worked with livestock and had 318 hired hands (Gen. 13:2—4, 14:14). Amos shepherded sheep and tended an orchard of fig trees (Amos 7:14). Luke was a physician (Col. 4:14). Paul worked his way from city to city as a tailor sewing tents (Acts 18:1—3; 1 Thess. 2:9). Peter, Andrew, James, and John worked as partners in a fishing business (Luke 5:1—11). Lydia owned her own retail business specializing in purple fabrics (Acts 16:14). Moses had been trained as a prince of Egypt to later rule Egypt as its king (Acts 7:17—53).

The first person listed in the Bible as being filled with the Spirit of God was a tailor, metalworker, stonemason, and carpenter named Bezalel—the craftsman responsible for designing and building the tabernacle (Exod. 31:1—5). God still anoints people for business and calls them to follow Him.

§

April 6

As we saw yesterday, God anointed many people for business including Abraham, Peter, Andrew, James, and John. God continues to anoint more people for business than for vocational ministry like Ward who made his hobby to help start a new business every month in his community and state.

God anointed Tim as an attorney so he could finance his ministry as an evangelist for Jesus. He brings more people to Christ on the golf course than in revival meetings. He combines his love for golf and his love for Jesus into a golf tournament every year. To enter the tournament you not only have to pay your fee but you also have to bring a non—Christian with you to play as well.

Steve worked as a financial investor deliberately living at a lower economic standard than what he earned so he could send more money to missions. God has anointed Steve for business so he can help reach the world with the message of Jesus Christ. When he speaks at mission conferences, he challenges the business owners to live simply so they can finance more ministries around the world. Has God anointed you for business? If so, he wants you on the front lines funding ministries all over the world.

April 7

Have you read the story of Abraham in Genesis 11—25? Through fourteen chapters spanning one hundred years, Abraham learns how to walk with God.

The first time God spoke to Abraham recorded in Genesis 12:1—3, Abraham responded by obeying only part of the way. God told him to leave his homeland and his family and go into another land. Abraham did leave his homeland but he left only most of his family. He took along his nephew Lot.

Shortly after they left, Lot's livestock and Abraham's livestock were too numerous for the land so Lot chose the better grazing fields. Lot got into some trouble and landed right in the middle of a war. Abraham loaded up his 318 hired hands and went into the midst of the deadly battle to rescue Lot. Later Abraham had to rescue Lot again when God destroyed Sodom and Gomorrah (Gen. 18:1—38).

When we obey God only partially instead of enjoying the consequences, it seems we consistently clean up messes. The consequences are negative and unpleasant instead of the wonderful plans and dreams God wants to pour out on us. He will not pour out His blessings because our partial obedience positions us outside His will for our lives.

APRIL 8

Take a look sometime at the story of Abraham in the Bible, especially Genesis 15:1—6. When God spoke to Abraham, He promised him all sorts of blessings in his future and in the future of his descendants, but Abraham told God all he wanted was a son. He told God he was more than willing to follow Him, but it had to be on his own terms.

Do you find yourself negotiating with God and making that same kind of commitment? Do you find yourself telling God it all sounds good, but you want to have a say in what happens? Many times we want to call the shots and have God just bless our plans and our efforts.

Often we go to God in prayer asking for blessings instead of merely reporting for duty. There's a joke that says many people want to serve God but only as advisors. Instead of telling God how we want it, what if we just told Him we are available and will abide by His plans?

When asked, "Why do you worship God?" one Asian pastor told about an elderly evangelist coming to his village praying for his blind sister who was then healed. Another Asian pastor pointed to the same elderly evangelist and told about a younger sister being born with legs different lengths and the evangelist prayed for her. Her shorter leg lengthened as her brother held it. Then the elderly Asian tribal evangelist answered through a translator, "Because He is God and I am not."

APRIL 9

The Bible records for us the story of Isaac and Rebecca and their twin sons, Jacob and Esau throughout Genesis 25—32. Today's standards and language would label this a dysfunctional family, with parents playing favorites between their sons and the mother teaching her favorite to lie, deceive, and manipulate.

Isaac favored Esau, who hunted and lived outdoors. Rebecca favored Jacob. He stayed near the tent and cooked the meals. His mother encouraged him to deceive his father and to cheat and steal from his brother. This family had significant problems brought about by their own manipulation and selfishness, by their own decisions.

In His amazing grace, God chose to work through this family to bring about His plan and purpose in history. He did that deliberately. He knew we have some destructive family situations. He wants us to know He will work through any family who will open themselves to Him. He does not overlook sinful attitudes or behaviors, but He refuses to give up on us. Have you opened yourself to God? Have you allowed God to work within your family? If you will allow Him to do so He will.

§

APRIL 10

Esau was a slave to his own appetite, as recorded in some detail in Genesis 25:19—34. He did not rule his body; instead his urges enslaved him. He did not have a problem with smoking or drinking or sex; his master was food. Esau was a slave to his stomach.

Esau ate when he was not even hungry. He ate when he felt tired or lonely, stressed or angry, and even more so if he was hungry. He came home empty handed from his hunt one day. The Bible records for us that his twin brother, Jacob had fixed dinner outside. As Esau neared their home a breeze floated the aroma across the hills. Already past hungry, Esau wanted food. He traded his part of the family inheritance for that one meal.

Esau was in bondage to his appetite. The Apostle Paul reported to the church in Philippi, "Many live as enemies of the cross of Christ, whose god is their appetite and whose glory is in their shame, who set their minds on earthly things" (Phil. 3:18—19). Are you in a similar bondage to food or to your appetite? God specializes in the bondage busting business. Talk to Him. He will strengthen you to overcome.

April 11

One aspect of our salvation reveals to us that God as a Judge invites us to receive forgiveness or pardon, a legal term. Years ago the United States president, Richard Nixon resigned from office because of his embarrassing participation in an event called Watergate. Moments after that resignation his vice president Gerald Ford took the oath of office and became the president. Not too long after that, Gerald Ford exercised his authority as president and pardoned Richard Nixon.

This pardon did not demonstrate Nixon was innocent. It simply meant he could not be arrested and prosecuted for those crimes. He was free to go, so to speak. This pardon did not eliminate his guilt, embarrassment, or shame but it did remove any fear of arrest and prosecution he might have had. He was officially forgiven.

Together guilt, shame, and fear can cripple us as we squarely face our sins and realize we have offended God and sinned against Him. Some people have even been hospitalized because of the emotional and psychological load guilt, shame, and fear can be. The Bible assures us in 1 John 1:9 that "if we confess our sins, He is faithful and just to forgive us our sins and to cleanse us from all unrighteousness."

Many of us struggle and strive to earn our forgiveness or to make peace with our violations of God's moral character. We want to believe His grace and we want to receive His grace. To many of us, His grace seems too good to be true. C.S. Lewis the great author read the four Gospels and concluded it was in fact too good to be true but he then set out to read them a second time. That second time through he concluded it was too good not to be true. If you are struggling with feelings of guilt, shame, and fear talk to God today. He stands ready to forgive you.

APRIL 12

Would you like to start all over again with a clean slate? With God you can. The Bible reveals that God, as our Heavenly Father offers us a new start. The Bible refers to this as the new birth or being born again.

When Jesus spoke with Nicodemus, recorded in John 3:1—21, He spoke about this new birth. Nicodemus was a good man, moral and upright. He believed in God and treated people well, but still Jesus told him he had to be born again. Nicodemus had not been born anew by the Holy Spirit. He had not experienced the supernatural touch from heaven.

Jesus explained that God wants to do a spiritual thing within us by entering and transforming us from the inside out. Nicodemus tried to understand it and even questioned how a grown man could be born all over again. Jesus explained it is not something that can be understood as much as it is something we must experience when we say yes to God. Jesus explained that we do not know from where the wind comes or where it goes but we see its effects and we hear it moving through the trees and across the meadow. So it is with everyone born of the Spirit.

Have you told God you want a new start? Ask Jesus to do this new birth within you. Ask Jesus to give you that new beginning. He will. He wants to do it today.

§

APRIL 13

God created the world. He splashed the stars across the sky and made the land and the sea, the animals and the fish, even the birds. God created it all super-naturally. He did not take what already existed to build the world. He created the world by speaking it into existence.

The Apostle Paul used creation language when he explained what happens to us when we turn our lives over to Jesus Christ. He wrote in 2 Corinthians 5:17 that we become a new creation. We kneel down one person and stand a brand new creation. This is not easy to understand or explain but millions of people throughout history have experienced this supernatural touch from God.

This facet of our salvation can be explained only with the supernatural language of creation. When we say yes to Jesus, the Holy Spirit works a new creation within us. The same Spirit introduced in Genesis 1:2, who hovered over the newly created world, is the One who creates within us what previously did not exist. We are not only changed; we are brand new. Have you experienced this yet? If not, why not ask Jesus to create you brand new today?

April 14

Do you ever wonder how to pray for someone to get saved? Do you ever wonder how to pray for someone to turn his or her life over to Jesus Christ? To exchange the guilt, shame, and fear for joy, peace, and hope is the very thing we want to happen in the life of an unbeliever.

We gain some insight into such prayer from Abraham as he sends his servant to find a wife for his son Isaac—a most intriguing story about a man who experiences the Lord's activity and guidance and then bows low and gives himself to the Lord in adoration and praise. Recorded in Genesis 24, the story is anything but boring.

Abraham influenced his oldest servant, Eliezer toward the Lord, his God. Abraham walked with the Lord daily. Eliezer witnessed this relationship between Abraham and the Lord. Over time Eliezer began to desire a similar relationship with the Lord.

So when you pray for persons to come to faith in Christ, one thing to pray is that God will order their activities in such a way to have them cross paths with coworkers or neighbors or friends who will influence them toward Jesus. Pray for those friends and coworkers who will share the story of Jesus. Pray for them to have a consistent attitude, speech, and temperament to authenticate their witness.

April 15

Have you ever wondered how to pray for non-Christians to get saved? Genesis 24 contains for us the example of Abraham's servant, Eliezer and his conversion to the Lord. At the beginning of the chapter, Eliezer prays to Abraham's God, but by the end of the chapter he is praying to the Lord who is now his God as well.

The circumstances in Eliezer's life pressured him to pray seeking guidance beyond his own common sense. Abraham sent him to find a wife for his son. The fear of failure or of choosing a selfish or harmful woman pressured Eliezer to pray to his master's god for success.

If we take that same principle we could pray that very same thing for our friends, coworkers, neighbors, or family members who are not believers in Jesus Christ. We could pray that God would organize the circumstances in their lives so they will feel pressured to pray for help or for guidance.

Now, this might sound somewhat harsh, asking God to pressure someone to pray. But it is similar to pressuring someone to take the medicine prescribed by a doctor. Prayer will not harm them, and neither will God.

§

April 16

Do you ever pray for someone to get saved and come to know Jesus as their Savior and Lord? Have you ever wondered how to pray such prayers?

The Apostle Paul gives us a hint in Romans 2:4. Paul wrote that it is the kindness or the goodness of God that leads to repentance. When we see God's kindness we are drawn to Him. We see difficulties, hatred, or war all over the world. But we find God to be kind and good. When we recognize that God blesses us, guides us, or encourages us, these expressions of kindness convince us to turn from our self—centered lives and turn toward Jesus—centered lives. God, the Holy Spirit draws us to Himself with His kindness.

You might have a friend or a family member who doesn't know Jesus as his or her savior. You might have a neighbor or a coworker who doesn't know about the blood of Jesus to wash away all the guilt, shame, and fear. So we pray God will speak to their hearts and show them all the ways He is kind to them.

In addition to God revealing His kindness, we also want to point out to them the various ways God has been kind to them knowing it is the kindness of God that will lead them to repentance.

APRIL 17

Did you know that a key to evangelism is simply telling your story? Instead of quoting the Ten Commandments, telling a person to repent, or arguing points of doctrine, simply tell the person how God has worked in your life.

Moses told his father-in-law, Jethro what the Lord had done on behalf of Israel, as recorded in Exodus 4—17, with his report recorded in chapter 18. Jethro was a priest of Midian. He was a professionally religious man. He led the people in worshipping Baal and Asherah, the main god and goddess of Midian.

In the ancient near east it is most common for gods and goddesses to be paired off in the religious development by each people group. That is one unique distinction about the Bible's self—revelation of the Lord. He does not have a female mate with whom He made the world. He created the world from nothing speaking it into existence instead of making it from materials already in existence. Jethro knew what he believed. A doctrinal discussion would have been pointless.

Moses did not argue various doctrines with Jethro. He simply told Jethro what the Lord had done for him and for the people. Jethro responded, "Now I know that the Lord is greater than all the other gods" (Ex. 18:11). After Jethro's statement he offered sacrifices, indicating he transferred his allegiance from Baal and Asherah to the Lord. For over three thousand years, Exodus 12:11 has stood to point to one fact: the Lord is supreme over all other gods of all people.

Instead of getting into doctrinal arguments about what you believe and do not believe, simply tell your family and friends what Jesus has done in your life.

April 18

Instead of telling a person to repent or discussing points of doctrine, a key to evangelism is simply telling your story. In spite of crushing agony, Naomi simply told her story to her daughter—in—law, Ruth, as recorded in Ruth 1:1—18.

Naomi had moved to Moab with her husband, Elimelech, because there was a great famine in Judah. Their sons grew up and married local girls. Then Naomi's husband died. Then both sons died.

Both daughters—in—law watched Naomi go through agony. Both watched her faith tested. Both watched and waited. Orpa returned to her people, but Ruth made a vow to go with Naomi to her land, to her people, and to follow her God. The Bible does not give us many details, but we can infer that the way Naomi handled her grief made allegiance to the Lord attractive to Ruth. Chemosh, the god of Moab, obviously could not support and encourage his followers in their times of trouble; however, the Lord proved His faithfulness throughout Naomi's pain. Naomi lived her faith through crushing agony. Ruth was convinced and turned to the Lord.

§

April 19

Andrew made a living as a professional fisherman. He was one of the first of the disciples to follow Jesus. He seemed to live in the shadow of his brother, Simon Peter, except for a few moments recorded in Scripture.

The Gospel of John records for us that Jesus was ministering to a large crowd when he told the disciples they needed to feed this crowd of thousands (John 6:1—15). No one knew what to do. Then Andrew introduced a boy to Jesus who had his own sack lunch with him. He had five small barley loaves of bread and two fish. The poor would use barley while the rich used wheat.

How much faith did Andrew have to have to think one boy's lunch would feed several thousand hungry people? Yet he brought it to Jesus. He brought this little bit to the Savior.

Jesus always honors real faith. He took that small lunch offered by a poor boy and fed the entire crowd, with baskets left over. If you put genuine trust in Jesus, He will honor your faith and cause your faith to grow. Do you have just a little bit of real faith you could offer to Him?

APRIL 20

Maybe you have read a book or two written by C. S. Lewis. In *The Chronicles of Narnia*, he presents the Gospel story in the fictional fantasy land of Narnia. In *Mere Christianity*, Lewis poses a logical defense of the Christian faith following Paul's similar logic in 1 Corinthians 15:12—34. He designs letters from the master demon, Screwtape, and his apprentice, Wormwood, in *The Screwtape Letters*. He taught medieval literature at Oxford University and at Cambridge University in England.

As a young man, Lewis read through the Bible books of Matthew, Mark, Luke, and John. He claimed the story of Jesus was just too good to be true, but he was intrigued enough by the Gospel account to read it through again. He decided the story of Jesus dying on the cross to bring salvation to the world was too good not to be true. He could not pass off the sheer logic of redemption.

Lewis reasoned that if God created this world, it was only right that He loves us with an incredible love and will go to any lengths to bring us back to Himself. So Lewis concluded Jesus shed His blood to reconcile us to God. He concluded that logic insists the Gospel story is indeed too good not to be true.

§

APRIL 21

After Jesus rose from the dead, John 21:1—14 records for us that He grilled a fish breakfast for His disciples over a charcoal fire. This word is translated from the original Greek manuscripts as "charcoal fire" in some English Bibles, but only translated "fire" in other English Bibles. In this case it matters. The only other place where that specific Greek word is used in the entire New Testament, is in John 18:18, when Peter begins to deny Jesus three times while warming himself beside a charcoal fire.

Jesus uses the sights, sounds, and smells distinctive to a charcoal fire to take Peter back, psychologically, to his biggest blunder, and then asks, "Do you love me more than these?" Three times Peter denied Jesus around a charcoal fire, and then three times, around a charcoal fire, Jesus asks him, "Do you love me?" giving Peter the opportunity to reaffirm his love and allegiance to Jesus.

Jesus, the master psychotherapist, takes Peter back to his biggest blunder and speaks about His plans for Peter. He doesn't throw Peter away. Sure, Peter blew it, and so have you. But Jesus's love and grace go past the failures and He stays focused on His incredible love for you and His amazing dreams for you.

April 22

Jack walked through the gate after twenty-six years in and out of prison. At the age of thirty-eight, he was getting another chance. About ten years earlier, Jack had asked Jesus to forgive him, to be his Savior and Lord and give him the life the Bible promised. Jesus honored that prayer.

Jack used those last ten years in prison to grow in faith. He read his Bible and prayed. He found the challenge and promise of Psalm 119:11: "I have hidden Your word in my heart that I might not sin against You." He memorized over forty chapters of the Bible.

A friend had made arrangements for Jack with a halfway house, a church and its pastor, and a men's accountability group. Jack married six months later, and together he and his wife had five children. Jack maintained a job. He and his wife bought a house and paid it off in less than ten years. Their five children grew up in that house.

God really does restore, reconcile, and make new. Do you need God to come into your life and work something new for you? He's the Master at fixing broken lives. Why not ask Him to fix your life today?

§

April 23

A mission team from Kentucky arrived in the Dominican Republic. Plumbers, skilled carpenters, and electricians planned to renovate a school. Sally knew God wanted her to go, but without any of these skills, she did not know why.

The local children were against the plan. In order to renovate the school, all the walls would have to be gutted, repaired, and repainted. Cartoons painted all over the walls would be torn out or covered forever. When the schoolteacher explained this to the mission team Sally began to weep. The team leader commented on her empathy for the children and suggested the team begin to pray for an answer.

Then Sally announced, "My hobby for the last thirty years has been cartoon art." The Apostle Paul wrote about the intentional variety of gifts the Holy Spirit gives people for ministry in 1 Corinthians 12:4—5: "Now there are a variety of gifts but the same Spirit. There are varieties of ministries and the same Lord."

So while the others renovated the school, Sally taught two hundred children how to draw cartoons. Later the children painted cartoons back onto the walls. Sally had resisted going because she was not a skilled plumber or electrician, but she became the key to their success.

APRIL 24

God caused the ground to bring forth all the trees, which were pleasing to the sight and good for food (Gen. 2:9). The Bible also records that God placed the tree of the knowledge of good and evil in the middle of the Garden of Eden.

There were hundreds, maybe thousands of fruit trees in the garden. Sweet limes, star fruit, oranges, cherries, apples, bananas, and coconuts all would have been found in the Garden. In contrast there was only one tree of the knowledge of good and evil.

God told Adam and Eve to enjoy the thousands of nutritious, beautiful trees. He told them the one tree of the knowledge of good and evil would kill them (2:17) and to avoid it at all costs.

God always wants life for us. God always wants us to enjoy this world. He created its abundance to be enjoyed; however, at the same time there are limits.

Sin is not logical. To eat from the one tree promised to kill us while there are thousands promising us nutrition and health simply is not logical.

Once Eve and Adam began to suspect God's character and to suspect His plans for their lives, their logic went crazy. They believed harmful lies and disregarded health and truth. Harming ourselves in any way is not the will of God. His will for us is good, and His will for us is life.

§

APRIL 25

You might have heard the story about the Garden of Eden from the Bible. In Genesis 2:9—17 God gives thousands of nutritious, beautiful fruit trees to Adam and Eve but tells them to avoid the tree of the knowledge of good and evil. He placed that lone tree right in the middle of the garden.

Why would God place that tree in the middle of the garden instead of out on the fringes somewhere? As a parent, if I do not want my children handling something dangerous, I put it in a place where it will be hard for them to find it and, consequently, hard for them to handle it and be harmed by it. However, God placed that one tree in the middle of the Garden, in the center of their home area, in the middle of their world.

Obedience to God is not a fringe issue in our lives. The tree was placed in the middle of the garden because trusting and obeying God is at the center of our lives. Trust and obedience is what determines life and death. God told them to choose life. We have the power to choose life. Will we trust God and obey Him? Life's choices might not be easy but they are simple.

April 26

Has anyone ever lied about you? If so, you probably have experienced a confusing variety of emotions in response. Maybe that experience will help you appreciate the steadfastness of a young man named Joseph who avoided resentment. Through it all he grew better instead of bitter.

As recorded for us in Genesis 39:1—23, the Egyptian palace guard unit had a commanding officer named Potipher, whose wife was a conniving woman. She tried repeatedly to seduce her main servant, a young, attractive man named Joseph.

Even though Joseph was single and available, and even though she wouldn't tell anyone, Joseph believed it was wrong. Nevertheless, she pursued him, but he refused to buckle under the pressure. One day she tore off his clothes, but he still avoided her and ran out of the room. She screamed.

When the Egyptian guards ran to her rescue, she lied about Joseph trying to assault her, and Joseph went to prison. While in prison, instead of growing bitter, Joseph grew better. He concentrated on getting to know God. In addition to this specific event, you can read his entire biography in Genesis 37—50 to discover his secret to happiness. His example and perspective has guided people for over 3000 years.

April 27

Allow me for a moment to use updated language to tell you about Joseph. Joseph's ten older brothers were all jealous and hateful toward him. He was Dad's favorite. So they planned to get rid of him. They threw him into a sinkhole on the family farm and left him for dead. They later sold him to a group of traveling salesmen who carried him out of the country and eventually resold him in the human trafficking slave market in Egypt.

How could anyone forgive his or her brothers for such things? But Joseph never held a grudge. Twenty-two years later he came face—to—face with his brothers and told them, "You meant to harm me, but God meant it for good" (Gen. 50:20). Joseph had learned that God always redeems the hurts, habits, and hang ups in our lives.

In Joseph's story, he talks about those days as a slave in Egypt, and he talks about his relationship with God. He talks about how God protected him and redeemed his situation.

Joseph points out a significant theological or religious distinction. He never says God caused this to happen indicating the common misunderstanding that God is in control of everything, but he talks about how God was in charge of the whole thing bringing good from the tragedy and how he drew closer to God during this time of troubles. It is a distinction the Bible makes repeatedly that God is in charge but not in control. He has given us a free will and in Joseph's case, his brothers used their free will to harm him. Joseph talks about how God can be trusted even among such tragic events. You can read Joseph's story in Genesis 37—50.

APRIL 28

Do you take responsibility for your decisions and for the consequences of your decisions? The Apostle Paul wrote in the love chapter, 1 Corinthians 13:11, that when he was a child, he thought like a child, but when he became a man he put away childish things.

I wonder if he was thinking about Adam and Eve when he made that statement. When God asked Adam if he had eaten from the forbidden tree, Adam blamed Eve (Gen. 3:11—12). And then Eve blamed the serpent (Gen. 3:13). Both Adam and Eve refused to take responsibility for their own decisions.

This pattern of passing the buck is childish. It is what children do. They lie. They confuse situations with excuses and try to justify or rationalize selfish or destructive behavior. Children try to deflect blame from themselves and place it on another person or on the circumstances of the situation. They reject the power of their free will and present their decisions as victimization. In contrast to this, as Paul wrote, adults put away childish ways of thinking and reasoning. Adults take responsibility for their decisions.

§

APRIL 29

Within the pages of the Bible, various persons succumb to peer pressure. As recorded in Exodus 32:1—35, Aaron, the first high priest for Israel, crafted a golden calf idol from the gold earrings and gold jewelry of the people. He used bellows to heat up the fire to melt the gold and then poured the gold into a mold, forming the golden calf. But why would a leader of Israel make an idol?

The people took a poll. They voted on the popular opinion. They made it clear to their leader what they wanted, and they wanted the leader to lead them away from the Lord. They wanted to reject the God who had set them free from Egyptian slavery. They wanted to turn their back on all the Lord had done for them. They wanted their leader to lead them away from what was right and what was true. They wanted self-interest and self-indulgence to rule and reign.

Aaron did just that. He led them according to the wishes of the popular poll. He lacked the courage needed to lead against popular opinion. His cowardice drove him to seek popularity instead of truth. Leaders need the prayers of the people for courage to avoid the cowardice temptation for popularity and for courage to lead in truth and righteousness.

APRIL 30

"Bitterness is like taking poison and hoping the other person dies." So the adage goes. If bitterness is our attitude, if we hold unforgiveness in our hearts, then we are actually poisoning our own bodies, according to modern research. Various toxins are constantly released into our bodies that can result in high blood pressure, diabetes, heart disease, and even some cancers.

Just as bitterness releases toxins into our bodies, joy and laughter release chemicals that strengthen our health and resistance to disease. We have discovered a greater chemical interdependence between our bodies and minds and spirits, proving Solomon knew something when he wrote, "A joyful heart is good medicine but a broken spirit dries up the bones" (Prov. 17:22). From this proverb of Solomon we formed our adage "Laughter is the best medicine."

We harm ourselves because of our own resentments. The Apostle Paul tells us in Ephesians 4:32, "Be kind to one another, tender hearted, forgiving each other just as God in Christ also has forgiven you." Do not be deceived into bringing more harm to yourself. Forgive that person who harmed you.

MAY 1

Robert Freeman points out that "character is not made in a crisis; it is only exhibited." This principle of life can certainly be seen in the life of Charles, a missionary to inland China around 1915.

Charles and his family relied on the financial support from home that would arrive in the mail to buy their food and other needs. One day they received double what they needed for the entire month, and Charles rejoiced. "Praise God forever. He knows what a bunch of grumblers and complainers we are. He sent us enough to keep us quiet for a few days."

Another time they received nothing in the delivery, and Charles rejoiced. "Praise God forever. We are close to heaven, for the Bible says the Kingdom of God is neither meat nor drink but righteousness, peace, and joy in the Holy Spirit" (Rom. 14:17).

Have you found this to be true in your life—that difficulties reveal the character you have developed to that point? When you have hardships, do you remain calm in your spirit and patient with others? Have you learned to trust God?

§

MAY 2

Few people in our world discover the secret of contentment. Have you learned what others seem to already know—that one of the most difficult things in life is to be content in any and every situation? The Apostle Paul wrote, "In any and every circumstance, I have learned the secret of being filled and going hungry, both of having abundance and suffering need" (Phil. 4:12).

After Paul revealed the secret, he wrote, "I can do all things through Christ who strengthens me" (Phil. 4:13). Paul made it clear that accomplishing all things through Christ has nothing to do with winning a championship ball game, becoming a millionaire, or even overcoming cancer.

The circumstances of life had nothing to do with whether or not Paul would be content. He found his contentment with God, who is good and trustworthy. In spite of any circumstances, Paul found his contentment in Jesus who died for his sins and who has risen again to give Paul new life. Try Paul's secret to contentment. A life hidden with Christ might work for you too.

MAY 3

Cletus Beam, a retired teacher and coach in Ohio, reminded his family and friends that "God is in the business of giving another chance. That's why we have Mondays."

Regardless of your blunder or mistake, don't grow discouraged. God has not given up on you. The Apostle Paul wrote this to the church in Thessalonica: "Encourage one another and build up one another, just as you also are doing" (1 Thess. 5:11).

Day after day, year after year, the prophets would call out to the people of God to stay faithful to Him. Many times we give so much attention to the message, we neglect to recognize what lies behind it; the incredible, amazing love God has for you. He refuses to give up on you. He believes in you. No matter what you do, He will not love you less, nor will He love you more. So if you've fallen flat on your face, even fallen repeatedly, don't give up on yourself, because God Himself will not give up on you. God always, always, always has hope for you.

§

MAY 4

One day years ago, a victory was confused with a defeat. When Jesus hung on the cross, the disciples ran away, scattered just as Zechariah had written centuries earlier (Zech. 13:7). The public thought Jesus had lost. The disciples went into hiding. They thought they had lost. They thought Jesus was gone forever.

What the disciples did not understand on that day but began to understand three days later was that in dying Jesus overcame sin and death. Isaiah 53:1—12 records for us that He overcame sin and sorrow. Then, three days later, came the extraordinary news: Jesus was alive. He had even overcome death.

Jesus had not been defeated at all. He had known the entire time that within just a matter of hours He would rise. If you had been there and had listened closely, you might have heard Him whisper, "Checkmate."

The match was over. Satan lost. Sin lost. Death lost. While Jesus was in the grave the Bible tells us He entered Hell to speak to Noah's generation (1 Pet. 3:18—20). Then with His resurrection Jesus stood victorious over Satan, sin, and death. Never be confused. Jesus is victorious.

MAY 5

So often we confuse our Christian faith with a list of rules and regulations. We put together our lists of doctrines. Individuals do this. Churches do this. We tell people they have to believe certain things in order to be Christians. We give them lists, and they have to align their lives accordingly, or we do not let them join our group. Philosophical agreement is not Christian faith.

As recorded in the Bible, Jesus told people, "Follow Me" (Matt. 4:19, Mark 1:17). He was inviting people into a friendship or a relationship with Himself. He did not give them a list to follow. He gave them Himself. Eternal life is not a mansion in heaven. Eternal life is to know Jesus (John 17:3).

In order to follow Jesus today, Christians have to read their Bible and pray regularly. By reading our Bible, we hear what God has to say. By praying we speak to God. Following Jesus primarily involves cultivating that relationship between Jesus and myself. It is so much easier just to have a list. You do not have to read much. You certainly don't have to pray. You just have to check it off each day. Jesus said, "Follow Me." Are you following a list, or are you following Him?

§

MAY 6

When I was growing up, I heard a lot of preaching about getting saved so you can avoid Hell or so you can go to Heaven when you die. The Bible spends very little time talking about Heaven and Hell.

Page after page the Bible offers the possibility of walking every day with the living God. The book of Genesis barely mentions the afterlife in any form. It focuses its fifty chapters spanning thousands of years on stories about seven men who walked with God in the here and now (Adam, Enoch, Noah, Abraham, Isaac, Jacob, and Joseph).

Jesus is not the lead character in a fairy tale or some statue you place in your meditation room. He did not start a religion somewhere but now lies comfortably in his grave. Jesus is the one true God (1 John 5:20). After writing that statement, John finished his letter with "Little children, guard yourselves from idols" (1 John 5:21). Guard yourself from false religions and false gods.

The opportunity to walk and talk with Jesus can be enjoyed day in and day out. It is a promise for the here and now—a lifetime adventure with God.

MAY 7

Are you satisfied with life? The old adventure of the 1960s and '70s of "finding yourself" is still alive today in many places.

The Bible can help us with this pursuit of self—fulfillment. Listen to the Apostle Paul's letter to the Galatians (Gal. 2:20) as spelled out in the New American Standard Translation: "I have been crucified with Christ. And it is no longer I who live, but Christ lives in me. And the life I now live, I live by faith in the Son of God who loved me and gave Himself for me."

In the Bible the number seven indicates completeness. In this verse Paul makes reference to himself seven times. He has died to himself, and Jesus Christ has taken up residence in Paul's life. Now Paul lives entirely and exclusively for Jesus.

Paul not only states this clearly but he also forms this nonverbal literary structure. He refers to himself seven times as a subconscious statement of self-fulfillment. Paul claims a life lived entirely and exclusively for Jesus is a life of self-fulfillment. I do not know about you, but I want self-fulfillment.

MAY 8

St. Francis of Assisi would tell us to "keep a clear eye toward life's end. Do not forget your purpose and destiny as God's creature. What you are in His sight is what you are and nothing more and nothing less. Remember that when you leave this earth, you can take nothing you have received, but only what you have given; a full heart enriched by honest service, love, sacrifice and courage." When St. Francis wrote this, it is possible he was pondering Hebrews 12:1—2: "Let us run with endurance the race that is set before us, fixing our eyes on Jesus."

With that list from St. Francis, it is hard to keep our eyes on the end goal. It is hard to stay focused on what is important. With so much life to live, work to accomplish, and ministry to undergo, who can stay focused on the end goal?

So often we turn our attention to what is urgent instead of what is important. Many successful business owners and executives regret investing more time in work than in family. I have never heard of anyone facing death wishing they had attended more committee meetings or filled out more paperwork. Do everything you can to focus your time and attention to the real priorities of your life.

MAY 9

Have you heard of the battle between David and Goliath recorded for us in 1 Samuel 17:1—58? It's possibly the most famous battle in history—and quite possibly the most misunderstood battle.

Goliath stood almost nine feet tall while David was a teenager of normal size. Goliath had been a warrior his entire adult life handling sword and spear, while David had shepherded sheep with a staff and a slingshot. Goliath spoke defiantly to the king while David spoke with respect. Goliath challenged anyone foolish enough to fight him. David took up the challenge. Goliath had insulted David's people and David's God with each taunt (1 Sam. 17:8-10). When Goliath cursed David in the name of Dagon and other gods threatening to give David's flesh to the birds, (1 Sam. 17:43) David no longer stood to listen. He made his reply and charged at Goliath.

David stood up for the Lord (1 Sam. 17:45). More than a battle between a giant and an opportunistic youth, the Bible records this as a battle to prove superiority between Dagon, the god of Philistia, and the Lord, the God of Israel. Consistently throughout the Old Testament, the Lord proves His superiority over the gods of other groups and nations. The living God, the Lord stands above all other gods.

§

MAY 10

The battle between David and Goliath recorded in 1 Samuel 17:1—58 is quite possibly the most famous battle in history—the trained warrior against the untrained man, pride and defiance against honor and faith. Each took his stand. Each chose his weapon. Each entered battle in the name of his god.

Goliath wanted to conquer and enslave the Israelites for his own honor while David wanted to defend the honor of his people and the honor of his God. David closed the distance, running toward Goliath. He placed a stone into his sling and swirled that sling at an increasing centrifugal speed. He released the sling, and the stone struck Goliath's head, sinking into his skull sending him to the ground. David needed to know Goliath was dead, so he took Goliath's own sword and cut off Goliath's head.

The Bible records that God gave David the victory that day, that God delivered David from the hand of Goliath and delivered the Israelites from the hands of the Philistines. David stood for the honor of the Lord. Maybe that is why he is listed as a man after God's own heart (1 Sam. 13:14). God still looks for men and women who will stand up for His honor. Obviously I am not suggesting killing other people, but maybe we stay quiet when God needs a champion to speak.

MAY 11

In 1981 a young man attempted to assassinate Pope John Paul II but failed. Later the Pope met with the man and pronounced forgiveness for him. Within what we commonly call The Lord's Prayer, we find the line "forgive us our trespasses as we forgive those who trespass against us" (Matt. 6:12).

After being shot, the pope forgave the man who shot him. This forgiveness is not natural. It is supernatural. To forgive someone who has harmed you is a supernatural thing, the result of having been touched by the supernatural God, transformed from the inside out by the grace of God.

The supernatural demonstration that we are Christians is the evidence of grace in our lives—not the demonstration that we have received grace but the demonstration that we offer grace. Jesus asked God to forgive his killers (Luke 23:34). Stephen forgave his killers while they stoned him (Acts 7:60).

When God has supernaturally touched us, forgiveness will be a way of life for us. Have you been touched by God? Is grace a way of life for you?

§

MAY 12

Have you heard of Daniel and the lions' den? Israel had been taken into slavery. After the Babylonian army besieged and conquered Jerusalem, the soldiers took Daniel to the foreign country of Babylon where he was identified as a youth with extraordinary leadership qualities (Dan. 1:1—7).

The Babylonians trained Daniel to give leadership in the foreign land even as a slave, and this he did for the rest of his life. About sixty-five years later, the Babylonian nation fell to the Medes and the Persians. Daniel was sixty-five years older, sixty-five years wiser.

The other advisors to King Darius the Mede connived against Daniel, convincing Darius to pass a law making it illegal to pray to anyone or any god except the king for thirty days (Dan. 6:1—28). Nevertheless, Daniel continued to pray to the Lord, and because he was caught praying to the Lord he was thrown to the lions.

You probably know the rest of the story. Daniel lived. He thrived. He excelled. When you experience pressure to compromise your religious convictions about Jesus Christ, do you remain faithful to God? If you have to make that choice today, what will you choose?

MAY 13

During America's war with Vietnam, a grenade exploded beside Dave Rievers. He rolled over in a mud puddle, looked up to heaven, lifted his arm, pointed his finger, and spoke these words to God: "I still trust You."

Dave had learned that God loves him. He had learned God is good. He had learned God offers grace so our sins can be forgiven, and he learned people could harm one another. So he found himself in a mud puddle at midnight in South Vietnam, realizing he really did believe God loves him and that he really did love and trust God—similar to Job's discovery: "Even though He slay me, yet will I hope in Him" (Job 13:15).

God's grace had permeated Dave to the point that his faith and loyalty to God stayed true in the most difficult of circumstances. He trusted God. His deep, deep joy remained in spite of the tragedies of life.

Have you learned this level of loyalty and love? God has the grace to work in your life at the same deep level He worked in Job's and Dave's lives. Ask God to do that deeper work in your heart. Ask Him to do it today.

§

MAY 14

In the 1950s Easter movie classic *The Robe*, a paralyzed woman sings about the love of Jesus. She sings. She smiles. She blesses everyone who comes to listen to her songs about Jesus.

Within one of those scenes, Tribune Gallio questions this joy of hers and points out that she is still paralyzed. Jesus could have healed her, but He did not.

An elderly man points out that previously she had been bitter and hateful. He points out that she had been shriveling up inside from her bitterness. Then Jesus touched her, and she became joyful, loving, and kind.

It is natural to be joyful, loving, and kind when your circumstances are positive and go your way. But when you are joyful, loving, and kind in spite of unpleasant circumstances, that is a touch from the supernatural God that goes beyond forgiveness. I realize this is a movie, but many people testify to such deep grace working in their lives. Many people testify that God not only has forgiven them but He has sanctified them entirely (1 Thess. 5:23). Paul makes such a hope and prayer for the Thessalonians. We can receive this level of grace also.

MAY 15

Tommy moved into a trailer park beside a Christian named Joe. The first night he used a flashlight as he tried to fix his car. Instead of offering help, Joe handed Tommy the keys to his own car and said, "Take my car for tonight and you can fix yours tomorrow in the daylight."

Tommy replied, "People don't do that." Joe smiled. "People who know Jesus might, and I am one of them."

Over the next several months, Tommy and Joe became friends. They ate a lot of spaghetti together because Joe knew how to boil water and open a jar of sauce. Joe concentrated on becoming an authentic friend to Tommy instead of using Tommy as his winter evangelism project. They went backpacking in the Smokies, and Joe trusted God to work in Tommy's heart.

Jesus told us to "make disciples," not "get decisions" (Matt. 28:19). It takes time and energy to make a disciple. Normally such a process will also result in a lifetime friend.

If you are a Christian, are you making friends of unbelievers? If not, try it for a year. You will not only be faithful to Jesus; you will gain a new friend.

§

MAY 16

Two Christians, David and Joe, invited Tommy on a hiking trip to the Smokies. They invited him for one reason: he was not a Christian, and they wanted an opportunity to witness for Jesus.

While on the trail, they told stories about each other, swung on vines, walked away from bear cubs further up the trail, avoided timber rattlers, and even stayed dry during the storms. Tommy, though a little suspicious of the invitation, enjoyed the time immensely. These Christians really were a lot of fun.

As they drove home, Tommy stayed quiet. Later he mentioned to Joe that he had never seen any two people love each other like David and Joe, and there was nothing sexual about it. "Even my own parents do not love each other like that." Tommy really did not understand such love between two persons.

Their evangelism had worked. Instead of preaching or demanding anything of Tommy, they simply enjoyed a backpacking trip together. Jesus said in John 13:34—35 that His followers would prove to the world they belong to Him if they love one another. Tommy would never be the same again.

May 17

In Genesis 1:26—27, the very first chapter of the Bible, humanity is created in the image of God. God created them male and female; He deliberately created opposites.

We are either female or male, not interchangeable, not a combination, as Plato tried to explain. God set us apart from all the rest of creation. He made the sun and moon, earth and sea, darkness and light. He deliberately created opposites.

God caused vegetation to sprout and even made the animals. Whether caterpillars, butterflies, lions, or bears, He made them all. He created the angels. He made the stingrays, barracudas, and sea turtles. He made the blue jays, penguins, ostriches, eagles, and yellow finches. He made it all, but only one thing He gave enough love and care, such intricacy and attention, to create it in His image. Only one thing carries the value of God's image.

Distinct within all of creation, God created men and women in His image. Did you know God holds you in such high esteem? Out of all of creation, He has placed the highest value on you. Above the birds and the whales, above the sun, Jupiter, and even the angels, you are created in the image of God. Let's treat each other and ourselves with respect and value.

§

May 18

Before their senior year of high school, Dan and Don attended a youth revival in a little country church where they met the living Christ. They asked Jesus to forgive them of their sins and to come into their hearts as their Savior and Lord. They vowed to live for Christ, pledging their loyalty to Jesus.

Two weeks later summer football practice began. The other players ridiculed Dan and Don, causing the locker room to become a hostile environment where the other players cursed the name of Jesus. As Paul wrote to Timothy, "Indeed, all who desire to live godly in Christ Jesus will be persecuted" (2 Tim. 3:12).

Toward the end of the twentieth century, the Roman Catholic Church published research indicating there had been more Christians martyred in the twentieth century than in the first nineteen centuries combined. The world had grown in its hostility toward Jesus and toward the people of Jesus.

Dan and Don relied on each other, and they kept their pledge to Jesus. They stayed faithful to Him even amid the persecution. Dan became a physician, and Don a helicopter pilot. Both faced persecution and stayed faithful to Jesus.

MAY 19

In Matthew 25:31—46, Jesus told His disciples that when we feed the hungry, clothe the naked, give aid to the sick, and visit those in prison, we are actually doing a ministry to Jesus. Likewise, when we neglect those people identified by Jesus, we neglect Him.

We know about Mother Teresa. She worked with some of the world's poorest people in Calcutta, India. The reports tell us that when the other nuns would speak of their fatigue, she would say something like, "Yes, you are tired. You have worked hard. Now go minister to someone lying in the street." She knew they could always find someone in need. She saw Jesus in the faces of the poor in the streets.

Standing less than five feet tall, she was one of the toughest people in history. A couple of biographers have written that she began every day at 4:30 a.m. on her face, in prayer to Jesus. She was madly in love with Jesus, who empowered her with His love. She knew Him, and she knew Him well.

Have you learned how to receive this empowering love from Jesus? He does not play favorites. He will empower anyone who will draw close to Him.

§

MAY 20

Not too many years ago, a reporter from America was sent to India to do a story on the Sisters of Charity, an order of nuns working among some of the poorest people in the world living in Calcutta. These are the nuns who take Jesus seriously when He said that when we feed the hungry, clothe the naked, give aid to the sick, and visit those in prison we are actually doing a ministry to Jesus (Matthew 25:31—46).

The reporter interviewed several nuns about their calling to that particular ministry. The reporter took photographs of leprosy patients standing in line. While smelling the stench of rotting flesh, the reporter commented to one of the nuns about her work, "Sister, I admire you. I wouldn't do that for a million dollars."

The nun looked up briefly from bandaging a leprosy patient, smiled, and replied, "I wouldn't either. But for Jesus I will do anything."

She had discovered the love of Jesus. Have you discovered how much Jesus loves you? His love for you is incredible, amazing, and complete. If you have not discovered the love of Jesus, why not talk to Him today?

May 21

When the University of Chicago recruited Karl Barth to come from Germany to lecture, he asked they arrange for him to preach at Cook County Jail. They did.

Late in Dr. Barth's life, a young reporter seemed annoyed at the idea of interviewing the elderly theologian for his newspaper. So he asked, "Dr. Barth, you have been teaching about God for many years throughout Europe and America. You have written immensely. You preached against the Nazi regime during the 1930s and 1940s. What's the most profound thing you have learned in your illustrious career?"

Without much thought Dr. Barth replied, "Jesus loves me, this I know, for the Bible tells me so."

Obviously disappointed, the young reporter asked, "That's it? That's the most profound thing you have learned?"

Dr. Barth replied, "If you understand how and why Jesus loves us, explain it to me. I stopped trying to understand it years ago and just decided to accept it and enjoy it. My life has never been the same since that decision."

§

May 22

A World War II France air force pilot named Antoine de Saint-Exupery, known for being a great writer, wrote one day, "If you want to build a ship, don't summon people to buy wood, prepare tools, distribute jobs, and organize the work. Rather, teach people the yearning for the wide, boundless ocean."

God shares this philosophy. Read John 3:16: "For God so loved the world that He gave His only begotten Son, that whosoever believes in Him should not perish, but have everlasting life." Or read Romans 5:8: "God demonstrates His own love for us in this while we were still sinners, Christ died for us." Or read the end of Romans 8:39: "Nor any other created thing will be able to separate us from the love of God which is in Christ Jesus our Lord."

God does not try to convert us with fear, guilt, or shame. The Bible teaches that God tries to win us over with His love. God's love motivates us more than anything else. God's love wins our allegiance. God's love draws us to Him stronger than anything else in all of creation.

MAY 23

When Jesus came, He came with a specific purpose. He came with a plan, a strategy laid out in detail from the heart of God.

The scholars tell us there are over three hundred different prophecies in the Old Testament fulfilled in Jesus and His life. They tell us He followed a well—crafted script that took the Holy Spirit more than a thousand years to speak from the mouth of the prophets. The scholars remind us that only God could have told us so many details centuries in advance about one person.

I am not convinced our society believes in God. The polls tell us as many as 90 percent of Americans believe in God. Acknowledging His existence and following His teachings are worlds apart.

Jesus said, "You are the salt of the earth" (Matt. 5:13). If I took a ten—ounce steak and put nine ounces of salt on it, that piece of meat would no longer taste like meat. It would taste entirely of salt. If 90 percent of our society believes, then by simple logic our society would look almost entirely like Jesus. Acknowledging His existence and believing, obviously, are very different.

MAY 24

On his twenty-first birthday, Thomas received a card from his mom. He was challenged and affirmed when he read her message. It went something like this.

My dear Thomas,

Twenty-one years ago, I gave you birth, but God gave you life. I have reared you the best I knew how. I took you to church and taught you to pray, to be honest, to be courageous, and to be compassionate. I encouraged you to become a man of integrity.

I will always be your mother, and I will always love you and support you, but today you turn twenty-one years old. You are now a man. I expect you to make your own decisions, earn your own way, and build your life as a man who honors God.

You are a man. Think like a man. Speak like a man. Treat others like a man. Act like a man. Put away all childish ways of thinking, of speaking, and of acting (1 Cor. 13:11). Be the man God created you to be.

I will always love you,
Mom

What a fantastic gift to give a son. Declare him to be a man. Give clear expectations regarding his thinking, speaking, and acting. Then send him into the world to soar.

MAY 25

The day came when the disciples of Jesus asked Him to teach them to pray just like John the Baptist had taught his disciples to pray (Luke 11:1—13). Notice they did not ask Jesus to teach them *how to pray* but instead to teach them *to pray*.

Why did they ask this? Why would a group of grown men who attended worship services every week ask someone, anyone, to teach them to pray? Why would they admit by their question that they did not make prayer a habit? Why would Peter, the one who seemed to think he had all the answers, risk looking like a child by asking such a question?

Was this question rooted in the fact that they had just witnessed Jesus at prayer? Was it because they noticed something in Jesus and in John the Baptist that they themselves were missing but wanted? Did they see an intimacy with God that was attractive to them? Did they recognize a lack of trust in their own lives but see that trust in John and in Jesus? Did they realize they really did not walk with God? Why would they ask this question? Why would you ask?

MAY 26

Do you struggle with a hang-up or habit? Have you ever been hurt and just can't seem to get past it? When you read about Jesus telling us He came so we might have life and have it abundantly (John 10:10), do you ask, "Where's my abundant life?" Do you wonder when, if ever, God is going to bless you with all these blessings from heaven He seems to shower on others?

Are you in a family that seems to drain the life from your very soul? Do you feel like you just cannot go on sometimes? Well, have I got good news for you.

If you are struggling with any hurt, habit, or hang-up, Jesus specializes in bringing healing, recovery, and reconciliation. The wonderful Counselor, the master Therapist who brings peace, joy, and hope into your life, Jesus wants to patch up the wounds, wipe away the tears, and mend your broken heart.

Sometimes we need people to help us connect with Jesus. Locate a church in your community. Speak with the pastor. Speak with twenty pastors if necessary until you find one who knows how to connect you with Jesus, who brings abundant life.

MAY 27

The Bible speaks of Job, who lost his ten children and every grandchild in one day as a wind burst (maybe a tornado or straight—line wind) exploded the house where they had gathered for a party. He lost all his livestock and all his farmhands to murdering thieves. He did not however, lose his integrity.

Later he came down with a massive case of shingle—like blisters and infected boils covering his entire body. We can read about the severe itch that drove him to bust a piece of pottery and use a broken shard to scratch himself.

Through all this heartache and disease, we hear about the patience of Job, how he endured. He did not stay happy. He did not maintain his joy. He sang no songs, nor did he entertain at any parties, but he did not turn from God.

Job had integrity. Blessings did not bribe him, nor did heartaches turn him away. He said, "Even though God slays me, I will hope in Him" (Job 13:15). One day Job announced, "I know that my Redeemer lives and one day will stand on the earth" (Job 19:25). Job knew he had no one else but God, nowhere else to turn but to God. His trust in God was real. Have you learned yet to have such a real faith? Have you learned to turn to God?

§

MAY 28

In the first two chapters of Job, Satan accuses God of buying Job's faithfulness with health and wealth: "You have built a hedge around him and around everything that he has" (Job 1:10). God's eyes narrow; His voice drops. He defends Job. Job is the real deal. He cannot be bought.

Good or bad, through health or sickness, Job is no hypocrite. He is not a fair—weather fan of God. He does not grow independent and self-reliant, thinking he is a self—made man. The blessings from God are not a payoff.

Job has integrity. His devotion to God cannot be bought. His loyalty does not go to the highest bidder. His allegiance is to his Maker and only to his Maker. Satan accuses Job of not caring for his children and caring only for his own comfort: "Skin for skin...touch his bone and his flesh and he will curse you to your face" (Job 2:4—5). That loyalty, that allegiance, is tested and tried.

God sends Satan home beaten, fully aware that Job is beyond his reach. Job wins. The battle is long and hard. But Job proves it is possible to have faith in God, genuine faith. Can you be bought, or can God trust you?

MAY 29

Many people confess they have asked God for a sign, something that confirms they are going in the right direction. Every so often we need a little boost, just a nudge of encouragement.

If you feel this way from time to time, you are in pretty good company. The Bible speaks of Moses, eighty years old, looking for a simple retirement with no drama. Instead the Lord told him to go back into Egypt and lead the nation of Israel out of slavery (Exod. 3:7—10).

Moses declared he was not the man God needed to go to Egypt, yet in Exodus 3:12 the Bible records God's reply: "You will know I have sent you when you are back here worshipping me at this mountain."

There is an old adage that says hindsight is always twenty—twenty, and that is the very thing God offered to Moses. To paraphrase his reply, he said when Moses looked back he would recognize how God had led him every step of the way.

So be encouraged if the Lord leads you with hindsight also. He did it with Moses. He wants you to step forward according to His proven faithfulness.

§

MAY 30

Steve stood on the sidewalk looking north up the coast at the rain. He looked south down the coast at the rain. He looked out over the ocean at the rain, and he looked up into the mountains at the rain, but it was not raining where he was standing. It was raining all around him, but it was not raining on him.

Steve was a heroin addict who had been invited to a barbecue. He thought it would be a great way to get some food, since all his money had gone for drugs. So, when he pointed out to another guest that it was not raining, the other guest replied, "We asked God to hold back the rain so we could have this barbecue." Obviously they trusted Jesus, who had stated, "Everything you ask in prayer, believing, you will receive" (Matt. 21:22).

Even though Steve decided to eat some food and keep a safe distance from these Christians, God had other plans for him. The host, Henry, shared the love of Jesus with Steve and spoke of His interest and plans for Steve. Henry then knelt down and prayed, weeping for Steve. Steve joined Henry kneeling and called out to God, and God met Steve that day, cleansed him, and rescued him.

May 31

Henry and Muriel drove their car into a drug commune in Australia. They had heard about a young mother and her difficulties and wanted to help her. So when they arrived at the commune, Henry, seventy years old, stepped out of his car and shouted, "Praise the Lord." The heroin addicts had all seen some pretty weird stuff, and Henry was no exception, praising God, car loaded with food and money for a homeless mother.

When Steve approached Henry and Muriel to ask them what they wanted, Henry told him of the young lady. Steve asked if he was her father, uncle, or cousin, any relation at all. Henry declined all those options and simply replied, "We are Christians, and this is what Jesus would do." Obviously Henry and Muriel took Jesus literally when He said, "Follow Me" (Matt. 4:19).

Steve was ready to argue philosophy or religious doctrine, but he could not argue with the simple truth of a Christian doing what Jesus would do. Years later, looking back on this as a Christian himself, Steve speaks of the sheer power of simply doing what Jesus would do: bringing God's love to people.

JUNE 1

Steve attended a party but tried to avoid contact with any of the Christians there. They were religious nuts, Jesus freaks. Then Henry began to talk to Steve about Jesus and about Jesus's plans for Steve.

Henry told Steve that God had made the world and had made Steve. Henry told Steve the Bible reports that Jesus came to seek and to save those who were lost (Matt. 18:11). Jesus came to seek and to save Steve.

This idea of God creating the world and Jesus seeking Steve was a complete reversal for Steve. He had studied Eastern religions where he had learned about a cosmic hide-and-seek sort of search for any god. God is out there, and you have to find Him, Steve had learned from other religions.

In a complete reversal of doctrinal thought, Henry told Steve that God was searching for him. Henry then knelt on the kitchen floor to pray for Steve. Steve knelt down beside him weeping and could only cry out to God for help. Steve felt overwhelmed and completely lost with no hope, but Jesus came to Steve that day. Jesus still comes to seek and to save those of us who are lost.

§

JUNE 2

In the classic story "The Tell-Tale Heart" by Edgar Allan Poe, the main character hears the heartbeat of his murdered victim coming from under the floor where he has buried the body. He has harmed another human being. He has sinned against God and against everything he believes to be ethically and morally right. His guilt has caused him to lose all balance psychologically. He cannot get past his guilt. He cannot rest.

Do you ever feel guilty? Usually we feel guilty because we have done something that is wrong. There really are right and wrong, and God has already decided what they are. As the Creator it is His right to determine right from wrong. As part of creation, we do not have that right. We live under God's authority.

The most fascinating part is that God will forgive us if we will own up to the wrong we have done. "If we confess our sins, He is faithful and just to forgive us our sins and to cleanse us from all unrighteousness" (1 John 1:9). He does not condone it or look the other way, but He does forgive us.

JUNE 3

Some men brought their paralyzed friend to Jesus hoping he would be healed. Instead Jesus announced the man's sins were forgiven (Matt. 9:1—8). People believed they suffered from illness as punishment for some form of sinful behavior.

We believe this still today to some extent when we suffer some form of hardship and ask, "What did I do to deserve this?" The belief today and the belief two thousand years ago are alike; good behavior gets rewarded while bad behavior gets punished.

When Jesus said, "Your sins are forgiven," some bystanders were offended, and He overheard their complaints. Jesus looked at them and asked, "Which is easier? To tell the man he is forgiven or to heal him of his paralysis? In order to prove to you that I have authority to forgive sins..." Jesus looked at the paralyzed man and said, "Stand up and walk."

The man stood up and walked away. The crowd was astounded that Jesus indeed had authority to forgive sins. He still has that authority today.

§

JUNE 4

Are you ever lonely? Do you ever wake up at night feeling alone? Do you wish you had a really good friend? Let me suggest two things.

First, get to know God. The Bible says our sin has separated us from God. Our sin has caused a wide gap between Him and us, but God bridged that gap by sending Jesus. God reconciled us to Himself, and such a ministry of reconciliation has been given to us according to 2 Corinthians 5:16—21.

Second, build bridges instead of walls with your neighbors or your coworkers. Invite them to your house to eat a plate of spaghetti or cook a hot dog. Meals are natural settings for conversations. Avoid watching TV or movies together. Instead, ask them to spend a couple of hours playing a board game around the dining room table. Use the meal or the game to cause some low intrusive level interaction. Then, a week or two later, do it again. Over time the talking and invitations to your home will build a friendship.

Other people are looking for friends also. So if you will take the lead and get to know God and get to know a neighbor, in time your loneliness will disappear.

June 5

God deliberately revealed Himself in two ways. He created the universe by piling on multiple layers of object lessons in order to reveal Himself. Some of these are recorded in Genesis 1—2, Psalms 139, Isaiah 45, and John 1, to mention just a few of the Bible passages that speak about creation.

God created the sun and the moon, the sea and the land, the earth and the sky as object lessons for us to learn about Him. The rhythm of the seasons, the orderliness of DNA strains, the water cycle, the interdependence of the oxygen and carbon dioxide cycle between plants and animals, and the overall interdependence of all living things only reveal that God is orderly, is intentional, and desires life.

God also has revealed Himself through the Bible. He has revealed His purposes and plans for humanity. Over a thousand times in the Bible, God endorses life. Jeremiah records God's intentions in 29:11: "I know the plans that I have for you," declares the Lord, "plans for good and not for harm, to give you a future and a hope." God has revealed Himself in nature and in the historical events recorded in the Bible. Get to know Him. Embrace His plan for life.

June 6

Is there a barrier or obstacle in your life, something blocking your progress or success? Do you believe that without some sort of miracle from God, you will not be able even to make progress? Maybe the barrier is only your imagination, and then again, maybe it is real.

About 3,500 years ago, the nation of Israel prepared to cross the Jordan River in order to enter the Promised Land (Josh. 4:1—17). The rains swelled the river to flood stage. God told Joshua to prepare the people to cross the river during the flood instead of waiting until the floodwaters flowed away and settled down. The people made a fresh commitment to God, packed up, and lined up. Once the feet of the first leaders stepped into the water, God split the flood, and they crossed on dry ground. The flood was real. It was not in their imagination, nor was it a philosophical idea. They faced a real barrier.

Only after they stepped into the flood, only after they trusted God and moved out in faith, did God move that obstacle. Only when you step forward into that obstacle in your life will God give you victory. Trust Him, and move forward.

JUNE 7

Within certain tribal communities of the African nations, when they talk about forgiveness, they use the phrase "to take the rope off," meaning to take a rope off of someone's neck, to set him or her free from slavery, from bondage. They use this image to mean forgiveness. You forgive by taking off the rope.

You might recognize a striking similarity in the story about Jacob and Esau recorded in Genesis 25:19—27:46. Jacob deceived their father and disguised himself to look, smell, and feel like his brother, Esau. In doing so he convinced his father, Isaac, to pronounce the family blessing on him. Isaac blessed Jacob instead of blessing Esau, as he had planned to do.

When Esau discovered what had happened, he vowed to kill Jacob, but his father told Esau, "You will be a slave to your brother until the day when you become restless, and when you become restless, you will break his yoke from your neck" (Gen. 27:40). The father knew that the bitterness and anger were nothing but slavery and that Esau needed to forgive, but he would not forgive until he grew tired of carrying the self-slavery of these emotions. You don't have to be in the slavery of these emotions either. You can break free.

§

JUNE 8

Solomon wrote, "There is an appointed time for everything. There is a time for every event under heaven" (Eccles. 3:1—8). He itemized a variety of opposites as those various times in the normal ebb and flow of any lifetime.

Solomon said there is a time to speak and a time to be silent. We get those mixed up at times, speaking when we should listen further. He actually started with there is a time to be born and a time to die. He mentioned there is a time to tear down and a time to build up.

Solomon said there is a time to heal and a time to kill, a time to weep and a time to laugh, a time to mourn and a time to dance. He did not identify what events determine the response. He simply said there are proper times, even ordained of God, to give the responses we give to the events in our lives.

Solomon finished with saying there is a time for war and a time for peace. All the other pairs listed seem to be aimed at an individual life and possibly at a community. This pair alone, war and peace, are not individual in nature but people against people, nation against nation. I guess there is a time to be an individual and a time to be part of a nation, a time to be part of something bigger than an individual.

JUNE 9

In the nineteenth century, the London Missionary Society received a telegram saying, "Baptizing eighty a day. Send help." When the local people saw the two missionaries the society sent row ashore, the entire island population came to greet them. They all knew of a legend of two men, one tall with black hair and the other short with red hair. The legend said these men would bring them the book of God.

The legend had been passed down through generations. The people hungered for God but knew no way to connect with Him. In Ecclesiastes 3:11 we read that God has placed eternity in our hearts. God has built a doorway for the Gospel in every culture and in every person, but often we rush in, arrogantly believing we already know what people believe and how they should hear the Gospel. So we present the Gospel from our point of view instead of getting to know them well enough to present the Gospel from their point of view.

Only God Himself can fill this eternal space. The island people knew the holes in their hearts. They knew the legend promising that two men would bring the book of God. When the men came, the entire population was ready for Jesus. When you share about Jesus, take the time to learn about the other person. You will be able to share with more discernment.

§

JUNE 10

King Solomon noticed that if a man or a woman found satisfaction with his or her work, that work in itself was a gift from God. He wrote this three times, in Ecclesiastes 2:24, 3:12—13, and 5:19. We can derive from this repetition that Solomon wanted to emphasize this point: that our work is a gift from God.

The wisest man who ever lived wrote that fulfillment or satisfaction from our jobs is in fact a gift from God. He seemed to understand what Moses told the nation of Israel, recorded in Deuteronomy 8:18: "It is the Lord your God who is giving you the power to make wealth." We can easily infer it is also God who is giving us the opportunity to work, because we were hired instead of the other applicant. God has given us the ability and the favor to do the work, resulting in us having dignity, earning our way, and providing for ourselves and for our families. God has provided the ability and the opportunity. We supply the effort and the attitude.

So do your work with an attitude of gratitude toward God. You will have great difficulty feeling angry, discouraged, or bored while you are working in gratitude to God. Instead of complaining, give God thanks for the ability to work.

JUNE 11

When Hurricane Mitch ripped through Central America, it dropped fifty inches of water on Honduras, Guatemala, and Nicaragua, killing over nineteen thousand people, with an additional 2.7 million people left homeless. In Nicaragua the rain filled the Casita Volcano, sending mudslides ten miles long and five miles wide along with great floods onto the region below.

Among the tragedies Pastor Carlos lost eleven family members that day. His brother Tomas lost his wife and all of his children. Ten—year—old Rebecca climbed high in a tree on a cliff and watched her neighborhood, her family, and many friends being buried beneath thirty feet of mud. With no safe drinking water for over three months, everyone was sick with dysentery. No plumbing. No power. Little help.

Many men left to find work. Pastor Carlos and Tomas stayed. They helped recover lost children. They protected women from roaming gangs. In the passing years, they have led the way in building and establishing over sixty churches, two health clinics, and two vocational colleges. Believing that "God causes all things to work together for good to those who love God" (Rom. 8:28) Carlos and Tomas are hand—in—hand with God rebuilding their home, their land, and their people.

§

JUNE 12

What do you value? If we were able to open your soul and look in, what would we see that you hold most dear in your life? Do you value entertainment or family? Are you most passionate about your comfort or your grandchildren? Our values lie at our very hearts and the very centers of our souls.

Instead of telling someone what you value, let me suggest a simple test. Look at your calendar and your checkbook. Where you give your time and your money reveals what you value.

Many people claim to be Christians, but when you look at how they invest their time and their money, their faith is shown as a sham. The IRS audited Dennis because his charitable contributions were unusually high. As he presented the receipts and records, it became very clear exactly where Dennis had his heart. He did "love the Lord with all his heart, all his soul, all his mind, and all his strength" (Deut. 6:5, Matt. 22:37). You could see it in the records of his life. You could see it in his calendar and in his checkbook.

JUNE 13

John Wesley had a personal slogan to pray as if everything depends upon God and work as if everything depends upon you and then at the end of the day you will be amazed at what you and God have done together. The Apostle Paul said it like this in 1 Corinthians 3:9, "We are fellow workers with God."

Bobbie Jean was a fellow worker with God when she organized an after school program for children at her church. Instead of going home to an empty house they could go to the church, get help with homework, and get some love and attention from some people in their neighborhood. She prayed every morning for guidance and success.

Amanda was a fellow worker with God when she bought a reading program and taught grown men to read. They had been arrested for domestic violence but could not read well enough to do the anger management homework. Amanda had them reading on a sixth grade level in four months. They secured jobs and paid their bills. They no longer harmed their families but provided a safe and nurturing home environment. She prayed before every class for the men to succeed.

Stacey was a fellow worker with God when she read the new census demographics and learned there were 459 single parent households in her zip code. She spoke with her pastor and with five ladies in her church. Together they developed a centralized place where single parents could find information on child support, job training, support groups, clothing supplies, and many other services. She had a twenty—four hour prayer phone line installed at the church and over a hundred people coordinated to help cover all the calls. They all prayed and worked.

JUNE 14

One of the recording artists from the 1970s Jesus movement was Keith Green. Keith was passionate in his demand for excellence in himself, his music, and the people around him.

During a recording session, a guitarist made several mistakes while playing a song. After the fourth or fifth mistake, Keith exploded all over this young musician and sent him from the studio. The producer called Keith to the side and told him that kind of temper would not be tolerated. Keith responded with an almost volatile explanation that he has always had passion. He expects a high level of excellence from himself and anyone playing with him. He then almost growled at the producer, "You cannot expect me to change."

The producer looked straight into Keith's eyes and replied, "That's exactly what I expect." After a moment of silence Keith's glare softened and he replied, "I'll try."

The producer knew "a gentle answer turns away wrath, but a harsh word stirs up anger" (Prov. 15:1). He knew that God can change people from throwing temper tantrums that destroy to using kind words that offer encouragement. Keith's willingness to allow God to do this work was the key. Willingness is the key for you too.

§

JUNE 15

One of the last songs Keith Green recorded went like this: "Jesus commands us to go, but we go the other way. It's no wonder we're moving so slow when His church refuses to obey, feeling so called to stay." He simply took the title from the Great Commission, where Jesus commanded, "Go, make disciples of all nations" (Matt. 28:19—20).

Keith sung about missions. He had written this song after a tour to visit various countries, meeting with missionaries and seeing the work they were doing. He had learned much more than expected. He had found where Jesus was bringing restoration and hope to the poor and the marginalized of His world.

Keith had been challenged by a friend who told him he was doing a great job, calling people to turn from their lives of self-destruction with drugs, selfishness, and greed, but he was not telling them what to turn their lives to. So he invested almost a year visiting mission posts.

Keith saw a world God desperately loves, a world for which Jesus died, a world where even Christians are selfishly keeping to themselves. Keith called on Christians to repent of their isolation and to go to the world Jesus loves.

JUNE 16

We often miss the privilege of witnessing for Jesus Christ. We say we need to earn the right to be heard, meaning of course we justify keeping quiet instead of telling someone about the incredible love of Jesus.

New grandparents never earn the right to talk about their grandchildren. Have you ever seen a person build a friendship for months before showing a photograph of his or her new grandbaby? Deuteronomy 6:5 records, "Love the Lord your God with all your heart and with all your soul and with all your strength."

We really don't need to earn the right to speak about someone we love dearly and are excited to have him or her in our lives. We are called to tell about Jesus. We are called to make Jesus look good. We are called to share how much we love Him and how excited we are that He is in our lives.

Just like a grandparent excitedly shows pictures of his or her grandchildren, we have the privilege to excitedly share how much Jesus loves us and to celebrate what He has done in our lives. We offer to another person the most wonderful part of our lives. Don't miss the opportunity and privilege to make Him look good today.

§

JUNE 17

Hope lifted Job. When he experienced his deepest despair, he whispered, "I know that my Redeemer lives. And one day, he will stand on the earth" (Job 19:25).

Hope is what carried Corrie ten Boom through those many hours standing in the rain at Ravensbrück, the Nazi death camp where she was held as a political prisoner for helping Jews escape Germany. You cannot imprison the soul of a person who has hope. Hope is what kept naval pilot John McCain focused as he was being held in a Vietnam POW camp for five and a half years.

Regardless of the pain, regardless of the odds, cancer survivors refuse to give up hope. John wanted to see his grandson graduate from US Marine Corps basic training. Sheila wanted to hold her first grandbaby. Malinda wanted to hold Mollie, her daughter born prematurely. The Apostle Paul wrote, "We also exalt in our tribulation, knowing that tribulation brings about perseverance; and perseverance, proven character; and proven character, hope; and hope does not disappoint because the love of God has been poured out within our hearts through the Holy Spirit who has been given to us" (Rom. 5:3—5).

June 18

In his darkest hour, Thomas Fuller could tell his friends, "If it were not for hope, the heart would break." After twenty—seven years in prison, Nelson Mandela continued the fight against apartheid in South Africa because he had hope he would see the day when racial equality would come to his country.

In Genesis 41:1—49 Joseph held to his hope as he waited in prison for the king of Egypt to set him free. He had been framed for a crime, and he knew that God would not let him suffer indefinitely. Then, in one afternoon, because he demonstrated to the king of Egypt that he walked closely with God, the king elevated Joseph to be in charge of the entire nation, second only to the king himself.

Even though she had buried a prematurely born son just one year earlier, Malinda never gave up hope as she held vigil by the bedside of her newborn two—pound baby daughter. She sang and prayed. After a few months, she took her Mollie home.

Earl kept his hope to grow his business, convinced if he gave a good product and he was honest with his customers, God would honor him with an increase.

§

June 19

Not too many years ago, a twenty—year—old sat at the bedside of his grandfather. With his father in prison, his mother relied heavily upon the young man. He had enlisted in the National Guard to cover the expenses of college. That night he called his pastor and asked him to come to the hospital. His granddad would soon die.

The family gathered around the bed. The monitors hummed in the silence. A guard brought the young man's dad from prison, but they stayed only twenty minutes. The pastor led the family in a prayer and then the guard took the father back to prison. At 7:00 p.m. the young man leaned over and whispered, "It's OK to go to heaven, Granddad. I've got it covered here."

Paul wrote, "When I became a man, I put away childish things" (1 Cor. 13:11). That twenty—year—old had put away childish things. He no longer thought like a child or spoke like a child or acted like a child. He had become the leader of the family. He knew it. The family knew it.

Five minutes later the granddad exhaled for the last time. It really was OK. The boy had become a man, not on some game field where older boys continued to play games, and not in the field of battle. Instead the boy became a man earlier when he had accepted the mantle of responsibility from his granddad—the responsibility of leading the family in the ways of God. Granddad had moved on and the twenty—year—old was the hand picked successor to lead the family.

JUNE 20

"When you see a Bible that is falling apart, it's a pretty good indicator of a life that is not falling apart." Joe used to hear that statement from his grandmother. She had not only memorized Psalm 119:11—"I have treasured Your word in my heart that I may not sin against You"—but had embraced this as her life's guiding verse.

As a man with a wife, children, and a job, Joe was just too busy to read his Bible. He valued it, so he assured his Sunday school class that he would read it the next week. But just like the previous week, each *next week* passed without Joe taking the time to listen to God from the pages of the Bible. Joe believed in God and attended church every week. Except for leafing through his Bible while at church, he had not read even a page for many years.

One day after Joe had written his child support check, he saw his Bible on a shelf under a pile of newspapers. Even after owning it for several years, it still looked brand new. So much had happened over the last couple of years. It all seemed like a blur. He thought about his divorce and about the present situation seeing his children every other weekend. He still believed. He still attended church, but what had happened? Then almost as if he could hear her voice, he remembered what his grandmother used to tell him: "When you see a Bible that is falling apart, it's a pretty good indicator of a life that is not falling apart." His Bible was like new and his life had fallen apart.

Joe's grandmother had been right. If Joe had worn out his Bible, gaining daily insight from God about how to cultivate his wife, how to encourage his children, how to listen to them all, maybe his life would not have fallen apart.

JUNE 21

In recent years many people have concluded that all truth is relative. That idea is a self-contradiction. If *all truth is relative* is true, the statement is presented as an absolute. Therefore this statement is a self-contradiction on truth being relative. In other words, this simple exercise in logic proves there is absolute truth.

Since there is absolute truth, how do we discover it? Where do we start? Throughout history people have started with creation, and creation led them to the Creator. They have realized there must be a Creator who has put the Milky Way galaxy, Halley's comet, Orion, Scorpio, and the rest of the universe into place.

The Apostle Paul wrote to the Romans about this: "Since the creation of the world His invisible attributes, His eternal power and divine nature have been clearly seen having been understood through what has been made" (Rom. 1:20). People argue over how God created, but throughout history there seems to be an agreement that God did in fact bring the world into existence.

$$\S$$

JUNE 22

If you are a Christian, you want to be comfortable with evangelism. So let me make two suggestions about witnessing. First, follow John's example: "What we have heard, what we have seen with our eyes, what we have looked at and touched with our hands" (1 John 1:1). Stick with what you have experienced firsthand, what you have seen and heard yourself.

Second, write down the name of one person who is probably not a Christian, someone you expect to see weekly. It is better if you see this person repeatedly than if you have only one conversation with him or her. Then, begin to pray for that person by name every single day for a month.

Include within your prayers to pray God will give you openings to invite that person into your life. You could invite him or her to a cookout, a picnic, a ball game, an afternoon of shopping, a fishing trip, or a double date to a movie. Pray for the person, and look for openings. Don't be in a hurry to invite him or her to church.

Invite this person into your life. Begin to deliberately build a friendship, and pray for openings to share your faith. Don't preach at him or her. Just share what Jesus has done for you.

JUNE 23

When Abraham was eighty—five years old, God made him a promise. Genesis 15:2 records Abraham's response as he tried to bargain with God: "O Lord God, what will you give me since I am childless?"

If God wants you to obey, isn't it fair to ask God about the payoff? Abraham certainly wanted to know what was in it for him. All he wanted was a son, an heir to whom to pass on his legacy. God was promising him the stars and descendants for a thousand generations but was not giving that first son Abraham could enjoy firsthand.

Do you have the same attitude about obeying God? Do you believe if God wants your allegiance, He had better come through with a big incentive? Do you believe if God wants your love and your obedience, then He had better give you and your family good health, plenty of wealth, and no heartaches? Maybe I have overstated the whole thing, but if you believe obeying God entitles you to His blessings, then what is your faith worth?

§

JUNE 24

In January 2002, while hiking to the jungle village of Mt. Olivos, Peru, a mission team stopped at a small hut. Eight poles held its sleeping platform eight feet from the ground. The thatched roof provided shade. Plants from a nearby garden hung from a rope extended between the poles, and a pot of water boiled over an open flame.

Wilma and her children lived there. Her husband had abandoned her. She asked why the team was traveling through. Larry, the team leader along with Wilkinson, the host pastor, explained to her about Jesus's love for her and invited her to receive Him as her savior, "for all who call on the name of the Lord shall be saved" (Rom. 10:13). She said yes. The team gathered around her for prayer.

The team then returned to relaxing in the shade while Wilma went about her chores. Only minutes later Wilma gathered up her largest chicken and presented it to Larry as her first offering to Jesus for His incredible love. She gave her best. She gave freely, with an overflowing, joyful heart. She had heard the good news of Jesus's love for her, and His love compelled her to give in response.

JUNE 25

Within the very first chapter of the Bible, Genesis 1, we find that God created the world and everything in it. God created human beings in His image. He created women and men as opposites and as equals.

Did you ever notice that God created man and woman as equals? The will of God is equality, and therefore God's will for society is for us to treat one another as equals—equal in value, equal pay for equal work, and equal in dignity.

Women's rights did not originate with some political movement in the United States in the nineteenth century. Women's rights originated in the heart of God and are the will of God established at the dawn of time, intended by God to involve equal educational opportunities, equal employment opportunities, equal advancement, and equal pay.

Hindus do not believe in this equality; neither do Muslims or Shintos or any other religion. Even Christians usually get it wrong when they claim Jesus honored women but Paul did not. Both Jesus and Paul rooted their teachings in Genesis 1, where God revealed His will for equality.

§

JUNE 26

In the Bible we read that God created man and woman in His image. This means many things, including that we have value even above the angels.

Speaking about angels, Hebrews 1:14 reveals, "that they are all ministering spirits sent out to render service to those who will inherit salvation." Angels are sent out to minister to us.

The Bible and church history teach that in the earliest days, after the angels were created, some of them sinned. Led by Lucifer, some of them rebelled against God and were thrown out of heaven. In speaking about these angels, Jesus explained that hell was created just for them— " prepared for the Devil and His angels" (Matt. 25:41). God never made any plans to offer them forgiveness and redemption.

In glaring contrast to that fact, when we humans, created in God's image, sinned, He loved us so much that He sent Jesus to die for our sins, purchasing our salvation with His own blood so we could live in heaven for eternity. Being created in the image of God makes us more valuable than even the angels.

JUNE 27

Do you ever look for heroes? Do you ever look for men who are strong physically, strong mentally, strong to stand, strong to lead, and even strong to suffer?

Since the 1950s several books have been written about Jim Elliot. An all-conference wrestler while in college, Jim did a lot of motivational speaking across the Midwest and the South. After college his work took him deep into the Amazon Jungle. There are early home movies of him fishing and building tree houses. He had a life slogan: "He is no fool who gives up what he cannot keep to gain what he cannot lose." In Romans 14:8 Paul wrote, "If we live, we live unto the Lord. If we die, we die unto the Lord. So whether we live or die, we are the Lord's."

Jim ended up becoming one of the most well known missionaries to be killed in the twentieth century. His story, along with that of the other four men—Ed McCulley, Pete Fleming, Nate Saint, and Roger Youderian—speared to death on January 6, 1956, by the Waodani hunting party, has inspired millions of Christians to become missionaries giving themselves totally to Jesus Christ. You can read about their ministry in books like *Through Gates of Splendor* and *Jungle Pilot* and *The Savage, My Kinsman*. In these books you will find stories of men worth having as heroes to follow their examples.

§

JUNE 28

After putting his fist through a cabinet door, Tony stormed out. He and his wife had just fought again. Tony walked about a mile and a half to the house of a friend, who listened to him proving Galatians 6:2: "Bear one another's burdens and so fulfill the law of Christ." The friend supported him and reminded him that regardless of what his wife did, every choice he made was within his control, and he had made many decisions to be less than a loving, encouraging husband. Truth matters.

Two hours later Tony walked home, thinking about the kind of husband he had become, which was a far distance from the husband God wanted him to be. So he made a decision to study the Bible and other books on marriage. He asked straight questions to men who had been married for at least thirty years about how they did it. He also asked their wives, hoping to learn about his wife. Finally he humbled himself and asked his wife, "How can I be a better husband?" He wanted to obey God. He wanted a great marriage, and he went for it 110 percent.

Have you gone for it? Or are you still coasting, hoping your marriage will work in spite of your potentially damaging attitudes and behavior?

JUNE 29

Ideas can change over time. An example could be the way we challenge people to become Christians. We have softened the requirements of discipleship to Jesus instead of using the simple, straightforward Gospel of Jesus Christ.

Do you remember what Jesus commanded of His early disciples? He said, "Repent, for the Kingdom of God is at hand" (Matt. 4:19). To *repent* means to turn from a life revolving around you and recalibrate it so it revolves around Jesus. "Come, follow me" (Matt. 4:17), Jesus said, but following Him is harder than simply believing certain doctrines. A relationship with the living God is more difficult than a religious checklist.

Jesus sets the direction and runs the show. He calls the shots. Jesus is Lord. He is the supreme commander in chief. No one outranks Him. He is not one option out of many. He is the one and only path to God. He is "the way, the truth, and the life," and no one comes to the Father except through Him (John 14:6).

Jesus said, "Follow Me." The call of God is clear: "Repent and follow Jesus." I guarantee you one thing. If you say yes to Jesus, you will never regret it.

§

JUNE 30

Are you a worrier? Would you like some peace of mind? Paul's letter to the Philippians promises "the peace of God which surpasses all understanding will guard your heart and your mind in Christ Jesus" (Phil. 4:7).

What could possibly deliver such a promise that results in having the peace of God in my heart and mind? Paul lists two things that, when done together as a package deal, do in fact deliver the peace of God so many long for in their hearts and minds. These two things are found in the preceding verse, 4:6: "Be anxious for nothing but in everything by prayer and supplication with thanksgiving let your requests be made known to God."

First, defiantly refuse to worry about any situation. Instead talk to God about that situation. Deliberately choose to trust Him with the outcome. Second, while you trust God with the outcome, thank Him for all the previous problems He has prevented from coming into your life. Itemize them. Remember previous problems you worried about that He diverted from your life, and give Him thanks for His extraordinary loving care toward you. His peace will come.

JULY 1

How often do you pray? Do you pray in the morning or in the evening? Do you pray about many things or just a couple of things? Do you pray daily or less often? The George Gallup organization and the Barna Group both have conducted surveys on prayer. They report that outside of religious services, the average Christian in the United States prays about five minutes each week.

Maybe the disciples of Jesus recognized a similar lack of communicating with God in their own lives when they asked Jesus, "Teach us to pray just as John taught his disciples to pray" (Luke 11:1). They did not ask Jesus to teach them *how* to pray but to teach them *to* pray. They seemed to recognize and desire a stronger, more intimate relationship with God. Possibly they saw this life of purity and power in Jesus, resulting from His relationship with God. Possibly this was the enticement that motivated their request.

Most Christians pray very little. The disciples asked Jesus to get them to the point where they prayed enough. So if you are like them, ask Jesus to do the same for you. Ask Jesus to teach you to pray. Maybe even ask Him right now.

§

JULY 2

An evangelist stood up during the early part of the revival service and said they were going to take up a second offering. He asked the congregation if they would be willing to put their gold watches into the plate and take stainless steel ones as replacements? He then announced a third offering. Would they be willing to place their jewelry into the plate for world missions? Then he announced a fourth offering. Would they be willing to stand, offering themselves for world missions?

Charles stood. His wife knew he was serious. The Holy Spirit was calling for Charles. He would leave her behind at home if her heart were not set with his. She did not have to have a separate calling from God. She was his wife. So, with some anger, some fear, and some panic, she stood.

Over the years they began a ministry that would reach into many countries. Each year One Mission Society reports starting hundreds of new churches and receiving thousands of new converts. If Leddie Cowman, author of *Streams in the Desert*, had kept her jewelry and her comfortable seat, thousands would have perished separated from Christ for eternity.

JULY 3

Many times people will have different opinions of themselves than the opinions God has of them. What God thinks about us and feels about us is usually different from how we think and feel about ourselves.

In the New Testament, we find Romans 8:16: "The Spirit Himself testifies with our spirit that we are children of God." John 15:15 records from Jesus, "I have called you My friends." In Romans 8:17 Paul wrote, "We are joint heirs with Christ."

Oftentimes people believe the New Testament records God as loving but the Old Testament records God as angry and punitive. So let's take a look at just a few Old Testament verses to see that God does not change. The loving God who sent Jesus to save the world is the same God who spoke through the prophets.

Isaiah speaks for God in 43:4: "Since you are precious in my sight, since you are honored and I love you..." God hid Moses in the cleft of the rock, passed by, and declared, "The Lord God, compassionate and gracious, slow to anger, and abounding in lovingkindness and truth" (Exod. 34:6).

God is consistent. He has not changed from angry and punitive to loving and gracious. He has been loving and gracious from the beginning. He chose mercy for Adam and Eve (Gen. 3:21). He developed the sacrificial system making mercy and grace a normal occurrence in Israel, (Leviticus 1—7). If you do not know this God of mercy and grace, speak to Him. He would enjoy introducing His love to you.

July 4

On July 4, 1776 the United States declared itself a sovereign nation with the signing of the Declaration of Independence, which refers to the Creator who has endowed all men with inalienable rights. This Creator who from nothing brings life into existence is unique to the Bible within the ancient religions.

Isaiah 33:22 states, "The Lord is our Judge. The Lord is our lawgiver. The Lord is our King. He will save us." Because reading the Bible was common practice among the founding fathers of the United States, it is no surprise that the Bible significantly influenced the way they thought. They designed a government with three branches: the judicial, the legislative, and the executive. This government design can easily be found in this one verse from Isaiah.

By a 1931 act of Congress, "The Star Spangled Banner" became our national anthem, with lyrics in the fourth stanza pointing to the God revealed in the Bible: "may the Heav'n rescued land praise the Power that hath made and preserved us a nation...and this be our motto: 'In God is our trust.'" This stanza leads the way to our national motto, which first appeared on our coins in 1864, made official by a 1956 act of Congress. It's a fact of history: our national conscience is built on the Bible.

§

July 5

An adage states that if you lend someone your ears, you will immediately open a pathway to that person's heart. We can listen with both the ears and the heart. When you are trying to key in on more than what a person is saying, you are also hearing that person's feelings and emotions.

The Bible mentions something like this in James 1:19, where James wrote, "But everyone must be quick to hear, slow to speak, and slow to anger." For generations mothers have told their children God has given us each two ears and one mouth, and we must use them accordingly.

Listening has become a lost art to many people. We live in the video age, with flashing images. Computer chat rooms and social media sites promise connection with others but have left us even more disconnected and lonely. We want human contact. We want someone to listen and understand. We need someone to listen. Will you be that someone, that solution in another person's life? We yearn to see "I understand" in a listener's eyes. Will you offer your ear to someone today and open a pathway to his or her heart?

July 6

As a graduating high school senior, Jay walked by the principal's office, where he noticed a sign on the wall reading "I have found the enemy, and it is me."

Jay married his high school sweetheart and divorced three years later. He stayed up late drinking a lot. He married another young lady, determined to make this marriage work, but after only five years he divorced again. Jay was getting more and more discouraged and depressed. He decided to go speak with his old high school principal.

As Jay entered the office, he again saw the sign: "I have found the enemy, and it is me." The principal shared with Jay that the Bible says in 1 John 1:8 "if we say that we have no sin, we are deceiving ourselves and the truth is not in us." On his way home, Jay walked by the river to think and to throw rocks.

Jay realized he was indeed his own worst enemy. He turned his life over to Jesus, who began to put the broken pieces of his life together again. Over the next several years, Jay experienced firsthand that Jesus is the eternal Master at putting together the pieces of broken lives.

§

July 7

A story is told of a homeless man during World War II who knocked on the door of a house in his home country of Russia. The lights were on, and the family was at home on that cold night. They allowed the man to stay in the basement, out of the winter weather, while they prepared the evening meal.

A few hours into the evening, they heard beautiful music coming from the basement. The family went to investigate only to find that the man had fixed the family's broken harp and he was playing a piece by Johann Sebastian Bach. They did not understand how a homeless man could fix such a classical musical instrument.

He told them, "I am the craftsman who made this harp. I made it. When it's broken, I can fix it."

This principle rings true throughout all of life and eternity. Whoever makes something can also fix it when it is broken. That is why "God is an ever present help in times of trouble" (Psalm 46:1). Psalm 139:13 records for us that God "wove me together in my mother's womb." Because He created you, when you are broken and in pain He can heal you and make you whole.

July 8

Do our attitudes really make a difference? Does a positive mental attitude make any difference at all? Paul seemed to think so when he wrote, "difficulties bring perseverance, and perseverance brings proven character, and proven character brings hope. This hope does not disappoint" (Rom. 5:4).

Powell Royster invested his life's energy and passion in a career as a missionary and a minister. During his retirement years, he and his wife, Helene conducted Operation Appreciation at Fort Knox, Kentucky. Using a church in Louisville, they hosted three hundred to four hundred soldiers every Saturday night, with food, games, and a worship service. They saw thousands of US soldiers during basic training give their hearts to Jesus as Savior and Lord.

One day, while in his nineties, Powell sat in a staff meeting of Hope Springs, a new church plant in Lexington, Kentucky. The worship leader asked, "Powell, you're ninety-three years old. Why do you want to help us start a new church?"

Powell pounded the desk and stated, "The adventure, man, the adventure!" People like Powell Royster embody the truth that one's attitude really does make a difference.

§

July 9

He wanted to scream when the prison door slammed against his foot, but Jacob DeShazer kept quiet. Days earlier he had been given a Bible and had practically read it all in a week along with memorizing verses. He had become a Christian, and he was working deliberately to live out Paul's instructions from Romans 12:21: "Do not be overcome by evil, but overcome evil with good."

Jacob had flown with Doolittle's Raiders to bomb Tokyo but was captured by the Japanese and treated harshly as a POW for the remainder of World War II. Instead of cursing his guard for slamming the door, he asked about the guard's family. He tried to speak kindly to him as well as treating all of the guards with kindness and respect.

About a week later, one guard slipped him a sweet potato—a rare delicacy in that POW camp. Jacob continued to read his Bible, to pray for his enemies, and to speak kindly to them. They began to give him better food. He tried to speak with them in Japanese. After the war Jacob was released and sent home to America, where he attended Bible College. Later he returned to Japan as a missionary.

JULY 10

Not long into World War II, Doolittle's Raiders carried out a bombing raid on Tokyo. They did little damage to the city itself, but they gave a giant boost to the morale of the American forces. Jacob DeShazer flew as one of the bombardiers. He did not make it back from that raid but sat out the remainder of the war in a Japanese prison camp.

While in that prison camp, he obtained a Bible and was genuinely converted to Jesus Christ. After the war Jacob returned to Japan as a missionary. One of the men he greatly influenced was Mitsuo Fuchida. If you don't recognize the name, he is the Japanese commander who led the aerial attack on Pearl Harbor on December 7, 1941.

Maybe the Apostle Paul was imagining about such things when he wrote, "There is neither Jew or Greek, slave or free, male or female. We are all one in Christ Jesus" (Gal. 3:29). DeShazer and Fuchida, two opposing warriors, humbled themselves together at the foot of the cross of Jesus Christ. Only Jesus Christ is grand enough to accomplish that feat.

§

JULY 11

One common mistake people make in trying to understand the Bible is to think that Noah saved the world from the flood when in fact Noah saved only his family from destruction. The Bible records that God was disappointed with the evil in each person: "Then the Lord saw that the wickedness of man was great on the earth, and that every intent of the thoughts of his heart was only evil continually. The Lord regretted that He had made man on the earth and He was grieved in His heart" (Gen. 6:5—6). The only exception to this was Noah.

God felt compelled to show Noah mercy by saving him and his family from the global destruction because of Noah's character: "Noah was a righteous man, blameless in his time; Noah walked with God" (Gen. 6:9).

Do you have a relationship with God that would save your family from destruction? One suggestion to help you save your family is to put your spouse first in your heart. God created Eve for Adam, not for Cain and Abel. Often parents put their children ahead of their spouses—and then lose them all. Put your spouse first, and save your family from destruction.

July 12

Many people believe Noah saved the world from the flood when in fact he saved his family from destruction. In the book of Genesis, God showed mercy to Noah because he was a righteous man who walked with God (Gen. 6:5—9).

This example found in Genesis gives us a brief but powerful insight into how to save our own families from destruction. Just like Noah we must live our lives in a way that proves we walk with God. We want to live as examples of what is right, what is true, what is honorable, what is pure and good.

Children learn to be honest by watching their parents being honest. Children learn to lie when they overhear Dad telling Mom how he called in sick to work so he could go fishing. Children learn to cheat when mom keeps the extra money given to her at the grocery checkout when the cashier gives her too much change. Children learn to destroy their own families when they hear Mom tell them, "Don't tell your dad" or Dad say, "Don't tell your mother." To help save your family from the destruction of drugs, divorce, abuse, deception, and even prison, be their example of truthfulness and honesty.

§

July 13

In January 2003 about three hundred pastors, evangelists, and church leaders met in Hyderabad, a small city in south central India, in a Bible conference to help them strengthen their reach to the tribal peoples of India.

The tribal peoples comprise eighty to one hundred million people who speak about seven hundred languages. They never converted to Hinduism many years ago when it was brought to India. They live in caves, in the jungle, and in other remote areas. Some have immigrated to Pakistan and Afghanistan.

The Bible teacher at the conference asked, "Why do you worship God?" One man spoke of his crippled brother being healed. Another spoke of himself being blind from birth and being healed. Another spoke of his entire family being saved and brought out of witchcraft.

Then the elderly evangelist replied, "I worship God because He is God, and I am not." He knew from his experience what Isaiah 45:5 records for us: "I am the Lord and there is no other. Besides Me, there is no other God." Still today God saves and heals, but we worship God because He is God, and we are not.

July 14

There is something supernatural about seeing into the future. The prophet Zechariah recorded for us centuries in advance that Jerusalem's king would come: "just and endowed with salvation, humble and mounted on a donkey, even on a colt, the foal of a donkey" (Zech. 9:9).

The Bible also records the story of Jesus doing this very thing, riding a donkey into Jerusalem on what we now call Palm Sunday (Matt. 21:5). The crowds cried out, "Hosanna in the highest. Blessed is He who comes in the name of the Lord" (Matt. 21:9). They put their coats on the ground, and the donkey walked over them. Children climbed the nearby trees to cut the palm fronds, threw them to their friends, and waved those branches as they celebrated Jesus coming into town.

I wish you could have been there. I wish you could have seen it. An old—fashioned New York City ticker—tape parade celebrating a war hero could not outshine the celebration of the people of Jerusalem that day. Their King was coming to them, just as the prophet Zechariah had written centuries earlier. They had waited their entire lives, and there he came. God had kept His promise. God keeps every promise He has made. What promises has He made to you?

§

July 15

On many days we remember the crucifixion of Jesus Christ. Almost two thousand years ago, the crowd demanded that Jesus be put to death. The ancient Romans had perfected the method of slow, agonizing death. We even get our word *excruciating* from them. It is a Latin word developed from the Roman execution procedure meaning "out of crucifixion."

The Romans took Jesus and beat him beyond recognition (Matt. 27:27—54). Out of deep respect, artists do not portray Jesus on the cross with wounds as severe as the Bible records. The Romans nailed His hands and feet to a cross, designed to have Him die slowly, but He actually died later that same day—sooner than planned.

Some witnesses challenged Him to save Himself if He really was the Son of God, but instead He chose to save you and me. He could not save Himself and die for our sins. So, out of His incredible love, He chose to stay on the cross and die so that we could have our sins forgiven, so that we could be born again by the Holy Spirit, so that we could be reconciled to God from our rebellion. Jesus paid the price for our sins. He died in our place. For Him it was a death sentence, but for us it is a day to celebrate the love and grace of God.

July 16

There is a hero in the Bible named David. Just like in our movies, he gets the girl, wins the battles, conquers evil, and seems larger than life. There is one difference, however, that sets David and the movie heroes at opposite ends of the spectrum.

Today's movie heroes do their heroic deeds thanks to their training, their abilities, or their raw determination. David, on the other hand, performed his heroic feats out of a dependence upon God (Ps. 23). David claimed he protected his sheep from the lion and the bear because God's hand was upon him (1 Sam. 17:34—37). He claimed he beat the giant Goliath because God gave him the victory (1 Sam. 17:37, 17:46—47). He claimed he won military battles because God was with him. David claimed he did all these things because God gave him the victory.

So when you face your difficulties, instead of trusting your abilities to see you through, instead of trusting your raw determination to carry you, instead trust God. He specializes in giving victory to those who trust Him.

§

July 17

Jamie woke up at 2:00 a.m. again, thinking about his life and his future. He has wondered if maybe there is something wrong with him. He is a good student carrying high grades. He is involved with various clubs at school, plays soccer, and works part time at the area grocery store. He just cannot figure out why there is a deep loneliness in his soul.

Jamie refuses to try drugs. His girlfriend doesn't fill the emptiness; neither do sports or studies. His friends have invited him to parties, but that excitement lasts for only a couple of hours. He wants more fulfillment, more meaning, more purpose.

Maybe he has discovered what Solomon wrote three thousand years ago in Ecclesiastes 3:11, that "God has set eternity in their hearts." Maybe Jamie is on the verge of discovering the eternal emptiness of his soul can be filled fully only by the eternal and living Savior, Jesus Christ. Maybe Jamie will also soon discover that if he kneels beside his bed and speaks to Jesus, the eternal Savior, Jesus will fill that eternal loneliness he feels deep in his soul.

July 18

Nick could play the trumpet and play it well, bringing down the house at jazz concerts with his impromptu runs and high—pitched finishes. As a college sophomore, he was first—chair trumpet in the stage band at the World Jazz Festival in New Orleans that backed up Doc Severinsen who served as the event's host for the week.

About midnight one night, he looked over at his college roommate and announced he was going for a walk. He strolled around campus for about thirty minutes and then headed for the chapel. Once there he sat under a light and opened a nearby Bible to 1 Samuel 16, where the story is recorded about King Saul's internal torment. Saul believed music would bring peace to his soul, so he called for a musician. Nick's eyes landed on verse 17: "Bring me a man who plays well."

It was undeniable. God was beckoning to Nick. That night he turned his life over to Jesus. He gave everything to Jesus: his music, his girlfriend, his college degree, his life, everything.

§

July 19

Years after God sent the angel Gabriel to Mary, Jesus found Himself in the Garden of Gethsemane, where He prayed for at least an hour. Matthew, Mark, and Luke recorded that Jesus asked God to possibly come up with another plan, but then concluded with "not my will, but Your will be done" (Matt. 26:39, Mark 14:36, Luke 22:42).

Jesus prayed for an hour, but we have only two sentences recorded. Is it possible that during His prayer, His mind wandered? Is it possible that Jesus remembered sitting at the table as a boy, listening to His mother, Mary, speaking about having to trust God with her life? She told Him that God had asked her to have the Messiah even though she was a virgin. She might have shared with Jesus that she didn't understand it all, but she did trust God. She might have even told Him that someday He would have to trust God with His life as well.

Is it possible Jesus drew strength in that hour from the story His mother might have told Him? Such complete faith shared with another person can strengthen him or her with faith at levels only understood from eternity.

July 20

The book of Proverbs stands full of great advice. Some of them are as short as one line. Some unpack over an entire chapter. When you take a particular topic and look at many proverbs, it can strengthen you in some amazing ways.

Here are a few lines from the proverbs regarding self-control, that last character trait on the list of the fruit of the Spirit from Paul in Galatians 5:22—23:

> "A short tempered man must bear his own penalty; you can't do much to help him. If you try once you must try a dozen times" (Prov. 19:19).

> "A man without self-control is as defenseless as a city with broken down walls" (Prov. 25:28).

> "A fool gets into constant fights. His mouth is his undoing! His words endanger him" (Prov. 18:6—7).

> "It is better to be slow-tempered than famous; it is better to have self-control than to control an army" (Prov. 16:32).

Over and over again, the book of Proverbs speaks about what a great feat it is to control ourselves. So it is no surprise when Paul includes self-control in that legendary list of character traits describing a life filled with the Holy Spirit. He is consistent with the Old Testament. If you have trouble with your temper, ask God to help you.

July 21

The goal of life is God. The goal is not to die with the most toys. The goal is not to become healthy, wealthy, and wise. The goal is not even life, liberty, and the pursuit of happiness. The goal is God.

About 3,500 years ago, when Moses led the nation of Israel from slavery in Egypt, they traveled to Mount Sinai. They saw the mountain quaking and on fire. They heard the trumpet of God and the claps of thunder. They heard God beckon Moses to go up on the mountain. At that time God told Moses and the entire nation, "You yourselves have seen what I did to the Egyptians, how I bore you on eagles' wings and brought you to Myself" (Exod. 19:4). For the nation of Israel, the goal was not even the Promised Land. The goal was God Himself.

In Jesus's High Priestly prayer, recorded in John 17:3, He starts with, "This is eternal life, that they may know You, the only true God and Jesus Christ whom You have sent." The goal of life is not even heaven. The goal of life is to know God. Often we get sidetracked into secondary pursuits and even give them our passions and our hearts, but, to emphasize it one more time, the goal is God.

§

July 22

As you have probably noticed, we are called human beings, not human doings, yet very often we divert our value to be based on what we do. We define our value by our accomplishments. We even get our self-esteem from what we do or do not do.

We put price tags on the others around us based on what they do. Sometimes we value people based on their positions in society, their jobs, or how they earn their paychecks. Sometimes we value people based on their net worth which simply means how much money they have. Sometimes we place value on someone based upon how little harm he or she has caused us. That is why we are so quick to discount criminals because they have harmed someone.

In stark contrast to the values of our society, Genesis 1:26—27 tells us God has created us in His image to reflect Him and to represent Him to the rest of creation. Animals are not created in His image. Angels are not created in His image. Only human beings are created in His image. Our value to God is not based on what we do but on the fact that He created us in His image.

July 23

When you read through Revelation, the last book of the Bible, you find some very dramatic imagery and stories. Many people find these passages hard to understand, but one thing can be understood.

In Revelation we miss the prayers recorded there because we are not expecting them. They are not prayed from duty or a sense of service. Instead the prayers in Revelation are full of force and energy. They seem to have lives all their own as they are collected, held securely near the throne of God, and saved for all eternity.

The prayers ascend to the ears of God on behalf of His people. God does not allow one prayer to fade away: "the four living creatures and the twenty—four elders fell down before the Lamb, each one holding a harp and golden bowls full of incense, which are the prayers of the saints," (Rev. 5:8). "And the smoke of the incense, with the prayers of the saints, went up before God out of the angel's hand" (Rev. 8:4).

Just like the prayers collected in Revelation, God collects every single prayer you pray. You might not feel like He listens, but He does. Your prayers are like love letters sent home. They are collected and kept forever.

§

July 24

Have you ever wondered what you should pray for? Let me offer a suggestion that you pray for your children in advance that they will learn in their own marriages to daily renew their love for one another.

Pray that your children will find spouses who will hold your children in great value and that your children will hold their spouses in high honor and value. Pray that they will respect each other with their attitudes and with their behaviors. Pray that they will set their hearts in exclusive loyalty to one another.

The normal struggles of life will bring stress and strain to their marriages, so pray in advance that God will teach them their spouses are not the ones causing the problems. The Apostle Paul wrote to the Ephesians that "we do not wrestle against flesh and blood but against principalities and powers" (Eph. 6:12), so their spouses cannot be the enemies. Instead pray that they learn to lock arm in arm and fight together against their common enemy: the devil who is trying to deceive, kill, and destroy their marriage (John 10:10). Pray also that they will live humbly before each other, always ready to apologize for offenses.

July 25

Some Christians believe you should never pray for yourself. I assure you praying for yourself is biblical and can bring great benefits to the people around you.

In Matthew's Gospel it is recorded for us that Jesus Himself provided a model prayer. Within that prayer He guided the disciples to ask God for things for themselves, like, "Give us this day our daily bread" (Matt. 6:11) or "do not lead us into temptation but deliver us from evil" (Matt. 6:13).

One unusual prayer recorded in the Old Testament is the Prayer of Jabez: "Oh that You would bless me indeed, and enlarge my border, and that Your hand might be with me, and that you would keep me from harm that it might not pain me" (1 Chron. 4:9—10). The next part of verse ten is "God granted him what he requested." So the Bible itself provides examples for us to pray for ourselves.

Ask God to open your eyes to see Him, to open your ears to hear Him, and to open your heart to recognize His presence in your life. Ask Him for the courage to speak up for Him. Pray for yourself, and pray strategically.

§

July 26

A young man once asked Ed if he expected to go to heaven. Ed replied, "Expect to go? Son, I live there." Ed had gained an intimacy with Jesus through his daily Bible reading and prayer. He knew God well. To go from here to heaven would be a very short step for Ed.

A high school dropout, Ed read many books and had worked outside his entire life. He landscaped, planting trees and shrubs. He dug streambeds and placed rocks. He pruned and harvested fruit trees. All the while he stayed focused on the fact that he was living, breathing, and enjoying life in the presence of God. Ed experienced what the Apostle Paul wrote to the church at Philippi: "For our citizenship is in heaven, from which also we eagerly wait for a Savior, the Lord Jesus Christ" (Phil. 3:20).

Ed had tuned his ear to God's voice and his heart to God's presence. He obeyed what he read in the Bible. He would raise his hand to heaven and whisper, "Bless the dear Master, lad." He always seemed to be tuned in to the presence of God. Ed had learned to live life in the shadows of the Pearly Gates. Are you learning these same things in your relationship with Jesus?

July 27

Do you read your Bible just to get information, like you would if you read the newspaper or the new issue of your favorite magazine? Do you search through the index to simply find a verse that might support your view on some subject?

Instead of merely searching for information, could you read it for personal transformation? Could you read the Bible in such a way that you place yourself into the hand of God, allowing Him to transform your life by His word? Would that decision benefit you personally or benefit your family? Would it benefit your coworkers or even your community?

Psalm 1:1—3, states it like this: "How blessed is the man who does not walk in the counsel of the wicked nor stand in the path of sinners nor sit in the seat of scoffers, but his delight in in the law of the Lord and in His law he meditates day and night. He will be like a tree firmly planted by streams of water which yields its fruit in season and its leaf does not whither and in whatever he does, he prospers." Is it possible to set your heart in a position to delight in the word of God? Does God have the grace to work in cooperation with you to bring about this result?

$$\int$$

July 28

We celebrate Easter, remembering the resurrection of Jesus from the dead. Many people believe His resurrection is merely a spiritual or philosophical thing we believe. They don't believe it actually happened at a specific place on a specific day.

It might be hard for you to understand this amazing historical event, but all of Christianity is built upon the historical fact that Jesus did physically and bodily rise from the dead.

You see, Christianity is not a religion like Hinduism and Buddhism. Those religions are centered on philosophy or abstract religious ideas. Christianity is centered on the person of Jesus living, dying, and rising from the dead.

If you could prove these events did not occur, you could completely wipe out Christianity. The Bible includes the names of the Roman emperor, the Judean governor, the various people involved, and the geographic locations so these events can be verified. An example is the Roman governor Pontius Pilate (Matt. 27:11—26), verified to have existed by documents and by an archeological discovery near the Mediterranean. It is a fact of history: Jesus is risen.

July 29

Often we stop believing an event occurred if it happened a long time ago. Some have tried to disregard the Holocaust because it happened long ago. Yet we have many books, diaries, and other documents describing those events. We have eyewitnesses, and we have objects to validate the stories.

We have the exact same categories of evidence for the resurrection of Jesus Christ two thousand years ago. We have books, diaries, and other documents telling the story of the crucifixion and resurrection and telling about the changes that took place in that city and region.

One such document is the letter from Governor Pliny to the Roman emperor Trajan in AD 111. In the letter Pliny wrote about the worship services taking place at dawn on the first day of the week by the followers of Christ. We have lists of the eyewitnesses of the resurrection (1 Cor. 15:5—8). We have other items from archeological discoveries validating the stories, such as the Moabite Stone, the Shroud of Turin, and the graves containing ossuaries. They don't make today's newspaper headlines, but we have this evidence nonetheless.

When I take the internal subjective change that happened to me when I accepted Jesus as my Savior and Lord combined with the thousands of pieces of objective evidence from archeology, history, and logic I find my faith growing stronger. God wants us to experience both the external evidence and the internal dwelling of His Spirit.

JULY 30

The Apostle Paul gives an argument for the resurrection of Jesus in 1 Corinthians 15. Along with Athens and Sparta, Corinth was one of the great cities of ancient Greece. The Corinthian church wanted to believe in spiritual things but they wanted to separate abstract philosophical religious ideas from actual physical events. They believed there was a clear separation between body and spirit, so they believed Jesus rose from the dead spiritually but not physically.

Paul addressed this in his first Corinthian letter, found in 1 Corinthians 15:1—58: "If Jesus did not rise from the dead, then you are still in your sins." He wanted people to recognize that the forgiveness and freedom they experienced subjectively was reliable evidence of the objective resurrection of Jesus.

Paul told them there is no forgiveness of sins if Jesus is not alive. There is no freedom from bondage and no liberty from sin's tyranny if Jesus is physically still in the grave. Paul rested the entire message of salvation on the crucifixion and actual bodily resurrection of Jesus. And you can rest assured of your salvation on the crucifixion and bodily resurrection of Jesus as well.

§

JULY 31

Christians are people of the resurrection. Jesus has risen from the dead, and this simple fact of history is the foundation for the Christian Church.

The Old Testament records how God commanded His people to keep the Sabbath Day holy, but the Feast of First Fruits was to be celebrated the day after the Sabbath (Exod. 23:16, 34:22; Lev. 23:9—22; Num. 28:16). The Apostle Paul identified Jesus with this Old Testament festival when he wrote, "Jesus is the first fruits of the resurrection" (1 Cor. 15:20—23).

It is no accident, nor is it a coincidence, that the four Gospel writers, Matthew, Mark, Luke, and John, recorded for us a total of seventeen statements that Jesus's resurrection occurred on either "the first day of the week" or on "the day after the Sabbath" (Matt. 27:62—64, 28:1; Mark 15:42, 16:1—9; Luke 23:54—56, 24:1—21; John 19:42, 20:1—19).

The day of worship changed for the people of God, from Saturday to Sunday, from the Sabbath to the first day of the week, because the resurrection of Jesus trumped the commandment "You shall keep the Sabbath holy." This is significant objective historical proof of the resurrection of Jesus. With that kind of historical evidence my faith is strengthened. How about yours?

AUGUST 1

Within the very first chapter of the ancient Hebrew songbook called the Psalms, we have a contrast between life and death, good and evil. The writer used the analogies of a tree and chaff. He wrote that the righteous person is "like a tree firmly planted by streams of water which yields its fruit in season and its leaf does not wither and whatever he does prospers" (Ps. 1:3).

He also wrote that the wicked person is "like chaff which the wind blows away" (Ps. 1:4). The writer contrasted a living, vibrant, fruitful tree with the dead husk or chaff from a grain. The tree is living and growing. The chaff is already dead and useless. The righteous person is living and growing. The wicked is already dead.

It's possible this was some of the imagery in the Apostle Paul's mind when he wrote to the Ephesians that they were dead in their trespasses and sins, "but God being rich in mercy, because of His great love with which He loved us, even when we were dead in our transgressions, made us alive together with Christ" (Eph. 2:5). Jesus's death on the cross and His resurrection are just that powerful. He can take what is dead and give it life. This is what He does when we call to Him. He gives us life. Have you called to Him for life?

§

AUGUST 2

Has God answered your prayers? Has He ever moved in a way that made you realize not only was He there, but He had heard you and given you what you requested?

In the Old Testament we have many genealogy lists. Some are simply a list of names in a rhythm. Some of those rhythms get disrupted with some treasured nuggets of theology or a biography. One of these nuggets disrupting the rhythm of a genealogy cadence is in 1 Chronicles 4:9—10, the prayer of Jabez. It includes a most intriguing final line: "and God answered his prayer" (1 Chron. 4:10).

Jabez asked God for four things. He asked that God would bless him and extend his responsibilities. He asked that God would anoint him with His power and presence and would keep him from all trouble and pain. In order to have those results, Jabez had to meet the conditions.

In order for God to bless Jabez and extend his responsibilities, Jabez had to be faithful with what God had already entrusted to him. For Jabez to have God's anointing for power and presence, Jabez had to live a life of obedience and faith. Jabez prayed a big prayer. He stepped out on faith, and God delivered a big answer to his prayer. God is ready to deliver a big answer to your prayer as well.

AUGUST 3

Human history began with a wedding, recorded in Genesis 2:22—25. This was when God escorted Eve and presented her to Adam. God made all the prearrangements for the wedding, officiated the service, and pronounced the blessing upon their marriage.

Revelation 19:7—10 records for us that human history ends at the wedding supper for Jesus and His bride, the Christian Church. The very next verse speaks about Jesus coming to retrieve His bride.

John 2:1—12 records for us that Jesus did His first miracle at a wedding in Cana. While at the reception His mother told Him they had run out of wine. After some discussion between Jesus and His mother, He turned the foot—washing water in the large stone pots near the door into wine—the best tasting wine of the entire reception.

When asked about fasting by John's disciples (Matthew 9:14—15), Jesus referred to Himself as the Bridegroom and His disciples as friends of the Bridegroom.

The Bible teaches that earthly marriage reflects the relationship between Christ and His Church. Maybe that is why God places such a high priority on us developing our marriages. When we make the effort to develop our marriage relationship, God is pleased.

§

AUGUST 4

About five hundred years ago, Reformers like John Calvin and Martin Luther coined a phrase: *Common Grace*. It means God shows us grace simply by giving us life and breath. God gives us sunshine and rain.

The Reformers developed this belief from verses like Proverbs 22:2: "The rich and the poor have a common bond, the Lord is the maker of them all," and Proverbs 29:13: "The poor man and the oppressor have this in common; the Lord gives light to the eyes of both." Peter refers to the impartiality of God in his first letter: "If you address as Father the One who impartially judges according to each one's work" (1 Pet. 1:17). God treats everyone equally.

The difference is found in how we respond to His common grace. Some people embrace what God has for them and consequently receive even more grace. Others reject God and His grace, which automatically prevents them from receiving additional grace. Life is not about who is God's favorite and who is left out. Life is about who will embrace God's plan and who will reject it. God has offered His grace. Are you receiving it or rejecting it?

AUGUST 5

The Bible uses a unique term, *grace*, which has been defined by many people as the unmerited favor of God. We have done nothing to deserve His favor and nothing to earn it. Grace is a synonym for mercy, and, just as mercy cannot be earned, neither can grace. If we earned it, it would then be our due payment, and God would be obligated. Instead God offers mercy; He offers grace.

Unlike the religion of Islam, where you earn God's favor by your performance, the Bible states that all of us are sinners. We all fall short of the glory of God (Rom. 3:23). We all miss the bull's—eye of behaving perfectly.

God believes somebody has to pay in blood for our sins. He knows you and I cannot pay such a high price. So He paid it Himself, with the blood of Jesus (1 Pet. 1:18—19). He did not take a vote or ask for our input. He simply made an executive decision to pay the exorbitant price. So give up trying to earn His favor or perform to a standard unattainable through your efforts, and allow the grace of God to transform you and empower you from the inside out.

§

AUGUST 6

Do you ask God for trinkets or for something more? Nehemiah found out that Jerusalem, his hometown, had been destroyed (Neh. 1:1—11). The news ripped his heart, causing him to weep and not eat for days.

After Nehemiah mourned, he prayed. He also prayed for days. As a slave he served as the king's taster, in order to protect the king from poisoning, but this also placed Nehemiah in a very strategic position right in front of the king. When the king noticed Nehemiah's mood was preoccupied, he began to suspect a plot against his life. So he asked Nehemiah what was wrong. Nehemiah explained about his hometown lying in ruins (Neh. 2:1—10). He then asked the king for permission to go home to rebuild the city. He also asked the king to provide the supplies from his own timber. The king gave Nehemiah everything he requested.

The Bible says God had given Nehemiah favor with the king. He asked God for big things. And God delivered through an enemy king. Dawson Trotman, founder of the Navigators which specializes in ministries on college campuses and military bases is quoted widely with this penetrating question: "When you pray, why ask God for trinkets when He wants to give you entire cities, countries, or even continents?"

August 7

After years of being a Christian and helping people in many ways, Peter found himself distant from God. He had grown so busy with his schedule of helping people that he had neglected his relationship with God for years. He felt the spiritual power draining from him every time he ministered to someone, yet because of his neglect of his relationship with God, he was not receiving a recharge or a refilling of his spirit.

Peter had been a pastor for years. Nevertheless he found himself sitting on the stairs to his basement pleading with God for forgiveness for having neglected their relationship for so long. He was empty and seeking a refill from God the way a deer seeks water from a river (Ps. 42:1).

You can do wonderful things for God. You can express your love and allegiance to Him in hundreds of ways, but according to Mark 3:14 the very first responsibility of a disciple is to be "with Jesus." Even the great Peter Marshall, chaplain of the US Senate, got so busy with his life that he neglected life with Jesus. He needed to turn back to being with Jesus.

§

August 8

When you think of the outlandish claims in the Bible—healings, babies born to old women, armies conquered in a day, entire seas splitting apart—do you laugh at God? Abraham laughed at God.

God had told Abraham repeatedly for twenty-four years that he would receive a son. Abraham was ninety-nine years old when God repeated this promise emphasizing that his wife, Sarah at ninety years of age would give birth to that promised son. Genesis 17:15—19 records that Abraham laughed so hard, he fell down and asked God just to work through Ishmael.

Many times we have that same lack of faith. God wants to do great things in our lives, but we are locked in to what we have already experienced. We tell God He has no clue. We flatter and compliment ourselves by telling ourselves we are realists; we live within the boundaries of our common sense when all the time, what we are really doing is calling God crazy and choosing to disregard any mustard seed—size faith within us. In spite of Abraham's laughter, God delivered on His promise. What outlandish miracle does God want to do in your life that might be blocked by your common sense?

August 9

The promised day was drawing near. Genesis 17:15—19 records for us that God told Abraham that Sarah would have the promised son, but Abraham fell on his face laughing at the ridiculous claim because he was ninety-nine years old. Sarah was eighty-nine. God told Abraham that Sarah would have the son the following year, and his name would be Isaac (Gen. 17:19).

In the Ancient Near Eastern culture, it was common to name a child in reference to the god the family worshiped. Many gods were worshiped throughout that region, and each area had its own set of gods.

The next chapter records for us that God showed up again only to repeat the promise that Sarah would have the baby and to specify it would be within the next twelve months. Sarah overheard the conversation and laughed, as did Abraham earlier. The name the Lord gave them, Isaac, was in reference to the god of the family, meaning "the Lord laughs." God greatly enjoys blessing His people. God laughed from pure and complete joy the day He gave Isaac to this couple.

§

August 10

Have you heard of Adam, Enoch, Noah, Abraham, Isaac, Jacob, and Joseph? You might recognize these seven men from the book of Genesis. They all had one thing in common—one thing that set them apart.

The book of Genesis will tell you each of these men had a very long life. It tells of their exploits and accomplishments. It tells of their failures. The Bible does not cover over the moral failures of its heroes. It tells it like it is, including all the good, the bad, and the ugly of its heroes.

In Genesis these seven men had one other thing in common too: they walked with God. Adam started the human race; Noah built an ark and saved his family from the global flood; Abraham became the father of our faith; Isaac was the promised son; Jacob wrestled with God to turn around a three—generational moral curse of cowardice; Joseph saved an entire generation from a great drought and famine; and Enoch walked so closely to God that he never died.

Each of these men communed with the Almighty. They lived in the hand of their Creator. They did it. So can you.

AUGUST 11

The last words spoken can be the most important, possibly more so if the separation will be for weeks or months. The importance is greater still if the separation will be because of death.

Jesus understood this point about relationships. In the Upper Room, just hours before his arrest, trial, and execution, He shared with His disciples one of the key factors for them to be successful in reaching the world with the Gospel.

Do you think the key was their knowledge of the message? Or maybe it was their ability to win theology debates. Maybe it was their connections to God. All of these might have been factors, but what Jesus actually said was, "By this will all people know you are my disciples, if you love one another" (John 13:35).

Maybe that explains why people are not flocking to our churches. Often we Christians will show compassion to one another during difficult times, and in other times we tolerate each other, but we still keep our relational distance. Maybe if we genuinely loved one another and liked being with each other, our communities would want that same connection with Jesus and with real friends. Make a decision today to be part of the solution for your church and your community.

§

AUGUST 12

Have you ever imagined being the answer to Jesus Christ's prayer that He prayed just hours before His death? As recorded for us in John 17:1—26, He prayed while in the Upper Room. The disciples overheard. God listened. At one point Jesus prayed, "I do not ask on behalf of these alone, but for those also who believe in Me through their word; that they may all be one; even as You, Father, are in Me and I in You, that they also may be in Us, so that the world may believe that You sent Me" (John 17:20—21). Jesus prayed His followers would be unified, have a singleness of purpose, a unified front toward one goal. He did not pray for one congregation but for a unified collection of followers.

The result of this unified attitude and purpose will be effective evangelism. Instead of spending thousands of dollars on a crusade, a well-known speaker, and a variety of special music, churches could get together on Monday and pray for each other and for their community. They could rally together on Friday at lunch to pray for each other. Jesus said He would bless unity among His followers; He would not bless competition, suspicion, and division.

August 13

Jacob grew up in a home where his parents worshiped the Lord. They believed, and they taught their children to believe, but Jacob simply pretended in order to keep his parents off his back. He did the right things and said the right answers to their questions. After all, he knew the drill. But as time passed, Jacob found himself in some real trouble.

Jacob's twin brother, Esau, was hunting him with intentions to kill him. Jacob left town and tried to run away. While on the trip to a foreign country, Jacob breathed this prayer to God: "If God will be with me and keep me safe on this trip. And if I have plenty to eat and plenty to wear, and if I can someday return home safely, then the Lord will be my God" (Gen. 28:20—21). Jacob offered to take the Lord as his God just as he had witnessed his father, Isaac worshiping the Lord as his God.

Jacob knew where to turn when in trouble, but he did not turn to God honestly. Instead Jacob turned to the Lord in a manipulative negotiation: "If God will bless all of my life and prosper me without adversity, then I will allow the Lord to be my God." Often we follow this same pattern to follow and worship God on our terms. And like Jacob, we do not connect with God.

§

August 14

Often we make our decisions backward, exposing our backward values. Leadership principles tell us the way to make the best decisions is to first determine what is right, not what is affordable.

Because we often get our decision—making procedure backward, we often refuse to do the right thing. This can result in some horribly uncomfortable situations.

In Matthew 17:24—27 Jesus asks Peter, "Who pays taxes?" Once Peter answers, Jesus sends Peter to the beach with these instructions: "Take the first fish you catch, and when you open its mouth, you will find a coin that will cover the expense for your taxes and mine."

If you believe your problems are bigger than God, then you will have problems trusting God with your money, but if you believe the Creator of the universe, the Almighty who gives life to everything and upholds all of creation in the palm of His hand, is greater than your problems, then trusting Him with your money only makes good sense.

AUGUST 15

Jesus had been up on the mountain with Peter, James, and John while a man brought his sick son to the other disciples. The disciples tried to cast out a demon from the boy but could not. Jesus Himself had given them such authority earlier, but it had dissipated for some reason, according to the story found in Matthew 17:14—23.

The man came to Jesus asking for help and pointing out that he had brought his son to the disciples, but they could not cure him. So the man brought his son to Jesus, and Jesus healed him and set him free.

Later, in private, the disciples asked Jesus why they could not bring healing to the boy. Have you ever noticed Jesus did not say, "Because we did not have enough money in the budget"? The answer Jesus gave to them to explain why they could not bring healing to the boy was startling to them: "Because of your lack of faith," (Matt. 17:20). They could not minister to a person in need because they did not trust Jesus. They had plenty of money, plenty of time, and plenty of desire to help. They simply did not trust Jesus to bring the desired result.

§

AUGUST 16

Do you believe in the supernatural? Do you believe the only things that exist can be seen and touched, or do you believe there is more? Jesus Christ believed there is more—a lot more.

He talked about this one day with the greatest teacher in Israel. We have this conversation preserved in John 3:1—21. Jesus told Nicodemus that Nicodemus could lecture on the Kingdom of God all day long to all of his students, but the only way into the Kingdom was to be born again. That is what Jesus called it. He called it being born of the Spirit, born from above, and born again. He said we can discuss it and think about it, but the only way in was for us to allow God to perform a supernatural experience within us.

Jesus said God loves us and wants to do this supernatural experience within each of us, making it crystal clear that there is no other way into the Kingdom of God except being born of God, born of the Spirit, born from above, born again. If you have not experienced this supernatural touch from God but would like to, talk directly to Jesus about it.

August 17

Cletus was sixteen days old when his mother died from childbirth complications. Her parents hated him for it but took over rearing him and his sister. His grandmother placed food in front of him and said something like, "Enjoy your lunch, boy. My daughter is dead because of you." Each morning she woke him by throwing a cup of water into his face and growling, "Get up, boy!" All the cards were stacked against Cletus; he was bound to grow into an angry, hate-filled criminal. But at the tender age of fourteen, he turned his life over to Jesus Christ.

Years later, as a married man with children, he remembered his childhood and chose not to repeat those tactics in his home. Rooted in the fact that we are created in the image of God (Gen. 1:26—27), God gives us the ability to think, to reason, to evaluate, and to choose how we will act or react in any situation.

Cletus certainly took advantage of that freedom and that power. He refused to give his power of choice over to any anger, hatred, addictive habit, or bad memory that would only cloud his judgment. God gives us each the power to choose, and Cletus used that power for good to benefit many people.

§

August 18

Not even God will interfere with the power He has given you to choose. Rooted in the fact that we are created in the image of God, He created you to have a free will, or the freedom and the power to make all of your choices. "Now, wait a minute, I never chose that one thing to happen," some might say. I'm not talking about what happens to you. I'm talking about how God has given you the power to make all of your own decisions.

You can choose to look for the good and positive, or you can choose to focus on the bad and negative. You can choose to eat healthy food or harmful food. You can choose to watch wholesome shows on TV or the Internet or choose to watch shows that promote harm and damage to your family. You can choose to forgive someone who has harmed you, or you can choose to hate them and think about them all day long, keeping them as the center of your attention.

Several times in the Bible, in one form or another, God says, "I set before you life and death, good and evil. Choose life" (Deut. 30:15—16). God gave you the incredible power of choice, a free will. Use that power wisely.

AUGUST 19

Do you ever get disappointed or discouraged and consider giving up? I have. We do not usually grow discouraged because of one big thing but because of a lot of little things that pile up: little complaints, people not doing their best, people criticizing you, or maybe your spouse being more interested in fixing you than supporting you. Life can get very discouraging at times.

When disappointed we sometimes stop attending church, cutting ourselves off from the social support designed by God to help us. We stop reading our Bibles and even stop praying because deep down we are also disappointed with God. We blame the pastor. We blame the church board, or we blame the entire church in general. As this process unfolds we become part of the problem.

Jesus sat outside Jerusalem and cried out, "O Jerusalem, Jerusalem, how often I wanted to gather you to me as a hen gathers her chicks, but you would not allow it" (Matt. 23:37). Wow. Jesus also struggled with disappointment and discouragement. When you struggle with disappointment, look to Jesus, and learn from Him to endure and not to quit.

§

AUGUST 20

Jesus told stories for many reasons, foremost to communicate something about God's character, His plans, and His desires.

Luke 7:40—50 records for us that sitting at the dinner table one day, Jesus spoke to His host, saying, "Two people owed a man some money. One person owed the man fifty dollars while the other person owed the man fifty thousand dollars. Neither one had the money to repay, so the man, feeling gracious, decided to cancel each debt. He forgave both persons, and neither had to pay back the man" (Luke 7:40-42 author's paraphrase).

Then Jesus asked His host which debtor was more grateful and demonstrated love more readily. His host replied, "That's easy. The one who owed more will be more grateful and love the man more" (Luke 7:43 author's paraphrase).

Jesus declared, "You are exactly right" (Luke 7:43 author's paraphrase). He told this story to help the respectful homeowner see some compassion for a prostitute seeking mercy and love from Jesus.

Why do we today deliberately try to keep out the thieves, drug pushers, prostitutes, adulterers, and at—risk children? Knowing the stories of Jesus as we do, why do we turn our backs on the very ones He identifies as the ones He wants us to reach?

AUGUST 21

Peter had worked third shift his whole life. He owned a fishing business along with his brother and two friends from the same town where he worked. He claimed to be a follower of Jesus Christ.

Now, most people in society expect a follower of Jesus to be a kind and gentle person. Not Peter. Nothing about him was gentle. He had an explosive temper; he was quick to say his opinion, and then later he would have to either apologize or even recant it.

One night in particular, after Peter had been a follower of Jesus for over three years, his temper got the best of him, and he pulled a sword out of its sheath and attacked another man. In the fight, according to John 18:10—11, Peter cut off the right ear of Malchus, the servant of the high priest.

If Jesus had not been right there, the Apostle Peter might have ended up dead, but instead he ended up being one of the best followers of Jesus, the leader of the disciples. Peter, a partner in a fishing business, who worked third shift every night and had an explosive temper—Jesus used him to change the world. Jesus is not looking for our ability but for our availability. Peter was available for Jesus.

§

AUGUST 22

Simon and the other disciples found themselves answering questions from Jesus one day. Jesus asked, "Who do people say I am?"

As recorded in Matthew 16:13—20, the disciples answered, "Some say John the Baptist and others Elijah, but still others Jeremiah or one of the prophets."

Then Jesus asked, "But who do you say that I am?" Simon jumped in. "You are the Christ, the Son of the living God" (Matt. 16:16).

Jesus seemed very pleased with Simon for his insight and eagerness. Jesus told him He would no longer call him Simon but would call him Peter. The word Peter literally means "the rock."

Changing a person's name in the ancient world was an indication of a change of inner character. From that day, Jesus declared this Simon would be known as the rock. Peter's inner character would become known for strength and stability, faithfulness and reliability. He would be the rock on which God could rely.

Scholars debate what this rock is, but it seems pretty clear that when Jesus supernaturally transforms a person from the inside out, that person becomes a rock who will stand even against the powers of Hell.

August 23

One day Jesus told Peter, "Satan has demanded to sift you like wheat, but I have prayed for you that your faith will not fail. When once you have turned again, strengthen your brothers" (Luke 22:31—32).

Jesus said He had just given Satan permission to attack, to bring hardship, and Peter was going down. No way was that good news; however, Jesus did include good news in the message, as preserved for us in Luke 22:31—32. He told Peter, "When you recover" or "turn again."

Yes, Peter would be attacked; he would be harmed; he would fall flat on his face, but Jesus had prayed for him. Peter would recover. He would get up. His faith would survive. He would stand firm again, and when he did he would strengthen those around him.

It is very possible you have been attacked, but Jesus has prayed for you also. Trust Him today for that strength to recover. Trust Him today for that strength to stand up again. Trust Him today to empower you to strengthen someone else in need.

§

August 24

Five historians from the first century AD reported a solar eclipse that lasted for three hours on the day Jesus was crucified. Biblical writers Matthew (27:45), Mark (15:33), and Luke (23:44) recorded this great darkness along with two Greek writers by the names of Thallus and Phlegon.

Before you say these five recorded a normal eclipse, remember that the day Jesus was crucified was also during the Jewish festival called Passover. This festival is always connected with the full moon. So what we have is a great darkness during the phase of the full moon, when an eclipse is impossible simply because the moon is on the wrong side of the earth to cause an eclipse.

What these five men recorded is the only eclipse—type event in history that has no explanation even from modern—day astronomers. Some skeptics dismiss it as a religious myth, which would work if only Matthew, Mark, and Luke documented it, but two unbelieving Greek historians also documented this event in history. Jesus's death and resurrection are the two most significant events in history, and God moved heaven and earth to help place these events on the historical timeline.

Such a piece of scientific and historical evidence as this one strengthens my faith. How about you?

AUGUST 25

About three years into His ministry, the Gospel of Luke records, Jesus "set His face" to go to Jerusalem (Luke 9:51). This means Jesus made His decision. He stood determined. Even though He still had several healings to do, even though He still had a lot of teaching to do, even though He still had many things to accomplish, He set His face to go to Jerusalem.

Jesus knew that Simon Peter, the leader of His disciples, would deny Him. He knew one of His own would betray him. He knew He would be beaten, stripped, and crucified naked in front of everyone. The artists who paint the pictures of Jesus wearing a loincloth are simply showing respect.

Jesus remained determined to see it through. He tapped in to the power of the Holy Spirit to stay focused on the task of getting to Jerusalem. He had a world to redeem. He had you on His mind, and He remained unwilling to waver. He set His face to suffer and bleed and die for you. He knew if He could prove His love for you by dying for your sins, He might win you over for all of eternity. He "set His face" with you on His mind.

§

AUGUST 26

When John the Baptist introduced Jesus, he stood at the Jordan River, baptizing all who came to him, and he knew Jesus stood in the crowd. In that first chapter of John's Gospel, various persons called Jesus "rabbi" (John 1:49), "the Son of God" (John 1:49), "Messiah" (John 1:41), and even "the king of Israel" (John 1:49). But when John makes the initial introduction, he does not refer to any of these lofty titles.

When John introduces his cousin and childhood playmate to the nation of Israel, John calls Him "the Lamb of God who takes away the sin of the world" (John 1:29). He calls Jesus "the Lamb of God" because Jesus will be the sacrifice of God to save the entire world.

Both John and Jesus knew full well why Jesus had come to earth, why He stood in front of the people, and how it would end. Because Jesus knew this, He stayed focused on His end goal: redeeming you and me. This was foremost on the mind of Christ as He healed the sick and preached to the poor. Redeeming you never left His mind. You are always on His mind.

AUGUST 27

Have you ever considered your potential, really sat down and thought it through? A few factors come into play that might help you to recognize you have great potential.

First, you are created in the image of God (Gen. 1:26—27). That alone places you above the animals and even above the angels.

Second, Jesus Christ died to provide forgiveness for the sins you have committed in your life. He offers a clean slate.

Third, in Romans 8:11 we read that the same Spirit who raised Jesus Christ from the dead is the Spirit who dwells in you. If you are a Christian, then you have been born of the Holy Spirit, and just as He raised Jesus from the dead, He dwells in you to give you supernatural power to obey God, to live life, and to reach those God—given dreams that reside in your soul.

Society says you have limits and many restrictions. God says the same Spirit who raised Jesus from the grave is alive in you. What does that say about your potential?

§

AUGUST 28

The Dead Sea is the lowest land point on the face of the earth, sitting a couple of hundred feet below sea level. You can drive down to the Dead Sea, and along the road is a sign identifying that you are dropping below sea level.

It is called the Dead Sea because nothing lives there. The various minerals in the water are at such high levels that nothing can live. Ocean water is 3 percent salt, and all the oceans in the world teem with life of all kinds. The Dead Sea is 30 percent salt—presently ten times saltier than the world's oceans—and growing saltier every year. The novelty of swimming in the Dead Sea is you cannot sink. The mineral level is so high everybody floats.

The Dead Sea is an object lesson in life from God for us. The Dead Sea only receives water from area streams. Nothing goes out. So if you only take and do not give, you are dead also. If you do not give of your time, talents, and resources, you are dead also. God is the giver of life and love. Having been created in the image of God (Gen. 1:27), you are designed to be a giver. God has created you for life, so make a decision today that you will be like God: you will be a giver.

AUGUST 29

King Saul had a problem with low self-esteem, according to 1 Samuel 15:17. He did not think highly of himself. He would hide from his responsibilities and his problems. He avoided the truth and pursued popularity with the people instead of choosing what was right. He practiced what today we call denial.

Saul chose to follow his feelings instead of the facts. The prophet Samuel told him God had made him taller and stronger than anyone else in the entire nation and had anointed him as their king, but Saul felt little. So he acted like less than God wanted him to act, choosing his feelings over the facts, and it cost him his throne. He would not trust God or obey God. He would not stick his neck out and lead the way God wanted him to lead. He pursued what was popular with the people. He simply believed he was not valuable.

Do you struggle with low self-esteem? Jesus says you are the salt of the earth and the light of the world. He does not say you will hopefully become those things someday. He says you are the salt and light. Do not be like King Saul; choose to believe the facts instead of believing your feelings. Choose what is right instead of what is popular.

§

AUGUST 30

King Saul suffered from low self-esteem, according to 1 Samuel 15:17. Not thinking highly of himself, he hid from his responsibilities and his problems. Denying what God thought of him, Saul was more interested in what the nation of Israel thought of him.

He chose deception over truth. God told him to conquer a nearby city, kill the enemy, and destroy the city. After the battle Saul's people kept the best of the spoils for themselves. When Samuel the prophet confronted Saul about this, Saul replied, "I have obeyed the voice of the Lord." Samuel pointed out that Saul had not obeyed and was now making excuses and believing a deception.

Today's denial can take many forms. We choose to believe deception instead of the truth. We stay entangled in unhealthy, even destructive personal habits and relationships because we refuse to believe the truth about them. Jesus said, "The truth will set you free" (John 8:32). By practicing denial we believe the deception. King Saul hid behind his low self-esteem, trying to gain and maintain the favor of the people instead of obeying God. Who are you trying to please, people or God?

AUGUST 31

Jesus said you are the salt of the earth (Matt. 5:13). He did not say you might be the salt of the earth someday. He did not tell you to strive to become the salt of the earth. He said, "You are the salt of the earth."

Salt is used to influence. It influences the food we eat. It is used to affect taste and for preservation. It keeps food from rotting over time. If we as Christians are the salt of the earth, would that mean we are to influence the others around us? Are we to influence the "flavor" of the society around us and preserve the very society in which we live?

Various Gallup polls tell us that over 90 percent of the people in the United States believe in God. They acknowledge His existence. The polls tell us that over one third of the population of the United States claim to be Christians. If you put one third of a pound of salt on a sixteen-ounce steak, it would no longer taste like steak at all. That amount of salt would cause the entire dish to taste like salt.

Maybe it's time for Christians to affect society so much that society looks and acts more like the Christ. After all, we are the salt of the earth.

SEPTEMBER 1

Jesus told his disciples they are the light of the world, recorded for us in Matthew 5:14. If you follow Christ, you are the light of the world.

Have you ever gone into a room and turned on the light, and the room became darker? That would never happen because even one light would influence the level of light in the entire room. You are the light of the world. Instead of the other people influencing you away from Jesus, Jesus expects you to influence other people toward Him.

Jesus fully expects you to have an influential effect on the part of the world in which you live. When He spoke about light, His followers thought of the sun or fire. Jesus expects you to bring warmth and illumination. He expects you to make a positive difference in your home, at your work, and within your community.

Jesus did not say that maybe someday you might become the light of the world. He did not say to work day and night, making workaholics look like slackers, and strive to become the light of the world. He said it simply and profoundly: "You are the light of the world."

§

SEPTEMBER 2

Some people never turn to God. Regardless of how God works in their lives—sending adversity and hoping they will cry out for help, sending blessings and hoping they will look up and give thanks, or providing just enough for survival so they consistently call out to Him for food and shelter—some people just never figure out that they need to turn their lives to God.

King Saul was this kind of person. Anointed by Samuel as the first king of the entire nation of Israel, Saul found himself with incredible authority in a very short time. After all, he was king.

Samuel consistently told Saul what the Lord wanted from him as king, but Saul consistently bowed his leadership to the pressure of popularity with the people. The turning point came when Samuel rebuked Saul for disobeying the Lord, and Saul replied, "I have sinned, but please honor me now before the elders of my people and before Israel" (1 Sam. 15:30).

Saul ignored Samuel's rebuke. Saul ignored the fact that he had rebelled against God. Saul focused exclusively on seeking the favor of the people. Don't concern yourself with pleasing other people more than concerning yourself with pleasing God.

SEPTEMBER 3

We have learned that the way a person speaks can reveal his or her true values and true beliefs just like a well—conducted lie detector test. A careful, attentive listener can pick up words or tones betraying the speaker's true values. The Bible has such statements by various persons throughout its pages. One example is when the Prophet Samuel and King Saul are arguing over Saul's sin.

Samuel tried to explain to Saul that Saul has rebelled against the Lord, and each time Saul defends his behavior or deflects the attention onto the people and off of himself. Three times Saul betrays his beliefs with the pronouns he chooses to use. Three times while Saul speaks with Samuel, Saul refers to the Lord as "your God" instead of "my God" or "our God" (1 Sam. 15:15, 15:21, 15:30).

By using the pronoun *your*, Samuel reveals he has turned away from following the Lord. Earlier in Saul's story, he followed the Lord, but those days are past. Saul has rejected the Lord, his God and three times in this one conversation he refers to the Lord as Samuel's God, not his own God. Don't follow Saul's example. Keep yourself true to God.

§

SEPTEMBER 4

Rachel was only four years old when a pattern began to emerge. Her mother would tell her to pick up her clothes or put away her shoes, and Rachel would run over to her, hug and kiss her, talk to her for a moment, and then return to her play.

Genesis 17:1 records for us that the Lord said to Abraham, "I am God Almighty. Walk before me and be blameless." Abraham responded by falling on his face in worship. As God continued to speak to him, he laughed at God's plan and argued with Him.

Many people have deliberately and consciously adopted a personal policy of decision—making behavior, and they even have a slogan for this policy: it is easier to ask for forgiveness later than to get permission now.

When King Saul explained he disobeyed God to keep the best of the sheep so the people could offer them in sacrifice to the Lord, Samuel the prophet explained the flaw in that decision: "to obey is better than sacrifice" (1 Sam. 15:22). Instead of planning to sin and seek forgiveness, simply obey. Instead of a façade of worship, God wants obedience.

SEPTEMBER 5

In the very first verse of the Bible—"in the beginning God created the heavens and the earth"—(Gen. 1:1) we find an interesting grammatical structure. We find the earliest beginning of God revealing Himself as a Triune Being.

The church fathers developed a new word, *person*, in the third century AD. They were trying to describe the Trinity as revealed in the Bible. The Trinity is the idea that there is one God, but three Persons. Those persons are the Father, Son, and Holy Spirit. They developed the word *person* as a descriptive term for the first person of the Trinity, God the Father; the second person of the Trinity, God the Son; and the third person of the Trinity, God the Spirit.

Genesis was written in Hebrew. So the first verse in Hebrew is *"Berry-sheet, bara Eloheem"* which when translated into English is "In the beginning, God created." The verb *bara* is the third—person masculine singular for "create." *Eloheem* is the plural form of El, "God," a grammatical structure revealing a plural God (three—in one) creating as one. It is the first indication we have of the oneness of God simultaneous with the three Persons.

§

SEPTEMBER 6

At the climax of the book of Exodus, we read that "the cloud covered the tent of meeting, and the glory of the Lord filled the tabernacle" (Exod. 40:34). Everything in the story of Exodus leads up to this climactic moment when God comes to His people and they worship.

God first reveals who He is by proving Himself greater than all the gods of Egypt (Exod. 18:11), conquering them with one plague after another. He protects Israel at the Red Sea and in battle against the Amalekites. The Lord provides Israel with guidance through the cloud and pillar of fire, provides food with manna and quail, provides water from the rock, and only then invites them into an exclusive covenant relationship with Himself.

The Lord gives them guidance on how to prepare the tent of meeting, the place where His glory will dwell and the place where they will gather for worship. All these things and a few more are in preparation for worship.

Once Israel has experienced the Lord's salvation by grace, protection, provision, guidance, and invitation, they bring it all to a climax with worship. Have you experienced His salvation by grace? Do you use His grace, protection, provision, guidance, and invitation to launch you to worship?

SEPTEMBER 7

The climax of the book of Exodus is worship. The cloud covered the tent of meeting, and the glory of the Lord filled the tabernacle" (Exod. 40:34) and Israel gathered for worship.

In John 1:14 we read this unusual statement describing how Jesus left His throne in Heaven and came to earth as a man: "The Word became flesh and tab-ernacled among us and we beheld His glory" (author's translation). One English translation of John 1:14 translates this Greek word as *dwelled*. One translation uses *pitched His tent*. Still another one uses *moved into the neighborhood*. I suppose all these scholars have their reasons for the words they chose to use in their translations, but the word John used is *tabernacled*.

John takes the noun *tabernacle* and uses it as a verb, but more importantly he uses the language and the imagery of Exodus 40:34—"the glory of the Lord filled the tabernacle"—by writing "The Word became flesh and tabernacled among us and we beheld His glory."

John identifies Jesus as the One who came down on the tabernacle and filled it with His glory. Jesus is the One worshiped in Exodus 40:34 and He is the One you are invited to worship now.

§

SEPTEMBER 8

Jacob had a dream where he saw God in heaven at the top of a ladder that stretched from heaven to earth. Angels were climbing up and down the ladder, receiving assignments from God and carrying them out throughout the world (Gen. 28:10—17).

Jesus had a conversation with Nathaniel one day where Nathaniel seemed fascinated with Jesus's ability to see things and people in other lands. Responding to Nathaniel's amazement, Jesus stated, "You will see the heavens opened and the angels of God ascending and descending on the Son of Man" (John 1:51).

Jesus was clearly connecting with that image in Jacob's dream about a lad-der reaching between heaven and earth, and even more than mentioning the imagery, Jesus was stating He Himself is that ladder.

In several statements in the Bible, Jesus indicates He is the one and only way to God. So it simply makes sense that Jesus would identify Himself with any Old Testament story or image where heaven and earth connect, identifying Himself as the part of each story that connects earth with God. He is the One who will connect you to God.

SEPTEMBER 9

Israel rebelled against God and complained about Moses. As preserved in Numbers 21:1—9, God responded to their rebellion by sending venomous snakes into the camp. The Bible records for us that many people died, and many others confessed to Moses, "We have sinned because we have spoken against the Lord and against you" (Num. 21:7). Then Moses prayed for the people.

God instructed Moses to make a bronze serpent and place it on top of a staff. God then promised that anyone who looked to the serpent would survive the snakebite and live. Is seems like a strange remedy for a snakebite, but it was a test of faith. Would they trust the Lord to deliver them from death? Moses obeyed the Lord and built the bronze serpent. Many looked to the serpent, and because they trusted what God had said, they lived.

When Jesus had His conversation with Nicodemus about being born from above, being born of the Spirit, being born again, at one point He stated, "As Moses lifted up the serpent in the wilderness, even so must the Son of man be lifted up; so that whoever believes will in Him have eternal life" (John 3:14—15). Jesus is still God's solution to any problem including death itself.

September 10

Jack had given his heart to Jesus as a nineteen-year-old college freshman. Over the following eight months he read through the entire Bible three more times and was within a mere three chapters of finishing it again when he read Revelation 19:11—16, describing Jesus as a warrior riding on a white stallion with the armies of heaven following Him, wearing a robe dipped in blood and a pile of crowns on His head, with a tattoo on His thigh reading "King of Kings and Lord of Lords." Jack read the paragraph several times, getting more anxious each time.

Jack knelt and prayed something like this: "Lord Jesus, I have seen many tough guys with many tattoos, but none had the audacity to wear one saying 'King of Kings.' Growing up I was taught You wore a robe and went about being kind and compassionate. I was never taught anything about how you are portrayed in Revelation 19:11—16. I am now scared I have been worshiping a figment of my imagination. I am going to read my Bible a lot to learn who You really are now. Would You please teach me who You are now? I do not want to follow and worship a figment of my imagination. I want to worship the one true and living God. Amen."

Some people read the Bible limiting their reading to certain portions only to validate their beliefs. You could read just parts of your Bible that validates your beliefs or you could read your entire Bible to discover the one true God.

September 11

The adage is a play on words, merely a changing of one letter between two words, and historically profound: choose to grow better, not bitter.

Joseph's brothers sold him into slavery, to a traveling caravan of merchants who resold him in Egypt. The total story of Joseph takes several chapters (Genesis 37—50) to unfold, and he repeatedly chooses to reject bitterness.

Twenty-two years later the brothers have to stand in front of Joseph, who never gives any indication of revenge. He realizes the brothers do not recognize him, so he introduces himself to them with this gracious statement: "I am your brother Joseph whom you sold into Egypt. Now do not be grieved or angry with yourselves because you sold me here, for God sent me before you to preserve life...God sent me before you to preserve for you a remnant in the earth, and to keep you alive by a great deliverance" (Gen. 45:4—8).

The twenty-two years that had passed had helped Joseph see God's perspective on his entire life. An integral part of that perspective was his decision to grow better instead of bitter.

SEPTEMBER 12

In trying to be gracious to people and trying to preserve relationships, we often say things that might make others feel better, but the statements are not true. We might say, "It's OK," "You didn't mean to hurt me," or something similar, removing responsibility from others.

Joseph was seventeen years old when his brothers sold him into slavery. Twenty-two years later they stood before him still cowards, still jealous, still planning cowardly deception. Joseph did not even respond to their statements or acknowledge their consistent deceptions.

Joseph had already chosen to grow better instead of bitter many times. So his decision to offer mercy and remain honest was consistent with his character. He chose to walk with God. The brothers were consistent as cowards and Joseph was consistently courageous expressing that courage with honesty and mercy.

When his brothers came to him with their latest deception, Joseph replied, "Do not be afraid, for am I in God's place? As for you, you meant evil against me, but God meant it for good in order to bring about this present result, to preserve many people alive" (Gen. 50:19—20). Because of his honesty, he knew he was not in God's place and he was not God. There is a God and Joseph knew he was not He. Because of this, Joseph was gracious.

God still can do such a deep abiding work of grace in your life. God wants to bring such profound grace to you also.

SEPTEMBER 13

The book of Genesis records for us that Joseph was sold into slavery in Egypt and purchased by Potiphar the captain of Pharaoh's bodyguard. Joseph was assigned as the chief slave to take care of Potiphar's house.

Potiphar's wife pursued Joseph for sexual favors. As recorded in Genesis 39:8—9, Joseph resisted her, stating that Potiphar, his master, had withheld nothing from him "except you because you are his wife. How then could I do this great evil and sin against God?"

Even though this was almost five hundred years before God gave the Ten Commandments to Israel, Joseph knew another man's wife was off limits. He did not have to have a commandment. He knew you do not have sex with another man's wife, because that would be a great sin against God. Without the commandment how did Joseph know this would be a great sin against God?

To follow the commandments is a stiff religious practice, a list of what to do and what not to do. Genesis presents Joseph as a man who walked with God, who cultivated his relationship with God so that he did not need a set of rules. He knew God. Because of that intimacy, he understood God's desires. Are you cultivating your relationship with God? Do you know God's desires?

§

SEPTEMBER 14

The worst part about being deceived is we end up making decisions and living life based on information that is not true. Consequently we will experience confusion and consistent discouragement.

Within our family relationships, *denial* is just a fancy word for believing lies. Denial becomes a breeding ground for emotional insecurity, envy and jealousy. It causes us to divide alliances and act selfishly. All of these weave tangled webs within our families.

These various character traits can all be found within the family of Isaac and Rebecca as they reared their twin boys, Esau and Jacob. Beginning in Genesis 25:19 and continuing throughout the remaining twenty-five chapters we see significant drama within their family. Parental favoritism results in multiple deceptions and even death threats among their children. The family is estranged from one another for decades. However, all of this can give us hope. If God chooses to work His wonders of salvation and reconciliation through such a family then there is hope for us all.

SEPTEMBER 15

Abraham placed his wife and any future children in grave danger more than once. At seventy-five years of age, he and his wife went to Egypt, where he announced to her one day, "I know that you are a beautiful woman, and when the Egyptians see you, they will say, 'This is his wife' and they will kill me, but they will let you live. Please say that you are my sister so that I may live" (Gen. 12:11—13).

The Egyptians did see Sarah and did see she was beautiful and did send word to Pharaoh. The Bible records that Pharaoh did take Sarah into his home and did pay Abraham sheep, oxen, donkeys, camels, and slaves. Pharaoh's understood intention was that Sarah would become one of his wives.

In all likelihood, regardless of where they live, most women would not be impressed with husbands who hand them off to other men. Most women are not looking to be married to such cowards. Women normally want secure relationships where they are safe from harm or treatment that would rob them of their dignity. In spite of such cowardice, God worked through this family. And God can work through you as well.

§

SEPTEMBER 16

One day when Abraham was ninety-nine years old, God came to him to announce that Sarah would have a son the following year. Abraham laughed and obviously did not believe God (Gen. 17:1—19).

After he had walked with God for twenty-four years, it would be reasonable to expect Abraham had gained some faith and some skill in trusting God. Reasonable, maybe, but Abraham made the same mistakes again nonetheless.

Abraham took Sarah and led his flocks to the grazing fields in the south country between Kadesh and Shur. There he gave her away a second time, telling people, "She is my sister" (Gen. 20:1—2). The king took her as a potential wife.

One simple question arises: how was Sarah going to conceive the promised child if she was sleeping in another man's bed? She would not be able to conceive Isaac by Abraham during this year, as God promised, if Abraham, the father of our faith, did not act faithfully to God and keep her for his own. Abraham clearly did not believe God. The extreme drama of this family still did not stop the faithfulness of God. He spoke to the king, who restored Sarah to Abraham, and later she conceived Isaac. God is faithful.

September 17

If sin is not interrupted by repentance, it just seems to advance to new levels. Abraham gave Sarah away twice to other men because of fear. Then Isaac was born, and Abraham did not turn from his cowardice.

The Bible records for us in Genesis 25:19—26 that Isaac and Rebecca had twin boys named Esau and Jacob. Similar to the previous generation with Abraham, the weather patterns repeated, and a drought came to the land, so Isaac took his family to Gerar, where the herds of livestock could graze for food (Gen. 26:1—7). Just like his father, Abraham, Isaac lived as a coward. So when he and his family arrived in the new land, he told everyone Rebecca was his sister.

Abraham handed over Sarah twice, telling people she was his sister. Taking the cowardice to the next level, his son, Isaac, handed over his wife, Rebecca, while their twin sons watched and learned. This family had some significant trouble with fear and deception, which is a breeding ground for denial, resulting in emotional insecurity, envy and jealousy, dividing lines of alliance, selfishness, and additional deception. Nonetheless, God chose to work through this family, and He will work through your family also. God is faithful.

§

September 18

Sin seems to have a mind of its own, growing more intense with each passing generation unless interrupted by repentance. Twice Abraham gave away Sarah out of fear. Isaac gave away Rebecca with their twin boys watching the entire drama, and they learned the lessons of deception and coercion well.

Jacob coerced Esau into selling his birthright for a bowl of food. Later, under the direction of Rebecca, Jacob deceived Isaac and stole the family blessing from Esau. Consequently Esau vowed to kill Jacob (Gen. 25:27—28:9).

By playing favorites, choosing Jacob over Esau, Rebecca, like a modern—day movie director, orchestrated the jealousy and stirred up the hatred that already existed between her sons. Esau saw that his mother did not like the women in the land where they lived, so he made a point of marrying one. For the remaining years of their lives, this caused pain and difficulties for Rebecca.

Rebecca's treachery resulted in Esau making a death threat against Jacob who left home. Rebecca's favorite was gone. When we aim at deception, no one wins.

SEPTEMBER 19

Because of Esau's death threat, Jacob ran from home to Paddan—Aram, which was a few days' journey away. He landed at the home of Laban, his mother's brother, where he spent the next twenty years of his life, gaining two wives, eleven sons, one daughter, and much livestock.

After those twenty years, God told him to return to his homeland, and he made plans to do so. While he was traveling to his homeland, a message came to him that his brother, Esau, was coming to meet him, bringing four hundred men with him (Gen. 32:6). Jacob suspected that Esau planned to kill him, so Jacob returned to the generational family curse or pattern of cowardice.

In preparation to meet Esau, Jacob divided his family into two groups and sent them ahead of him along with a large gift of livestock. Maybe between receiving the animals and killing the family, Esau would gain satisfaction and allow Jacob to live.

Abraham had endangered his family by giving away his wife. Isaac had endangered his family by giving away his wife in front of his sons. Taking the cowardice to the next level Jacob now endangered his family by using them as shields as he entered battle. Sin multiplies.

SEPTEMBER 20

Jacob heard that Esau was coming to meet him with four hundred men. Jacob divided his family into two groups and sent them across the Jabbok River.

In the ancient world, a person's name often reflected internal character. *Jacob*, when translated, means "supplanter, deceiver, or fraud."

That night God wrestled with Jacob, who demanded that God bless him. So God asked for his name, and he replied, "Jacob." God stated, "Your name will no longer be Jacob, but Israel, for you have striven with God and with men and have prevailed" (Gen. 32:28).

By changing Jacob's name to Israel, God was changing Jacob's core character from a cowardly deceiver to one who walked with God. In a moment the supernatural touch from God changed Jacob from the inside out, transforming his core inner nature from fraudulent to honest, from cowardly to courageous. We might think an all—night wrestling match is a long time to change a core character trait, but it is a miraculous moment for the man who had already invested sixty years to developing his cowardly character. Unless transformation happens, sin multiplies over time.

SEPTEMBER 21

In addition to growing within individuals, sin seems to multiply from generation to generation unless interrupted. Sin seems to have a destructive power all its own that only grows when passed on to the next generation.

Because of cowardice, Abraham gave away Sarah twice. Because of cowardice, Isaac gave away Rebecca in front of his twin sons. Because of cowardice, Jacob divided his wives and children and offered them to Esau as the first line in an expected battle.

Even today men continue to consistently jeopardize their wives and children because of their own cowardice. Globally we have a crisis of manhood, but God has a solution (Gen. 32:24—32).

We see how God intervened with Jacob. In the dark, attacking from behind, Jacob could not run. He had to fight. Jacob thought he had pinned God, but God had Jacob right where He wanted him. Then, as Jacob cried out of his selfishness for a blessing, God did in fact bless him by transforming his core nature from cowardly to courageous. And God wants to transform you also.

§

SEPTEMBER 22

The Bible teaches that debt is a form of slavery (Deut. 15:4—6, 28:1—2, 28:12—15, 28:43—45; Proverbs 22:7; Romans 13:8). Research reveals the average American spends $1.26 for every $1.00 we earn, possibly because of our beliefs around happiness and contentment.

Jesus asked a question one day recorded in Luke 16:11: "if you have not been faithful in handling worldly wealth, who will entrust the true riches to you?" So immediately I want to know, are the true riches the things money cannot buy?

For instance money can buy a bed but not a restful night's sleep. Money can buy medicine, but it cannot buy health. Money can buy people's time and attention, but it cannot buy a friend. Money can buy a book, but it cannot buy wisdom. Money can buy food, but it cannot buy satisfaction. Money can buy entertainment, but it cannot buy joy and happiness. Money can buy land, a house, a car, but it cannot buy a family who supports, encourages, and loves you.

Maybe we would find happiness, friends, and loving families if we used money according to the guidelines of the Bible. God seems to know all about it. Will you trust Him with your money?

SEPTEMBER 23

Jesus challenges all of us with three tests recorded for us in Luke 16:10—13. You will benefit greatly, personally and professionally, by passing these three tests. Try them, and be ruthlessly honest with yourself.

First, the person who is faithful with a little money will be faithful with much money. The person who is unfaithful with a little money will be unfaithful with much money. Often we look at wealthy people who are generous and say, "If I were wealthy, I would be generous too." This statement betrays our ungenerous hearts revealing that we are not generous presently. Without an intentional change of our hearts, we will not be generous at any income level.

Second, can God trust you with money? Throughout history we have many persons who have shown themselves generous, and with each passing year God has them earning more money than the previous year. Can God trust you with money?

Third, does money own your heart, or does God have your heart's attention and passion? Here is where we want to be ruthlessly honest. We cannot fake it. If we are not generous, now is a great time to turn our hearts toward God.

§

SEPTEMBER 24

A pastor preached on tithing one day at church. Afterward a member approached the pastor and stated, "Pastor, tithing is Old Testament law. We are New Testament people. We give what we can according to 2 Corinthians 8:3."

To that the pastor replied, "Joe, that is wonderful. Thank you. Thank you. Thank you. Acts 4:32—35 in the New Testament indicates that within the early church, the landowners sold their land and homes and brought the money to the Apostles to be given to the poor. When can we expect the money from the sale of your farm?"

Joe responded, "You know, Pastor, ten percent is a great pattern to follow."

Abraham, the father of our faith, paid a tenth of everything to Melchizedek, priest of God Most High, as recorded in Genesis 14:20. God had delivered Abraham in battle. God had sent Melchizedek to bless Abraham, and Abraham's response was the first recording of the tithe. Properly we follow Abraham's lead.

Often we erroneously believe the Old Testament is law and therefore no longer in force when in fact Jesus came to fulfill the law, not discontinue it. We "leap" over the law, being a people "from faith to faith" (Romans 1:17) from Abraham's example to fulfillment in Jesus.

SEPTEMBER 25

Jacob was on the run from his brother, Esau, who had vowed to kill him because Jacob had deceived their father, Isaac, and stolen the family blessing from Esau. This family blessing involved all the intangibles of heaven's favor, the earth's produce, and ruling over many peoples around the area.

In his fatigue Jacob lay down and had a dream where he saw angels ascending and descending on a ladder that stretched from earth to heaven, with God standing in heaven at the top of the ladder. When Jacob awoke in the morning, he took the stone he had used for a pillow and set it upright, poured oil over it to consecrate the area, and made a vow.

Genesis 28:10—22 records Jacob's dream and his vow. Jacob vowed that if the Lord would bless him in five specific ways, then he would worship the Lord as his God, and he would pay the Lord one tenth of everything he earned.

Abraham paid tithes. Jacob vowed to pay tithes. Paying tithes is a formal acknowledgment with which we recognize God has provided it all. This is not paying bills. Just like prayer, this 10 percent tithe is an expression of our faith.

§

SEPTEMBER 26

Old Testament prophets would explain how the problems people faced were rooted in their disobedience to God. Malachi 3:1—15 explains Israel's rebellion against God caused several effects including witchcraft and adultery. He lists the economic oppression of employers paying low wages to employees is rooted in the fact that they had turned aside from God's statutes.

Malachi called the people to return to the Lord and asked, "How shall you return?" At that point Malachi explained that the problem that had manifested these earlier symptoms was a holding back of the tithe.

Malachi used harsh language, saying that men were robbing God. They were not bringing the entire tithe into the storehouse. Consequently they had oppressive sin throughout their communities.

Today there are all sorts of questions around this tithe, but the instructions are clear. We are expected to place 10 percent of our gross earnings into the offering plates at our churches. Only after the tithe is paid are we to give extra to other ministries or to the poor. People say they cannot do this. God challenges us to test Him in this very way, to test His faithfulness by paying our tithes.

SEPTEMBER 27

Retirement can be a difficult time financially, especially if you have not saved properly for many years. The Bible gives some instructions about saving for retirement.

Preserved in Genesis 41:14—37, Joseph advises Pharaoh to place a discerning man in charge of the agricultural area of Egypt over the years of harvest and the years of famine.

Many people have used this time line identified by Joseph as a principle of retirement savings—a season in your life when you are working and receiving a harvest followed by a season when you are not planting or harvesting.

Joseph instructs Pharaoh to hold back 20 percent during the planting and harvesting years (Gen. 41:34). The principle is to save 20 percent of your gross pay during the years of labor so that you will have enough during the years of retirement. Most people do not do this and consequently they have financial difficulties during retirement.

Centuries after Joseph King Solomon wrote, "Cast your bread upon the waters and after many days it will return to you. Divide your portion to seven or eight for you do not know what misfortune will occur on the earth" (Eccles. 11:1—2). We usually view bread as the results of our work—"he's the primary breadwinner." Solomon urges people to diversify their assets because of the uncertainty of future events.

§

SEPTEMBER 28

The Great Commission of Jesus—"go, make disciples of all nations, baptizing them in the name of the Father, the Son, and the Holy Spirit, teaching them to obey all that I have commanded you" (Matt. 28:19—20)—began when God told Abraham He wanted to bless every family on earth through him (Gen. 12:3). In order to do that, God would have to give Abraham descendants, and twenty-five years later He gave Isaac to Abraham and Sarah.

When Isaac was a youth, God told Abraham to take Isaac to Mt. Moriah and offer him there as a sacrifice. Abraham made the arrangements and was to the point of having Isaac tied up and lying on the altar the two of them had built when God intervened, calling out not to harm the boy and providing a substitute ram. Because Abraham proved he trusted God that day, God said to him, "In your seed all the nations of the earth will be blessed" (Gen. 22:18).

About eighteen centuries later, the Apostle Paul wrote that God did not say "seeds meaning many, but 'seed' pointing to Jesus Christ" as the way He planned to bless all the nations of the earth (Gal. 3:16). Jesus is the One through whom God plans to bless every family on earth including yours.

SEPTEMBER 29

God really does want us to understand His plans and purposes, even among difficulties. For instance, during the plagues on Egypt, when the Lord was revealing Himself as superior against the gods of Egypt one by one, He took the time to explain to Moses that He still had His sights set on world evangelism.

God's overall plan, the big picture, is preserved in Exodus 9:14—16: "For this time I will send all My plagues on you and your servants and your people, so that you may know that there is no one like Me in all the earth. For if by now I had put forth My hand and struck you and your people with pestilence, you would then have been cut off from the earth, but indeed, for this reason I have allowed you to remain, in order to show you My power and in order to proclaim My name through all the earth."

Why did God send all those plagues on Egypt? The Lord wanted to show He was greater than all the gods of Egypt (Exod. 18:11), and He wanted to get His name proclaimed throughout the entire earth including proclaiming His name throughout your community.

§

SEPTEMBER 30

Have you ever played a game of question and answer? The question was "why did the nation of Israel cross the Jordan River?" Normally the answer would be "to reach the Promised Land." However, the Bible indicates the answer really is much larger than simply reaching the Promised Land.

As Israel crossed the Jordan River, they collected twelve stones they used to build a pillar, a pile of stones to commemorate their crossing the river. They crossed during a flood (Josh. 3:7—17). When the feet of the first priests touched the water, God split the river, similar to how He split the Red Sea when Israel crossed over that in front of Egypt's army.

God pointed out that the children would ask for an explanation of the meaning of the pile of stones. When the children asked, the adults were to answer, "Israel crossed this Jordan on dry ground. For the Lord, your God dried up the waters of the Jordan before you until you had crossed...that all the peoples of the earth may know that the hand of the Lord is mighty, so that you may fear the Lord your God forever" (Josh. 4:22—24). They crossed the Jordan for world evangelism.

OCTOBER 1

Occasionally a group of Christians at a local church will argue over the purpose of the church. Twenty-seven centuries ago the prophet Isaiah outlined the purpose of the temple: "My house will be called a house of prayer for all the nations" (Isa. 56:7). When Jesus cleared the temple from the merchants, overturning their tables and releasing the animals, He then quoted this very verse from Isaiah: "Is it not written, My house shall be called a house of prayer for all the nations? But you have made it a robbers' den" (Mark 11:17).

Jesus not only quoted Isaiah about the purpose of the temple, but He also pointed to the very same idea God had been trying to get across to His people since the days of Abraham. God wants to bless every family on earth.

The purpose of the ancient temple and for each church today is world evangelism. If we practiced this, what would happen to our families? What would our marriages look like? Would illegal drug use decline? Would domestic violence diminish? Would our public schools still suffer regularly from violence? What would our communities look like? What would the world look like if we were to rearrange our agenda to be in step with God in reaching His world?

§

OCTOBER 2

We hear many stories about David versus Goliath—possibly the most well known battle in history. Philosophers try to make it represent the battle between the giant and the common man, the battle between the trained warrior and the untrained shepherd, the battle between good and evil, but what does the Bible record give us for the reason behind the battle?

When Goliath saw David, he cursed him in the name of his gods, including Dagon, the chief of the Philistine gods. David responded that the battle belonged to the Lord, the God of the Israelites, and the Lord had delivered Goliath into David's hands. God would give David victory that day by conquering Goliath and the Philistine army, and then David made that unbelievable statement explaining why the Lord would do this: "that all the earth may know that there is a God in Israel" (1 Sam. 17:45—47).

World evangelism is the reason for the most famous battle in history, the reason to reach all the peoples of the earth. How are you engaged in reaching the world for Jesus?

OCTOBER 3

You have probably heard the old adage "honesty is the best policy." In the 1920s, Columbia University conducted a study with sixth, seventh, and eighth graders. They wanted to discover the level of honesty among the preteens and early teens of the United States. So they conducted this study throughout the public schools of New York. The university personnel traveled to the schools and received permission to conduct the study. They handed out the Number 2 pencils and the test booklets. The students were asked to mark the answer that best described their beliefs and conduct. The test had one hundred questions that all went something like this.

1. When at the grocery store, the clerk gives you too much change. Do you (a) point it out to the clerk and return the money, or (b) keep quiet and keep the money?

2. When asked by a friend if you like her new sweater, do you (a) tell her you do like it regardless, or (b) tell her even though you don't like it, it does look pretty on her?

After the university scored the tests most of the students, teachers, and administrators were astonished to learn that only about 7 percent of the students tested were honest. When many school districts asked to see the results, they were sent a note that read something like this.

"Dear Principal:
Recently Columbia University conducted a study at your school to learn about the honesty level of your students. Even though many (over 94 percent) reported on the questionnaire that they were indeed honest, only 7 percent returned the pencils used. The questionnaire was a distraction. The only test score was to see how many students would return a borrowed pencil. Your school district scored 7 percent."

Jesus said, "He who is faithful in a very little thing is faithful also in much, and he who is unrighteous in a very little thing is unrighteous also in much" (Luke 16:10). This is a principle of life.

OCTOBER 4

The Bible opens the pivotal chapter recording the downfall of a hero with a mundane, routine statement: "Then it happened in the spring, at the time when kings go out to battle, that David sent Joab and his servants with him and all Israel, and they destroyed the sons of Ammon and besieged Rabbah, but David stayed at Jerusalem" (1 Sam. 11:1). One sentence. One decision.

David made one decision to ignore his responsibilities. He decided to disregard where he was supposed to be. When evening came he decided to walk on the roof of his home. As a great warrior, he knew the darkness would hide his stealth as he looked into his neighbor's bathroom window, with the light illuminating the nude bathing figure of Bathsheba. David knew when to walk. He knew where to look. Obviously, this was not his first time to watch and linger.

David decided to use his position as king to force a sexual evening with her. Make no mistake. This was not consensual on Bathsheba's part. She was a Gentile living in Jerusalem. She did not dare refuse the king. David decided to cover up his sin by having Bathsheba's husband killed. David used his own army to kill a key commander.

David decided to multiply his sin, causing an accumulation of guilt and shame, all because he decided to stay home from work one day. Make a conscious point to meet your responsibilities. Your decisions matter.

OCTOBER 5

We often equate moral or ethical failure with being human. We sin and then make the statement, "After all, I'm only human." This statement simply is not true. What about the many times we obey God, when we have moral and ethical victories? Are we not human during those days as well?

We read about Abraham telling people that Sarah was his sister in order to protect himself, but Hebrews 11:8—19 lists a few events where Abraham proved his faith in God. Was he not only human on those days also?

We read about the deception and treachery of Jacob, but Hebrews 11:21 records his faith. Was he not only human on that day also?

We read about Moses killing the Egyptian and arguing with God, but Hebrews 11:23—29 lists a few things Moses did proving his faith in God. Was he not only human on those days as well?

We read about the cowardice, the deceptions, the failures of Gideon, Barak, Sampson, Jephthah, David, Samuel, and the prophets, but Hebrews 11:32—40 lists their obedience and faith. Were they not all only human on those days as well? Quit using the statement of being human as an excuse for your sin. Instead use it as motivation to trust and obey God.

§

OCTOBER 6

They called him Sarge because of his time in the army. He lived in a trailer along the road. Sarge never aspired to greatness. He lived his life simply alongside his neighbors and friends, telling his stories about World War II and especially the Battle of the Bulge. His heart—gripping tales of tank battalions, explosions, and flamethrowers entertained men and children for hours.

Sarge was in his early eighties when his younger brother was badly burned in a garage fire. Sarge traveled to the hospital to visit his brother. His brother lived for only a few hours, but during that time he turned his attention to Jesus Christ and received forgiveness and grace (1 John 1:9).

Sarge listened to his brother tell him to get right with God. "Do not wait," he urged. Sarge confessed his sins to Jesus and asked Jesus to come into his heart to be his Savior and Lord. Jesus forgave Sarge and changed him immediately that day. Previously Sarge had used profanity with every sentence, but when he finished that prayer, he never used another word of profanity for the rest of his life. From then on Sarge made a point to tell people, "When Jesus cleans up a man, He really cleans him."

OCTOBER 7

Ray opened the door only to see a man clearly high on heroin and desperate, asking, "Are you the preacher at the city square who claims God can work miracles if we will just pray and trust?" Ray assured the man, "I am. Do you want to pray?" The man lifted his eyes to glare at Ray. "I am a heroin addict. I am also an assassin for a cartel in this city. I have killed over twenty judges and legislators. I want out of the cartel, and I want free from the drugs. I came to pray. If this doesn't work, I am going to kill you and your family, and then I am going to kill myself."

Ray was stunned and replied, "Then we need to pray." After about fifteen minutes, Ray saw that the man was still high, so they kept praying. After thirty minutes they kept praying, and the same thing after sixty minutes. After about ninety minutes, they broke through. God not only forgave the man but also kept His promise to deliver the man from the power of sin: "If the Son sets you free, you are free indeed" (John 8:36).

In churches today we often believe that God offers only forgiveness, but we have stopped believing He offers freedom. Jesus frees us from the power of sin.

§

OCTOBER 8

John was at a conference. He would be away from home for a few days. While he was there, his wife and four children went to Nana's house to visit. Their five—year—old son, Alexander, was acting exactly like a normal excited five—year—old would act. When John talked with him on the phone, John asked him, "Are you behaving yourself?"

Alexander paused and then replied, "A little bit." As cute as such honesty can be, it raises a question: how often do we behave ourselves just a little bit with God?

God called Abraham to leave his home and his family and go to a land God would show him later. Abraham left his home and his family just as God said to do, but, as the Bible records for us, "Abraham took his nephew, Lot along with him" (Gen. 12:5).

Much of the next few chapters record story after story of the negative and dangerous situations Abraham encountered by taking along his nephew, Lot. Abraham obeyed God part of the way, causing several difficult consequences to come his way, endangering his life and putting his wife at risk. How have your decisions to obey God only part of the way brought unpleasant consequences? You can change this. You can begin to obey God fully today.

OCTOBER 9

We have a common practice of keeping our struggles and sins secret. Our chosen isolation gives us an inaccurate perception that we are alone in our struggles. The Apostle Peter must have understood this when he wrote, "Be of sober spirit, be on the alert. Your adversary, the devil, prowls about like a roaring lion, seeking someone to devour, but resist him, firm in your faith, knowing that the same experiences of suffering are being accomplished by your brethren who are in the world. After you have suffered for a little, the God of all grace, who called you to His eternal glory in Christ, will Himself perfect, confirm, strengthen and establish you" (1 Pet. 5:8—10).

Peter understood that every man faces the same struggles. Every woman faces the same struggles. Many struggles are common to all people. No struggle is unique to only one person.

Peter understood that others face the same struggles and overcome them consistently. He offered this for encouragement, pointing out that we too can be victorious. A trustworthy friend can strengthen you in your struggle. Look for a trustworthy friend.

§

OCTOBER 10

Matthew 14 preserves the story of John the Baptist being executed by Herod. John's disciples tell Jesus about it. Then Matthew records what Jesus does with His grief over the next two to three days, possibly giving us a pattern to follow when we experience our grief.

First, Jesus went away to a "lonely place" (Matt. 14:13). He wanted to be alone. He did not even want to pray. Often our first response to news of tragedy is to go off alone and try to make sense of it.

Second, Jesus busied Himself with caring for other people by feeding five thousand. In order to burn off the internal energy of stress generated from our grief, we often need to be busy caring for others with something that takes little thought or reflection.

Third, Jesus went away again, this time "to pray" (Matt. 14:23). He was ready to connect with God. Because "to pray" is explicit here, we can infer that earlier Jesus had not tried to connect with God when he went away alone.

Fourth, He wanted to be with His friends and walked on the water to join His disciples. All these aspects of grief we can use to help us grieve in a healthy way.

OCTOBER 11

God fulfills many roles in our relationship with Him: sovereign King, righteous Judge, loving Father, etc. When we look at the different roles and attributes, we can understand more fully the relationship into which God invites us.

One of the roles Jesus fulfills is the role of priest—the one who mediates between God and us. Paul tells us in 1 Timothy 2:5, "there is one mediator between God and man, the man Jesus Christ." In Hebrews 7:1—28 we are told Jesus is a priest according to the order of Melchizedek. Jesus is described as similar to Melchizedek.

Further into Hebrews (10:11—12), we read, "Every priest stands daily ministering and offering repeatedly the same sacrifices which can never take away sins, but He, after He had offered one sacrifice for sins forever, sat down at the right hand of God." Jesus offered one sacrifice: Himself. He was without blemish, perfect. His sacrifice was complete while previous sacrifices were temporary. In contrast to other priests who were never finished standing all day every day, Jesus sat down. Jesus has finished the work of your salvation. Instead of holding back waiting for more, embrace the finished work Jesus offers to you.

OCTOBER 12

Jesus is described as a priest according to the order of Melchizedek (Hebrews 7:1—28). What does that mean?

First, like Melchizedek, Jesus has no beginning or end. He is eternal. He is actually labeled as the beginning and the end: "I am the Alpha and the Omega, the beginning and the end" (Rev. 22:13). Second, Melchizedek is a Hebrew word meaning "King of Righteousness" and he is titled as the King of Salem, which is a Hebrew word for "peace." Hebrews 7 records for us that these same two titles are attributed to Jesus, who is the King of Righteousness and the King of Peace, "a priest forever according to the order of Melchizedek."

Other priests offer up lambs and cattle as sacrifices for sin, but Jesus offers Himself as a sacrifice for sin. This is why John the Baptist introduced Jesus at the Jordan River calling Him "the Lamb of God."

On the annual Day of Atonement when the nation gathers to receive forgiveness and salvation on a national scale, the high priest recites the national sins over the head of the scapegoat and sends it into the wilderness to separate the sins from the people (Lev. 16:6—26). Jesus serves as the scapegoat on the Day of Atonement by suffering outside the city (Heb. 13:11—12). He is both the Lamb of God (John 1:29), and He is the scapegoat who takes away the sin of the world (John 1:29, Heb. 13:11—12). Jesus has completed your salvation. Embrace Him.

OCTOBER 13

When the Lord told Israel they were to be a "kingdom of priests," He intended the Levites to serve as priests to Israel and Israel to serve as priests to the rest of the world (Exod. 19:4—6). Earlier, when Moses tried to serve as a priest, his father-in-law, Jethro, provided some guidance: "Now listen and I will give you counsel and God be with you. You represent the people before God and bring their problems to God. Also you teach them the statutes and the laws showing them the way in which they are to walk and the work they are to do" (Exod. 18:19—20). Here we find the two functions of a priest God expects of every believer today.

First, as priests, we are to represent the people before God. Today we call this prayer. We pray to God on behalf of other people. We invest time with them, getting to know them, learning about their families, their work, their hopes and dreams, then praying for them properly.

Second, as priests we are to teach the people about God, His character, His plans and purposes for them, and His heart for the world. Embrace God's will for you. Be a priest to someone else.

§

OCTOBER 14

In Genesis 14:18—20 we have preserved the story of when Melchizedek, priest of God Most High, brought bread and wine to Abraham. This was the beginning of the holy meal we now call Holy Communion.

Abraham is the father of our faith, through whose seed (Gen. 22:18; Gal. 3:16) God is going to bless every family on earth. The Apostle Paul tells us the Gospel comes from faith to faith (Rom. 1:17) meaning that Abraham followed God by faith and we walk in his footsteps also following God by faith. The law served as a tutor (Gal. 3:24), but the Gospel connected Abraham to Jesus.

Abraham was the servant of God Most High while Melchizedek was the priest of God Most High. Melchizedek brought bread and wine to Abraham. In contrast to other priests and prophets throughout the Old Testament who brought food and drink or meat and drink, Melchizedek was the only priest in the Old Testament who brought bread and wine presenting them to Abraham.

Melchizedek was the king of Righteousness and the King of Peace. Because he had no beginning or end of days, many believe he was Jesus in an earlier form and offered the holy meal to His servant. So when you receive Holy Communion you participate in a meal that stretches back almost 4000 years.

OCTOBER 15

Joseph became a national hero in Egypt (Gen. 37—50) ruling as second to Pharaoh for about eighty years. After naming the family of Jacob, who moved to Egypt, the book of Exodus opens with the line, "Now a king rose over Egypt who did not know Joseph" (Exod. 1:8).

This king looked over Egypt and the growing people of Israel and feared that Israel might become too numerous for Egypt to control. So he took measures to put Israel into slavery (Exod. 1:8—14). Even more dangerous to the future of Israel was that the king also passed a law ordering that all boys born to Israelite families must be thrown into the Nile (Exod. 1:15—22), but this led to a significant theological crisis.

In his ignorance the king of Egypt declared holy war on the Lord of Israel. If the king had succeeded in killing the newborn boys, the nation of Israel would have ceased to be distinct, would have intermarried with the nation of Egypt, and God's promises to Abraham would have faded away over the generations. So the king's decree forced the Lord to act. God is faithful, and God will keep His word. He will keep His word to Israel and He will keep His word to you.

OCTOBER 16

In the Old Testament, God reveals Himself by name. Most English translations do not use the name Yahweh. Instead we have *LORD* or *GOD* in all uppercase letters. Each time you see these two words in all uppercase letters in the Old Testament, you are looking at the divine name Yahweh. Many stories in the Old Testament record Yahweh revealing Himself as superior to the god of another people.

When Moses returned to Egypt to lead the people from slavery, Pharaoh declared, "Who is Yahweh? I do not know Yahweh, nor will I let the people go" (Exod. 5:2). In order for Yahweh to answer Pharaoh's question *Who is Yahweh*, He had to reveal Himself, and He chose to do so in comparison to the gods Egypt worshiped, one by one.

Yahweh did not address all thirty-seven gods Egypt worshiped but just a few, all shown to be inferior plague by plague. Yahweh shut off Egypt's sun god, Amun—Ra, when He brought three days of darkness (Exod. 10:21—29). Yahweh is greater than Egypt's national god. In each plague Yahweh is superior to each god of Egypt.

Throughout the world today, Yahweh continues to show Himself superior to each of the gods of the other nations. In Thailand Buddhists pray but Buddha does not answer. Christians pray and Jesus Christ brings healing to diseased bodies. The same thing happens in India. The people pray to the Hindu gods but the gods do not answer. Jesus proves Himself all over the world by answering prayers, by healing, and by salvation. Jesus alone is Lord.

October 17

Holy Communion has its main roots in the Passover meal Israel celebrated every year to remember the night when the Lord brought judgment on all the gods of Egypt (Exod. 12:12) as He sent the death angel to kill the firstborn of each house in Egypt (Exod. 12:1—51).

On that night the firstborn from each house of Egypt was to be killed while the firstborn of each house of Israel was to be spared. The Israelites distinguished their homes by taking an unblemished one—year—old male lamb, killing it, and smearing the blood on the sides and tops of their doors. As long as the family stayed inside under the blood of the lamb, they would be safe from death. If they stepped out of the house, out from under the blood of the lamb, they would be in danger of death.

During the evening each family ate bitter herbs to remember the years of bitter slavery in Egypt. They ate the unleavened bread of haste not taking the time to let the bread rise. They ate with their sandals on and their robes cinched up for traveling quickly.

They did not know it at the time, but every year from then on life for them would revolve around remembering that evening. Life for them would revolve around the night when God delivered them from bondage by His grace. Does that sound familiar, that all of life revolves around salvation by grace? It really does and the holy meal is the reminder of that fact.

OCTOBER 18

The holy meal began with Melchizedek handing bread and wine to Abraham (Gen. 14:18—20). God revealed much more about the meal with the Passover inaugurated on the night the Lord brought judgment on all the gods of Egypt (Exod. 12:1—51, especially 12:12). The meal came into its fullest meaning at the hands of Jesus during the Last Supper (Matt. 26:20—30, Mark 14:12—31, Luke 22:1—23, John 1—17).

Instead of speaking about the unleavened bread as the bread of haste, instead of speaking about the urgency to pack up to leave Egypt, Jesus changed the tradition when He said, "This is my body which is given for you" (Luke 22:19).

Instead of speaking about the blood of the lamb being spread around the doorway, spread up and down and across the door frames, providing safety from death, Jesus brought further clarity when He said, "This is my blood of the covenant which is poured out for many for forgiveness of sins" (Matt. 26:28).

Jesus brought the meaning of a fourteen—hundred—year tradition into greater focus forever by having the meaning of the holy meal be Him and His sacrifice for the salvation of the world. Jesus has offered Himself for the world, especially for you.

OCTOBER 19

For over a century, missionaries had served in the Solomon Islands of the South Pacific. These missionaries preached the Gospel of Jesus Christ, ministered the sacraments of baptism and Holy Communion, visited the people, and provided some medical care and education.

Each morning and each evening, the Christians in the Solomon Islands met for singing and for prayers, but once every three months the entire population gathered for a Sunday morning worship service. On a quarterly basis, the bishop of the church would lead a service of Holy Communion. Then one day an anthropologist asked the tribal leaders to explain why the entire population attended Holy Communion.

This population in the Solomon Islands was previously cannibals who believed if they ate their enemies, they would ingest and receive their enemies' spiritual power. So when the bishop offered the body and blood of Jesus, they believed they would receive the power of Jesus.

Even though the Gospel of Jesus had been preached there for over one hundred years, even though they had seen many converts to Jesus, they still had not changed their core beliefs about religion and eternity. The Apostle Paul wrote about "having the form of godliness but not the power" (2 Tim. 3:5). The people of the Solomon Islands had taken on the form, but just like many Christians worldwide, they never had changed their beliefs.

OCTOBER 20

When Bruce Olsen began his work among the Motilone people living in the Andes Mountains of South America he made a conscious choice to befriend the medicine man instead of treating him as an enemy. As they grew in their friendship, Bruce introduced him to modern medicine, especially antibiotics. Over the years the medicine man came to believe in Jesus Christ and miraculously changed his religious beliefs.

Before his conversion to Jesus, the medicine man would give an oral potion to a tribal patient, raise his hands over the patient, and chant an incantation to ancestral spirits, asking the spirits to restore health to the patient. After his conversion to Jesus, the medicine man gave an oral medication or potion to a patient, raised his hands over the patient, and chanted a prayer to Jesus, asking that He restore health to the patient.

If you look closely, the form the medicine man used both before and after his conversion was absolutely identical, but the meaning was significantly different. Bruce had avoided the pitfall of many Christian witnesses who look at the form but miss the meaning. He focused on helping the medicine man change his beliefs, not his actions.

We act out of our beliefs. What beliefs is Jesus calling you to change?

§

OCTOBER 21

On the day of Pentecost, the Apostle Peter stood up and declared that the prophet Joel had foretold what they were experiencing on that day (Acts 2:16). He explained Jesus was the long—awaited Messiah spoken about throughout the writings of Moses and the prophets.

Often we get sidetracked by the miraculous proclamation of tongues, which is speaking fluently in languages not learned naturally. But what about Peter, who was speaking to the crowd in his native language? What miracles had happened to him?

In a moment of grace and power, Peter understood about the suffering of Christ and about God pouring out His Spirit in the last days on all people. Previously, when Jesus had spoken about going to Jerusalem, suffering, dying, and rising again, Peter had argued with Him (Matt. 16:13—23), but on the day of Pentecost Peter understood.

When God pours out His Spirit on a person, one miracle that happens every time is the miracle of understanding the plans of God for salvation. When God pours out His Spirit on you, you can expect to understand salvation in ways you previously did not.

OCTOBER 22

On the day of Pentecost, the Apostle Peter taught all of Jerusalem the prophet Joel had foretold what they were experiencing on that day (Acts 2:16). Many Christians today focus on the miracle of tongues. But Peter experienced so much more. He experienced God's grace and power in a moment that brought supernatural understanding of the plan and purposes of God.

In a moment of grace and power Peter was transformed from a coward to a man of courage. Previously, when in danger, he had denied knowing Jesus (Matt. 26:56—75). He had run away. He had denied knowing Jesus three times. Even though Peter was a big, strong professional fisherman, in his soul he was a coward, but that all changed on the day of Pentecost.

Just weeks after Jesus had been crucified, Peter stood in the public square and declared to all who could hear that Jesus is the Christ, their sins had put Him on the cross, and God had raised Him from the dead. Peter did not run. He did not deny. He stood courageously, having been filled with the Holy Spirit.

§

OCTOBER 23

Many prophecies tell us about God pouring out the Holy Spirit on the day of Pentecost. All of them seem to be partial in explaining what will happen and what we can expect. Scholars and church leaders debate if all these promises are still available to us today as God made these promises available to the first— century church. Dennis raised one important point in the debate, "I need what happened to Peter. I need the understanding and the courage. I need it."

Ezekiel 36:22—32 provides a very important promise about the coming of the Spirit: "I will put My Spirit within you causing you to walk in My statutes." Ezekiel prophesies that when you are filled with the Holy Spirit, you will be supernaturally empowered to obey God.

Some Christians misunderstand this statement. It does not mean you are perfect. It means you now live a life of obedience to God. Where you could not obey before by your own power and ability, the Holy Spirit comes to empower you to obey God. So for those Christians, who believe they have to sin every day, be encouraged. Be filled with the Spirit, and receive the promised super- natural power to obey God every day.

OCTOBER 24

How do we keep first things first? What is the most important thing or the most important relationship? The Apostle Paul wrote about this to the church at Corinth: "I delivered to you as of first importance what I also received, that Christ died for our sins according to the Scriptures, and that He was buried, and that He was raised on the third day according to the Scriptures, and that He appeared to Cephas, then to the twelve. After that He appeared to more than five hundred brethren at one time, most of whom remain until now, but some have fallen asleep: then He appeared to James, then to all the apostles; and last of all, as to one untimely born, He appeared to me also" (1 Cor. 15:3—8).

Luke records for us that there were 120 persons in the Upper Room waiting for the Holy Spirit to come, but Paul mentions over five hundred had seen the risen Christ. Why did so many stay away from the promise? Why do so many Christians today stay away from the promise? Why did only 24 percent of the witnesses choose to go all the way with Jesus? Why do so few Christians today choose to go all the way with Jesus? If you are not going all the way with Jesus, why not choose today to receive from Him all He wants to give you?

OCTOBER 25

Each Gospel writer seems to have had his own purpose in writing his specific Gospel. Matthew's is labeled the Gospel to the Jews. He began with a genealogy tracing three periods of fourteen generations of Jews from Abraham to Jesus tying Matthew's Gospel with Genesis and its genealogy lists. Matthew also records more prophecies from the Old Testament writings. He points out that these prophecies all find their fulfillment in Jesus Christ identifying Him as the Messiah.

Church tradition identifies Mark as the John Mark who joined Barnabas and Paul in their ministry who later abandoned them from Pamphylia and went home (Acts 15:38). He was later taken on again by Barnabas and traveled with Peter (1 Peter 5:13). He was the translator for Peter during Peter's time in Rome and finally wrote down his Gospel record.

Luke tells us he made a specific investigation about all the stories of Jesus. He was not an eyewitness. Using his investigative and observational skills as a physician he was reporting specifically about Jesus (Luke 1:1—4).

John wrote his purpose: "Many other signs Jesus also performed in the presence of the disciples, which are not written in this book; but these have been written so that you may believe that Jesus is the Christ, the Son of God; and that by believing you may have life in His name" (John 20:30—31).

When you take all the Gospels together, each one offers great insights into Jesus's life. They are not merely reporting from different vantage points, they are reporting with different purposes. Read them all for a more complete picture.

October 26

Each genealogy list in the Bible has a grammatical rhythm. Some of these rhythms are interrupted for vital points of history and theology. Within the genealogy that begins Matthew's Gospel (Matt. 1:1—18), the rhythm is interrupted at several points to provide some insight into Matthew's purpose.

Five times Matthew interrupted his genealogy by listing the name of a woman he believed is significant in the story. It makes sense to mention Mary, the mother of Jesus, at the end, but why did Matthew mention the other four women?

All four women—Tamar, Rahab, Ruth, and Bathsheba—were Gentiles. To have these women listed so prominently in a Jewish genealogy list does not bring honor to a Jewish family. Listing Gentiles in the family tree brings embarrassment and possible shame especially the stories around Tamar (Gen. 38:1—30) and Bathsheba (2 Sam. 11:1—27). However, mentioning these women becomes significant if we remember Jesus is sent to bring salvation to all the peoples of the world and forgiveness to the guilty, to restore dignity to the shamed, and to reconcile every person to God.

§

October 27

Matthew presents Jesus as having authority from God. In addition to what he wrote, it is the way he wrote using a special literary structure: "Jesus was going throughout all Galilee, teaching in their synagogues and proclaiming the gospel of the kingdom, and healing every kind of disease and every kind of sickness among the people." This verse is almost identical in both Matthew 4:23 and Matthew 9:35. Matthew seems to be using this verse as front and rear parentheses around all the examples of His teaching, healing, and miracles contained in the chapters between those verses.

The key lens through which we can see what Matthew wanted to communicate is when he repeatedly presented Jesus as the One who had authority.

When Jesus finished the Sermon on the Mount, the multitudes were "amazed at His teaching because He taught them as one having authority, and not as the teachers of the law" (Matt. 7:28—29). Jesus did not refer to the Bible repeatedly, as other teachers did and still do. Instead He would cite a law or a recognized guideline and then continue, "But I say to you," placing Himself in a position of authority (Matt. 5:17—20, 5:22, 5:28, 5:32, 5:34, 5:39, 5:44). By doing this Jesus taught about the moral and ethical standards placing His teachings even above the historic teachings in the Old Testament.

OCTOBER 28

Jesus had authority to teach morals and ethics, as seen throughout Matthew 5—7: "When Jesus had finished these words, the crowds were amazed at His teaching, for He was teaching them as one having authority, and not as their scribes" (Matt. 7:28—29). Most people throughout history agree that Jesus was a great moral teacher, but His authority did not stop there.

A Roman army officer sent word to Jesus one day (Matt. 8:5—13) that he had a paralyzed servant at his home. Jesus offered to go to his home to heal the servant. At that the centurion mentioned that Jesus did not need to go to the house. He only needed to give the order. The centurion implied he understood the chain of command and recognized that Jesus had authority over illnesses like paralysis because Jesus was within the chain of command. He recognized Jesus was under the authority of another.

With this recognition and explanation, Jesus praised the man for his faith. He pointed out to his disciples that He had not found anyone in Israel who understood this principle of authority within a chain of command. He then gave the order for the servant to be healed. Ask Jesus. He has authority to heal you as well.

§

OCTOBER 29

We have seen that Jesus has authority for moral teaching and for healing a paralyzed man, but His authority is wider still. Matthew used several stories in his Gospel to itemize the areas of life where Jesus has authority. One of those has to do with His authority over sin.

The friends of a paralyzed man brought him to Jesus (Matt 9:1—8). When Jesus saw their faith, he declared to the man, "Your sins are forgiven" (Matthew 9:2). At that point some bystanders who were trained as scribes mumbled to each other about the audacity of Jesus thinking He had authority to forgive sins. Jesus recognized this and asked them which is easier to do, heal a paralyzed man or to merely declare his sins forgiven.

Then Jesus made a startling statement that He would heal the man to prove He had authority to forgive sins. The healing was not a blessing but a proof of authority to offer grace and pardon. When the man stood up, the people were all amazed not that he was healed but that God had given authority to Jesus to forgive sins. He has authority to forgive you also.

OCTOBER 30

Matthew made a point of teaching us that Jesus has authority over all kinds of illnesses and diseases (Matt. 4:23—9:35).

We have the stories of Jesus healing a man with leprosy (Matt. 8:1—4) and Peter's mother-in-law who suffered with a fever (Matt. 8:14—17). Many people came to her home for healing also (Matt. 8:16). With the centurion's servant (Matt. 8:5—13) and the man brought by his friends (Matt. 9:1—8), Jesus showed He has authority over paralysis and authority over sin to provide forgiveness and cleansing. In Matthew 9:27—33, Jesus showed the crowds His authority over blindness and muteness.

While during a strong storm (Matt. 8:23—27), the disciples woke Jesus, who calmed the storm, proving He has authority over the forces of nature. At the end of chapter 8, Jesus delivers a man from demon possession, demonstrating His authority over evil, and in 9:18—26 Jesus raises Jairus's daughter from the dead, proving He has authority even over death itself.

Not only does Matthew mention that Jesus has authority, he provides at least one example of Jesus in several different situations demonstrating Jesus has authority over *every kind* of difficulty we face. Whatever you need from Jesus, He has authority to provide the solution.

OCTOBER 31

According to Numbers 12:3, "Moses was a very humble man, more humble than anyone else on the face of the earth." You remember Moses. At the age of forty, he killed a man and escaped Egypt as a fugitive. For forty years he worked as a shepherd in the desert of Sinai. At the age of eighty, he walked into Pharaoh's court and ordered the king to release the nation of Israel from their slavery so they could worship the one true God.

When the Bible talks about humility, it does not mean an inner attitude of the soul, like you and I might mean. What the Bible means by humility is living a life in obedience to God, realizing we are not God, the Creator, or the Redeemer.

In Philippians 2:5—11, when Paul wrote about Jesus's attitude or mind, he mentioned Jesus humbled himself "by obedience." The original Greek grammar here is a specific grammatical structure called a *dative of means*. Some English translations have Jesus doing two things, "He humbled Himself *and* became obedient" (Philippians 2:8 KJV). Paul is presenting the Greek term in such a fashion that it tells the means by which Jesus did this: "Jesus humbled Himself *by means of* obedience" (Philippians 2:8).

Biblical humility is not a self—insulting or self—effacing attitude as commonly believed. Instead, it is simple obedience to God. He is God. I am not. I answer to Him. I obey Him. This is humility.

NOVEMBER 1

In the second chapter of his letter to the Philippians, the Apostle Paul gave two absolutes: "do nothing from selfishness" (Phil. 2:3) and "do all things without grumbling or complaining" (Phil. 2:14). The first one had to do with their motives in initiating actions while the second one had to do with their reactions to what happened to them.

Showing compassion, fulfilling responsibility, and honesty are all difficult enough without removing all self-orientation from decisions, but maybe the self-orientation is what makes such decisions so difficult. Paul did not speak from theory but from experience. When we are focused on how we will benefit or what we will gain from any deal, we become resistant or manipulative. Paul wrote, "Do nothing in reference to yourself" (Phil. 2:3 author's paraphrase). Give of yourself for the benefit of others.

Often people will say, "I don't want to be taken advantage of." Fair enough, but Paul was not referring to that either. He was discussing the motives of our hearts that drive our initiative. What drives us to initiate actions? Are we honestly trying to do the very best for other people? Are we setting aside our agendas and helping others to reach their dreams?

§

NOVEMBER 2

When Paul wrote his letter to the Philippians he wrote two absolutes in the second chapter: "do nothing from selfishness" (Phil. 2:3) and "do all things without grumbling or complaining" (Phil. 2:14). *Do nothing* had to do with their motives when they initiated actions while *do all things* had to do with their reactions to what happened to them.

Life is partly what happens to us but mostly how we respond. Usually we complain only if we are receiving less than our fair share or less than we think we should receive. We never complain if we are receiving more than we hope to receive. Paul was not writing from a sense of theory but from personal experiences. He was writing about our reactions.

A pastor once asked an old farmer, "Do you ever get angry?" The farmer giggled and said, "I get angry in only one situation: when I don't get my way." Paul wrote about the way we react to unfair situations. Will we react with courage, with compassion, with patience or understanding? In other words, will we react like Jesus, who did not open His mouth when criticized? Or will we simply react like everyone else and complain?

NOVEMBER 3

As the Apostle Paul wrote his letter to the Philippians he focused on two absolutes: "do nothing from selfishness" (Phil. 2:3) which had to do with their motives in initiating actions, and "do all things without grumbling or complaining" (Phil. 2:14) which had to do with their reactions to what happened to them.

Those verses are Paul's sermon points while the main illustration lies between them (Phil. 2:4—13). The illustration is of Jesus, who did nothing from selfishness and did not complain in response to how He was treated. He laid down His rights to the throne of heaven. He had been born from a common virgin and placed in a feeding trough designed for cattle. Yet He obeyed His Father in heaven by laying down His life for the benefit of the entire world. He initiated nothing from selfishness or from a self-orientation.

Jesus did all things without complaining or arguing. He laid aside His rights to a fair trial and was slandered by liars and frauds. He was beaten and ridiculed by the Roman guards and even by the thieves crucified on both sides of Him, but He did not fight back or demand they treat him with proper respect. He is our example.

§

NOVEMBER 4

When Paul wrote to the Philippians, he wanted to address their motives and their reactions. He gave two absolutes: "do nothing from selfishness" (Phil. 2:3) which addressed their motives when they initiated actions and "do all things without grumbling or complaining" (Phil. 2:14) which had to do with their reactions to what happened to them.

Even though Jesus is the main illustration of these two sermon points, Paul gave two other examples in this same chapter by pointing first to Timothy and second to Epaphroditus.

Paul described Timothy as being the only one traveling with him who would not seek his own interests but instead seek only the interests of Jesus Christ for the benefit of the Philippians (Phil. 2:19—23). Timothy was doing nothing from selfishness but doing all things for the honor and glory of God.

Epaphroditus (Phil. 2:25—30) had been sent by the Philippian church to carry supplies to Paul. He almost died in the process (Phil. 2:27). Paul told the Philippians they were to treat Epaphroditus with high honor because he came close to death in his service to Christ. In this chapter Paul gave three examples of Godly character indicating that Godly character following the pattern of Jesus is expected for the Philippians. It is also expected for you and me.

NOVEMBER 5

The Bible uses the number seven repeatedly in such a way that scholars agree it considers seven to be the number of completion.

In Genesis 1—2 we see seven days of creation. We see God call what He created "good" seven times. The seventh time He looked over all of creation and called it "very good" (Gen. 1:31). God not only gave a completion statement but also emphasized it with *very*.

Throughout the fifty chapters of Genesis, all the stories revolve around seven men: Adam, Enoch, Noah, Abraham, Isaac, Jacob, and Joseph. Genesis records that each of these men walked with God.

Matthew itemizes the generations between Abraham and Christ as three specific periods of fourteen generations (Matt. 1:17). This is a multiple of seven indicating a complete history from the time God made the promise until the time God fulfilled the promise.

The Bible is crystal clear that we are in absolute control of every one of our decisions. We have a free will. The Bible also is crystal clear that God is directing all of history toward a climax. This pattern in Matthew 1:1-17 indicates how the Bible holds these two facts in a cooperative tension. Both are true. We have a free will and God is directing history. Make sure your choices line up with His plan.

NOVEMBER 6

In preparation for the transition in leadership from Moses to Joshua, God told Joshua three times to be strong and courageous (Deut. 31:6, 31:7, 31:23). After Moses died and Joshua was clearly the new leader, God told him four more times to be strong and courageous (Josh. 1:6, 1:7, 1:9, 1:18), bringing the total to seven times. The number seven is the number of completion in the Bible.

Joshua had been the general of the army of Israel for forty years but then God made him the new leader of the nation. Joshua needed some advice. A modern—day general, Norman Schwarzkopf, told his officers that leadership is a combination of character and strategy, and if you have to go into battle without one, go without the strategy. God focused on Joshua's character, and the core trait God wanted was courage.

Peter was told to love people, but God wanted courage from Joshua. Courage is the root of gentleness. Courage is not bullying your way to the top. God did not tell Joshua to be compassionate or respectful. He did not tell him to be patient and kind. Courage fuels these traits as well as many expressions we normally admire in people. Honesty, compassion, and responsibility are all expressions of courage. Courage is the foundation of godly character. God wants you courageous as well.

NOVEMBER 7

When Jacob the coward heard that Esau, his brother, was coming to meet him with four hundred men (Gen. 32:6), he divided his family into two groups and sent his wives and children ahead of him. He hid behind his wives and children for the anticipated battle. In his cowardice it was only natural to put his family in grave danger.

That night, while Jacob was alone in the dark, God jumped on him. They fought all night until dawn, at which time Jacob demanded God bless him before he released Him. So God changed his name from Jacob ("deceiver") to Israel ("one who walks with God"). It was evident that God changed Jacob's core character.

Genesis records the next morning, Jacob ran ahead of his family, no longer hiding behind them but standing as their protector and guard as they entered into possible battle. He was no longer a coward. God had changed him. He was now courageous and did not put his family at risk (Gen. 33:1—3). He stood in front of them to face Esau.

As Jacob ran ahead of his family to meet Esau, he bowed himself to the ground seven times (Gen. 33:3). He apologized to Esau completely. He humbled himself before Esau completely. He sought a complete forgiveness from Esau. Jacob's example of a complete change is incentive for you and me to wrestle with God until He changes us, even all night if necessary.

NOVEMBER 8

Because Genesis clearly presents seven as the number of completion, we can gain significant insight into the power of our free will in the story of Pharaoh hardening his heart. Many people misunderstand this story as an example of predestination, but to the contrary, it champions the fact that we have a free will. So let's take a look at the story.

God told Moses twice He will harden Pharaoh's heart (Exod. 4:21, 7:3). These are prophecies regarding the future action of God, however the first seven times it actually happened Pharaoh hardened his own heart (Exod. 7:13, 7:14, 7:22, 8:15, 8:19, 8:32, 9:7). Seven times in the Bible means Pharaoh hardened his own heart completely.

The King James translation takes liberties with Exodus 7:13. While the original Hebrew has the verb in this verse in the passive voice, *his heart was hardened,* the KJV adds to the passage crediting God with the action, "the Lord hardened Pharaoh's heart." The KJV is incorrect and inaccurate in this verse. The original Hebrew does not mention the Lord in 7:13. When it comes to the doctrinal distinction of predestination or free will, the original Hebrew must be followed even above the commonly preferred King James Version of the Bible.

In Exodus 8:32 the word *also* indicates that the five earlier times Pharaoh hardened his own heart which includes 7:13. God prophesied to Moses that He would harden Pharaoh's heart, but the Bible clearly records that God did not fulfill that prophecy until after the first seven hardenings done by Pharaoh himself. Pharaoh completely hardened his own heart first exercising the free will God gave him. We have a free will. We are responsible for every single decision we make.

NOVEMBER 9

Genesis clearly presents seven as the number of completion. Because of this we can gain significant insight regarding the sheer power of our free will by looking deeply at the story of Pharaoh hardening his heart contained in Exodus 4—14 side by side with the divine revelation of the Lord showing He is superior to the gods of Egypt with each of the plagues. Many people misunderstand this story of Pharaoh's heart as an example of predestination, but to the contrary, it champions the fact that we have a free will.

The Bible clearly presents that Pharaoh hardened his own heart completely seven times. Then for the next three mentions of Pharaoh's heart there seems to have been a struggle of sorts between the Lord and Pharaoh (Exod. 9:12, 9:34, 9:35). But then the passage turns painful as God fulfilled His two prophecies.

The last seven times that Pharaoh's heart is mentioned it is absolutely clear that the Lord hardened his heart every single time (Exod. 10:1, 10:20, 10:27, 11:10, 14:4, 14:8, 14:17). The Lord hardened Pharaoh's heart completely.

God told Moses He would harden Pharaoh's heart, but He did not do so until after Pharaoh completely hardened his own heart. Only then did God fulfill His prophecy and harden Pharaoh's heart completely. Pharaoh's free will hardened his own heart.

This story is normally misunderstood to point toward predestination. Since Pharaoh hardened his own heart seven times before God hardened his heart seven times, we can accurately conclude that Pharaoh exercised his free will to completely harden his heart before God fulfilled His prophecy.

God has given you the sovereign power of a free will. Use that sovereign power wisely.

NOVEMBER 10

In 1 Samuel 16:7 we find an interesting description of God's ability to discern the character of a person: "God does not see as man sees, for man looks at the outward appearance, but God looks at the heart." In Isaiah 11:3—4 we see this developed more fully: "He will not judge by what His eyes see, nor make a decision by what His ears hear, but with righteousness He will judge."

In the Garden of Eden, God called Adam to account by asking if he had eaten from the forbidden tree of the knowledge of good and evil (Gen. 3:11—12). Instead of taking responsibility for his decision, Adam blamed Eve. Then, when God confronted Eve, she blamed the serpent.

We usually do not like accountability, especially if we have disobeyed God. We are told a responsible person faces the music even if she or he does not like the tune. God loves us enough to hold us accountable. He looks beyond what He can see and hear to judge. He looks at our hearts so He can discern our motives and intentions, which for Him outweigh the results. God looks at the heart, at the motivation, instead of looking at the performance.

§

NOVEMBER 11

"While the cat's away, the mice will play" is repeated whenever children play instead of focusing on homework while their mother steps out of the room or to describe the relaxed atmosphere at work among the employees when the boss is gone for a few days.

Moses had gone up onto Mt. Sinai to receive the two tablets containing the Ten Commandments, and he had been gone many days. Israel demanded that Aaron shape a god (idol) for them while Moses was gone. Aaron guided them to bring forward their gold. He put it all into a fire, melted it down, and shaped it into a golden calf and declared, "This is your god, O Israel, who brought you up from the land of Egypt" (Exod. 32:1—35, especially 32:4).

When Moses came down from the mountain and saw the golden calf, he confronted Aaron, who replied, "I told them to bring me their gold. I threw it into the fire and out popped this calf" (Exod. 32:24) refusing to take responsibility for his decisions. He blamed the people. He even spoke as if the calf were alive and had a mind of its own.

God is looking for people who decide for Him. Can God depend on you to be faithful to Him even when no one is watching you?

NOVEMBER 12

If you do not have a prayer partner or an accountability partner, you might want to consider finding such a person. All of us have blind spots, so when you locate a person who will pray for you daily, watch out for you, and protect you morally and ethically, your trust and obedience to Jesus will grow rapidly. Consider this idea as you read these verses.

"As iron sharpens iron, so one person sharpens another" (Prov. 27:17).

"Two are better than one because they have a good return for their labor. For if either of them falls, the one will lift up his companion, but woe to the one who falls when there is no one to lift him up. Furthermore, if two lie down together they keep warm, but how can one be warm alone? If one can overpower him who is alone, two can resist him. A cord of three strands is not quickly torn apart" (Eccles. 4:9—12).

"Now after this the Lord appointed seventy others, and sent them in pairs ahead of Him to every city and place where He Himself was going to come" (Luke 10:1).

We have well—known pairs in Moses and Joshua, Elijah and Elisha, David and Jonathan, Peter and Paul, and others. Begin now to pray for God to bring you an accountability partner. Then also begin to seek the person who has the same desire to grow in their faith.

NOVEMBER 13

Many parents tell their children, "If you can't say something nice, don't say anything at all." We have a powerful choice regarding what we choose to say.

James explains this power of choice like this: "The tongue is a small part of the body, and yet it boasts of great things…from the same mouth come both blessing and cursing" (James 3:5—10). He tells us we have a choice.

Solomon wrote, "There are six things which the Lord hates, yes seven which are an abomination to Him: Haughty eyes, a lying tongue, and hands that shed innocent blood, a heart that devises wicked plans, feet that run rapidly to evil, a false witness who utters lies, and one who spreads strife among brothers" (Prov. 6:16—19). Within the seven things the Lord hates, three are done with our mouths in how we speak in a harmful way to one another.

The Apostle Paul addressed this: "Do not get drunk with wine, for that is dissipation, but be filled with the Spirit, speaking to one another with psalms, hymns, and spiritual songs" (Eph. 5:18—19). When we are filled with the Holy Spirit, the way we speak to one another will be encouraging, equipping, and kind.

§

NOVEMBER 14

In the days of the early Church, Peter and John were arrested and brought before the very group of leaders who had earlier arranged for the crucifixion of Jesus (Acts 4). They threatened Peter and John with beatings, implied death, and then released them.

Peter and John returned to a gathering of Christians who recognized the threats and prayed for courage to stay faithful to Jesus in spite of the threats and possible fulfillment of them. Please notice the Christians did not go door to door with petitions trying to change the laws. They did not lobby their politicians in the Roman senate trying to gain changes in the law that would show tolerance for their cause. Instead they prayed, demonstrating their determined dependence upon God.

The Bible records, "When they had prayed, the place where they had gathered together was shaken and they all were filled with the Holy Spirit and began to speak the word of God with boldness" (Acts 4:31). What would happen today if we would pray for boldness instead of lobbying our elected officials?

NOVEMBER 15

Modern psychology teaches us that within the average person, the fear of failure is stronger than the desire to succeed. Thank God not everyone is an average person. Thank God some of us humans act courageously in spite of our fear.

Acts 9:1—31 preserves the story of Paul's dramatic conversion to Christ. After his conversion we read about Ananias going to Paul and praying over him, and Paul receiving the Holy Spirit and having his eyesight restored. Afterward Paul preached in Damascus, proving Jesus of Nazareth was the Messiah. Then he traveled to Jerusalem, where he tried to meet with the apostles.

The Bible records that none of the twelve apostles would meet with Paul. In fact, they were all fearful of him, convinced he was putting on an act to deceive them until he could find their leaders and their hiding places (Acts 9:26). At that point Luke, the physician, the author of Acts, wrote, "But Barnabas took hold of him and brought him to the apostles" and defended Paul to the apostles (Acts 9:27). In glaring contrast with all the cowardly apostles, Barnabas exercised unique courage to approach Paul and then bring him to the twelve.

God still needs courageous believers who will place themselves in potential danger in order to advance the cause of Christ.

§

NOVEMBER 16

World demographics tell us if we live in our own homes, drive cars, and have three days' worth of clothing and one week's worth of food we are in the top 10 percent of the world's wealthiest people. There are over twenty nations on earth where the average household income is less than $5,000 per year, with one third of the world's population living on two dollars per day.

How many hours of each day does it take you to earn enough money for that day's food? Most of us in America already have today's food in the house.

Maybe this is why Jesus spoke about giving to the poor. The tithe is the basic requirement of giving (Gen. 14:20, Mal. 3:8-12). This is to be placed into the offering plate at church. Giving alms to the poor (Matt. 6:1—4) is in addition to the tithe. Jesus tells us to give to the poor secretly, not announcing it or drawing attention to our generosity. The poor have dignity. No one wants to be our religious project. Instead Jesus wants us to live simply and give generously so others can simply live.

NOVEMBER 17

Jesus told His disciples that one of the actions practicing righteousness is prayer (Matt. 6:1, 6:5—15), and it is to be done privately. We have examples scattered throughout the Bible where someone prays publicly during a religious festival or a worship service, but the daily act of prayer to God, Jesus said is to be done in a way that does not attract attention to us.

At some times prayer is easy because you are speaking with God, who loves you with an incredible love. There is nothing you can do to earn His love or to have Him love you more than He already does. Likewise, there is nothing you can do that will cause Him to love you less. He simply and profoundly loves you with all His heart. Sometimes this makes prayer easy because you are simply conversing with the One you love and who loves you.

At other times prayer can be difficult because you are speaking with God, asking Him to use His power to change situations; the power to heal a diseased body; the power to move people to sorrow, leading them to repentance (2 Cor. 7:10); and the power to show a person His kindness, also leading to repentance (Rom. 2:4). Prayer can be a struggle but it is a struggle worth every effort.

$$\oint$$

NOVEMBER 18

One of the practices observed throughout Christianity's history that has been lost to most Christians today is fasting. Jesus fully expected fasting when He spoke about it to His disciples, as He said "when you fast," not "if you fast" (Matt. 6:16—18).

Fasting is when we restrict our eating actually not eating a meal at all. Sometimes we might fast two or more meals in succession. Then we usually invest that time in additional prayer. Fasting is a spiritual discipline to focus, concentrate, and intensify our prayers. In our society of self-indulgence and excess, Christians usually ignore and seldom practice this exercise in self-control. We set aside this self-sacrificing expectation of Jesus.

The Bible implies a command to fast. We often turn it into a philosophical idea, like avoiding entertainment or chocolate or placing some other secondary restriction upon ourselves. Biblical fasting is doing without food and investing that time in additional specific, targeted prayer.

Fasting twice per week was common for the ancient Jews and for the early Christians (Luke 18:12). Try it. Skip the preparation for a meal. Skip the meal. Then use all that time in additional prayer. Try it once a week for seven weeks praying for someone having difficulties and see what God will do in response to your prayers.

November 19

One of the spiritual disciplines practiced by Christians throughout history is fasting. Most Christians today do not fast regularly. Some do not fast at all. Jesus fully expected us to fast when He said, "When you fast," not "if you fast" (Matt. 6:16—18). Jesus expects us to live sacrificially for the benefit of others.

Fasting is when we sacrifice food and water or go without food for a period, to dedicate that time more purposefully to prayer. Daniel practiced a "partial fast," as reported in Daniel 9—10. He abstained from meat and bread, eating only vegetables, and drank only water.

Daniel was heavyhearted confessing his individual sins and the sins of his nation, having been a part of that nation. He asked God for mercy toward His people and himself. On the twenty-first day of his fast, the angel Gabriel appeared to Daniel with a message from God. He told Daniel how long Israel's captivity in Babylon would last. He told Daniel about the coming Messiah. He told Daniel about the battle raging in the heavens that could be won only through prayer and fasting. That battle is still fought today, and only through prayer and fasting today will we win.

§

November 20

Fasting is a spiritual discipline practiced by people in the church for many centuries. In the Bible there are three reasons to fast.

First, we fast simply to grow closer to God, to seek Him and build our faith. This is the fasting Jesus spoke about in the Sermon on the Mount, recorded in Matthew 6:16—18. We avoid eating for a meal or more and use the time for prayer normally given to preparing and eating the meal.

Second, we fast to intercede for another person or situation. This is what Daniel did in asking God for forgiveness and mercy for himself and for the nation of Israel. You can read about this in Daniel 9—10.

Third, we fast as a means of returning or turning to God: "Return to Me with all your heart, and with fasting, weeping, and mourning" (Joel 2:12). Joel called on Israel three times to return to God by fasting (Joel 1:14, 2:12—14, 2:15). The nation was experiencing four swarms of locusts, which were clearing the entire land, leaving it barren. Joel called the nation to fast as a way to intensify and solidify their decision to turn back to God.

It is still a great way to return to God today. Skip a meal. Invest that time to intensify your prayer.

NOVEMBER 21

One common cause of divorce is when one parent is more oriented toward the children than toward his or her spouse. In Genesis 1:26—31 God makes it clear that He created people, both male and female, in His image. They are to work together side by side in wonderful, harmonious partnership.

In Genesis 2:18 God gives us more details: "It is not good for the man to be alone." So God began to work to create a customized partner for the man. He created Eve for Adam. Please notice, God did not create Eve for Cain and Abel.

Problems arise in a marriage when either the man or the woman is more oriented toward the children instead of oriented toward his or her spouse. "My children come first." Many parents say this not realizing such a statement puts the child in grave danger of growing up in a divorced home where they cannot be disciplined, encouraged, and nurtured to reach their full potential by both parents. When parents are oriented toward each other, they provide secure relationships within the home, where the children can grow to their full potential, and that is what we want for our children.

NOVEMBER 22

Many people believe if they had more money, they could be happy. We all chase that moving target of inner contentment. The Apostle Paul knew something about that when he wrote to the Philippian church, "Not that I speak from want, for I have learned to be content in whatever circumstances I am. I know how to get along with humble means and I also know how to live in prosperity" (Phil. 4:11—12). He chose inner contentment based solely on a relationship with Jesus Christ instead of on his circumstances.

He described a similar contentment to the Corinthian church: "Since you excel in so many ways—you have so much faith, such gifted speakers, such knowledge, such enthusiasm, and such love for us—now I want you to excel also in this gracious ministry of giving. I am not saying you must do it, even though the other churches are eager to do it. This is one way to prove your love is real. You know how full of love and kindness our Lord Jesus was. Though He was very rich, yet for your sakes He became poor, so that by His poverty he could make you rich" (2 Cor. 8:7—9, NLT). Contentment with Jesus is enough.

NOVEMBER 23

The classic doctrine of sanctification is much more than an ongoing process of chasing after a goal that will never be reached until we enter heaven.

Look at 1 John 1:9: "If we confess our sins [actions], He is faithful and just to forgive us our sins and to cleanse us of all unrighteousness" [heart cleansing]. At salvation God forgives us of our sins. At sanctification God cleanses us of our sinfulness. The first one addresses our actions or lack of action. This second work of grace addresses the condition of our hearts.

A purified heart is not only possible in this life; it is expected. A heart purified by the Holy Spirit is the standard for which God always looks. "Blessed are the pure in heart for they shall see God" (Matt. 5:8). This is not something that somehow happens at death, which is never presented in the Bible as a soul-cleansing agent. The Holy Spirit applies a deeper level of grace to us, purifying our hearts from sinfulness, our bent toward sin.

Many Christians believe God has the grace to purify our hearts so we can love Him wholly and genuinely love our neighbors as ourselves. Do you have the ability to do this? No. Does God have the grace to purify your heart wholly? Yes. Talk to Him about it.

§

NOVEMBER 24

We can see the distinction the early church made between salvation and sanctification if we look at the ministry conducted in Samaria by Phillip, Peter, and John, preserved for us in Acts 8:4—24.

Phillip went to Samaria and preached "the good news about the kingdom of God and the name of Jesus Christ" (Acts 8:12). The Samaritans turned to Christ and were baptized. When the home church in Jerusalem heard the news about Samaria, "they sent them Peter and John who came down and prayed for them that they might receive the Holy Spirit. For He had not yet fallen upon any of them, they had simply been baptized in the name of the Lord Jesus" (Acts 8:14—16).

Some Christians believe we are filled with the Holy Spirit when we are saved. They do not believe in two distinct events. They believe salvation is a once—and—for—all event, and they believe sanctification, heart cleansing, or infilling of the Holy Spirit is an all—at—once event.

Acts 8 has two distinct moments, and in recording them Luke made sure he was clear. He was not ambiguous. He recorded what was said and what was done. He listed two distinct events. God wants to do more in your life.

NOVEMBER 25

Just like salvation is conditioned on repentance and faith, so is sanctification. The repentance is different. This is clear in the record of Phillip going to Samaria and being followed by Peter and John, who went to Samaria to pray over the Samaritans, who had become believers in Jesus but had not been filled with the Holy Spirit (Acts 8:4—24).

With salvation we repent of and receive forgiveness for our sins. These sins are the actions we do or the actions we fail to do. With sanctification we repent of our sinfulness, our sinful nature, our inclination toward sinful actions. In addition to receiving forgiveness, we also receive cleansing or purifying from our sinfulness or from our sinful nature.

Simon the sorcerer believed in Jesus, repented, and was baptized in the name of Jesus. Luke's account is clear: Simon became a Christian, but later, when confronted with his bent or inclination toward his self—interest, Peter declared, "Your heart is not right before God" (Acts 8:21). Then Peter continued to instruct Simon to repent of his sinfulness: "repent of this wickedness of yours, and pray if possible the intention of your heart may be forgiven you" (Acts 8:22). Peter did not tell him to seek forgiveness for an action. He directed Simon to seek forgiveness for an inclination or an intention.

This is the "cleansing from all unrighteousness" John wrote about when he wrote, "If we confess our sins, He is faithful and just to forgive us our sins, and to cleanse us from all unrighteousness" (1 John 1:9). This is also the heart purifying mentioned by Peter in Acts 15:7—9, "Brethren, you know that in the early days God made a choice among you, that by my mouth the Gentiles would hear the word of the gospel and believe. And God, who knows the heart, testified to them giving them the Holy Spirit, just as He also did to us; and He made no distinction between us and them, cleansing their hearts by faith."

God wants to cleanse your heart, to purify your heart. He will not harm you. Trust Him. Turn from your inclination to sin, from your sinfulness and receive this purifying grace from God.

NOVEMBER 26

When we remove Stephen's speech from Acts 6—7, there are only twenty-three verses left to describe Stephen and his ministry. Within those twenty-three verses, Luke recorded four times that Stephen was filled with the Holy Spirit (Acts 6:3, 6:5, 6:10, 7:55). That is clearly an emphasis by Luke who wrote Acts.

Being full of the Holy Spirit, Stephen had a purified heart. He served others and put them first instead of putting himself first, even to the point of, like Jesus, asking God to forgive his killers while he died (Acts 7:59).

Being full of the Holy Spirit, Stephen had a power for ministry, attending to the needs of the widows for daily food. He also performed great wonders and signs among the people (Acts 6:8) and saw many of the Levitical priests turn their hearts and faith to Jesus (Acts 6:7).

Being full of the Holy Spirit, Stephen walked in the presence of God. He lived in intimacy with God so much that as he died, he saw heaven open and Jesus standing at the right hand of God (Acts 7:56). Unsurprised by what he saw, he stepped into heaven—a very small step for him.

When you are filled with the Holy Spirit you can expect a purified heart, a power for ministry, and an intensified sense of the presence of God.

NOVEMBER 27

Jesus commanded His followers: "Therefore you are to be perfect as your heavenly Father is perfect" (Matt. 5:48). Many Christians see the word *perfect* and categorically dismiss anything Jesus says about it. A more responsible approach would be to say something like *if Jesus commands it, then it is possible, even expected, and I'd better find out exactly what He means because I want to obey Him with all of my life.*

Grammatically we have a little help here with the word *therefore*. This is a conjunction always indicating "result." We use the word in a statement of the result of material covered previously.

So what did Jesus say previously? Reading Matthew 5:42—48 can help us figure that out. There we find Jesus talking about the way His Father loves contrasted with the way sinners and Gentiles show their love. They love others in a manipulative way considering only what they can get from them. Jesus states God loves all people unconditionally and sacrificially. This is Jesus's definition of *perfect*, and He commands we love according to this standard set by His Father.

It's very possible Jesus had in mind the promise recorded by Moses, "The Lord will circumcise your heart and the heart of your children to love the Lord your God with all your heart and all your soul so that you may live" (Deut. 30:6). It's certain Paul is referencing this when he wrote to the Romans "circumcision is of the heart, by the Spirit" (Rom. 2:29).

We cannot generate this pure and complete love on our own. God the Holy Spirit generates this kind of love and by His grace He purifies our hearts so that we do indeed love that same way. He wants to do this wonderful work in your heart and life. And He wants to do it today.

November 28

The Bible uses the words *holiness, sanctification, perfect, filled with the Holy Spirit*, and *baptized with the Holy Spirit* interchangeably. Paul helps us understand this second work of God with the way he uses the Greek word *telios* in his letter to the Philippians.

The first time Paul used *telios* in Philippians, he wrote, "Not that I have already obtained it or have already become perfect [telios], but I press on" (Phil. 3:12). Paul refers here to his performance, his actions, and states he has not been perfect in his performance.

The second time Paul used *telios* in Philippians, he wrote, "Let us therefore, as many as are perfect [telios], have this attitude" (Phil. 3:15). Here Paul referred to an internal attitude of the heart. He stated he not only was at that point himself but also implied there were other persons who had their hearts sanctified or purified in this way with his statement "as many as are perfect."

Paul made it clear he had not been perfected in his actions and performance. He made it just as clear that he had been perfected in the inner disposition of His heart. He did not live for his own benefit. He lived for others. Today God still offers this gracious work to purify your heart.

NOVEMBER 29

According to Genesis 3:1—7, Adam and Eve made a clear choice to sin. They were not forced into it. Tempted, sure, but not forced. They did not walk into it blindly. They knew God had said to leave it alone; nevertheless, they took the fruit and ate. They made a calculated decision to dismiss the command and disobey God.

Contrary to popular beliefs, the Bible teaches that the nature of sin never changes to become some irresistible force that overrides our free will causing us to sin. Sin cannot separate us from the power we have with our free will. God never removed the power of our free will. Never. Never. Never.

Many Christians misunderstand the verse "if we say that we have no sin, we are deceiving ourselves" (1 John 1:8). They believe erroneously the false idea that we are going to sin in thought, word, and deed every day and there is not a thing we can do about it because we are only sinners saved by grace.

Only three verses later, the Apostle John wrote "Little children, I am writing these things to you so that you may not sin" (1 John 2:1). Sin is a choice. Jesus not only forgave us of our sin but also delivered us from the power of sin. We cannot be delivered from the power of sin and simultaneously be enslaved to sin forced to sin each day.

You cannot drive your car in reverse while simultaneously driving it forward. You cannot throw a ball into the air while that same ball simultaneously falls to the earth. You cannot stand on a chair while simultaneously walking across the room. You cannot obey God and disobey God simultaneously. Therefore, enjoy the freedom God has given you and the sovereign power of your free will and make your choice to obey.

November 30

Acts 4:36—37 introduced Joseph, a Levite priest who had studied the Bible and who was trained in the worship procedures of the temple. The apostles nicknamed him Barnabas because, more than just giving pats on the back, Barnabas poured courage into people, equipping them to live faithful Christian lives. His nickname literally means *Son of Encouragement*.

Barnabas equipped Paul by bridging the gap between him and the apostles (Acts 9:26—30) and by providing on—the—job training for Paul to grow into a full disciple of Jesus (Acts 11:19—26) while Paul assisted Barnabas in leading the church at Antioch. Barnabas poured courage into the church there. Under his leadership the Antioch believers were first called Christians (Acts 11:26).

Barnabas poured courage into John Mark after John Mark deserted Barnabas and Paul in Pamphylia (Acts 12:25, 15:36—41), even to the point of splitting with Paul in order to focus his attention on John Mark. We can see how Barnabas succeeded in equipping John Mark.

John Mark later traveled with Peter (1 Pet. 5:13) and with Paul (Col. 4:10). John Mark learned his lessons well from Barnabas. Paul testifies how John Mark had poured courage into him (Col. 4:11). We need more people like Barnabas today.

DECEMBER 1

The leaders of the Protestant Reformation discovered a specific doctrine in the Bible and called it *Common Grace*. It is the grace offered to us by God, providing life, sunshine, soil, water, and treating everyone the same whether they are kings or peasants (Ps. 139:13—14; Prov. 22:2, 29:13). God treats everyone as a beloved child (John 3:16).

John Wesley was a priest in the Church of England during the 1700s. He is best known for starting the Methodist Church and leading that church to bring reformation to England. He identified a golden thread that stretched through Common Grace from a person's conception to his or her conversion to Christ. He called this *Prevenient Grace*, pronounced similar to *convenient*. Prevenient grace is the grace of God that leads a person to the point of salvation.

After Adam and Eve rebelled against God, they received a sinful nature that is now passed down generation to generation, called *Total Depravity*. This means we are totally lost and unable to respond to God: "we were dead in our transgressions" (Eph. 2:5). Through the cross of Jesus, God adjusted that total depravity so we could respond to His grace. Logic requires that adjustment.

All commands in the Bible imply the ability to obey or disobey. This requires us to have the ability to choose. We have a free will.

December 2

Prevenient grace works as the saving grace for persons who cannot choose Christ for themselves, as with infants who die and mentally handicapped persons. Prevenient grace also works in arrears for salvation. This explains why Jesus descended to Hell to preach to the generation destroyed with Noah and the flood (1 Pet. 3:18—22).

The conversions recorded in the Bible reveal at least four common aspects to this prevenient grace where God, the Holy Spirit, works in the lives of unbelievers, bringing them to repentance and conversion.

First, God uses people to influence us toward Him. Every one of us has experienced some person or persons influencing us toward God. Second, God capitalizes on the circumstances of life to squeeze us toward Himself. "God causes all things to work together for good" (Rom. 8:28) does not say He causes all things, but He redeems or takes advantage of the circumstances to reach out to us. Third, we think of things that do not originate with us but open up our thoughts toward God. Fourth, we come to see the activity of God in our lives, confirming that God does indeed care for us.

When we see the individual components of prevenient grace that worked in our lives we can then discern them more accurately in the lives of unbelievers. We can also pray more strategically for them.

December 3

God, the Holy Spirit, works His prevenient grace in the lives of every person, drawing him or her to Jesus. He does use unique details in the lives of each person; however, He also uses common tactics that can be identified.

In the case of Zaccheus, a chief tax collector based in Jericho (Luke 19:1—10), the Holy Spirit used Jesus as the person of influence to draw Zaccheus to God. Moses influenced Jethro (Exod. 18:8). God used Naomi to influence Ruth (Ruth 1:16—17).

The circumstance that squeezed Zaccheus was Jesus offering to spend the day with him. Zaccheus's honesty implied by his challenge—"if I have cheated anyone" (Luke 19:8)—led him to seek God instead of seeking a fortune.

The idea that came to Zaccheus, which did not originate with him, was the voluntary offer to give half of his fortune to the poor. Unlike the story of the rich young ruler recorded for us in the previous chapter of Luke who was enslaved to his possessions (Luke 18:18—34), Zaccheus was free from possessions.

The fourth tactic the Holy Spirit uses consistently is to reveal to us God's work in our lives. For Zaccheus, Jesus staying at his home was proof of God's attention, confirmed by Jesus' statement "today, salvation has come to this house" (Luke 19:9).

Look back over your life to see how God, the Holy Spirit used these four tactics to bring you to salvation. Begin to pray for unbelievers asking God to work these four tactics in their lives. Begin to pray today for the Holy Spirit to work in your family and among your friends and coworkers.

December 4

How can we pray for someone to become a Christian? The Holy Spirit works God's prevenient grace in the lives of every person, drawing him or her to saving faith. He uses unique situations in the lives of each person, He also uses four common tactics that can be identified and prayed for.

In the case of Naaman the Aramean general (2 Kings 5:1—27), who was suffering from leprosy, the person of influence was a household slave, a young girl he had captured in a raid on Israel. She mentioned to his wife one day, "I wish that my master were with the prophet who is in Samaria. Then he would cure him of his leprosy" (2 Kings 5:3).

The circumstance that squeezed him was the leprosy itself; nevertheless, he received permission and support from his king and left to find the prophet. The idea that did not originate with him, opening his mind to unknown possibilities, was the idea that he could have his leprosy healed.

When he dipped himself seven times in the Jordan River, he came up healed proving that the Lord was active in his life. He gathered soil from Israel, indicating he would be worshiping the Lord, the God of Israel, from that point in his life. He completely washed in the Jordan River and was healed. He turned away from the Aramean god, Rimmon (2 Kings 5:18) and turned his allegiance to the Lord.

Begin praying for unbelievers that the Holy Spirit would work these four aspects of prevenient grace in their lives and help you to see these aspects in their lives. This will strengthen your witness.

DECEMBER 5

When an older man invests his time, energy, knowledge, and character into a younger man, only as history unfolds will we see the full impact of his investment. Barnabas invested in Paul and John Mark. Paul invested in Luke.

When Barnabas recruited Paul to join him in ministry in Antioch (Acts 11:22—26), Paul was learning not only by experience but also from Barnabas, as the more seasoned disciple was there to explain, guide, and challenge Paul. When God healed a man through Paul, the people believed the gods had come to them, calling Barnabas Zeus and Paul Hermes because he was the chief speaker.

Paul was the front man, the stronger teacher, but Barnabas was the leader, and the people discerned this fact. Later Paul invested his time and energy in a similar way in the life of Luke, the physician (2 Tim. 4:11). Barnabas also invested in John Mark, restoring him to faithfulness (Acts 15:36—38, Colossians 4:10—11). Barnabas knew what investments would pay off the most.

We know little about Barnabas, but he invested in the men who wrote the Gospel of Mark, the Gospel of Luke, Acts, and Paul's thirteen letters. We need more people like Barnabas who are willing to sit to the side while training leaders for the Kingdom of God.

§

DECEMBER 6

Many years ago, a Roman Catholic priest in Germany named Martin Luther read the Apostle Paul's letter to the Romans. He read it over and over, and then he studied it. He studied each word, each phrase, and the sequence of ideas Paul discussed.

Luther noticed that Paul wrote in 3:23, "For all have sinned and fall short of the glory of God." He began to understand Paul's message in 6:23: "For the wages of sin is death, but the free gift of God is eternal life in Christ Jesus our Lord." Luther also saw Paul's statement in 5:8: "But God demonstrates His own love for us in this, that while we were still sinners, Christ died for us." Then, one afternoon as Martin Luther sat hunkered over his Bible, he saw 1:17: "but the righteous shall live by faith," and 10:13: "Everyone who calls on the name of the Lord shall be saved."

Martin Luther read his Bible, especially Paul's letter to the Romans, until it exploded within him. Do you read your Bible enough for God to light a fire within you, or maybe even another explosion?

DECEMBER 7

Creation is such a fascinating thing to observe, to ponder, and to enjoy. The clouds, stretched like cotton candy across the horizon, ablaze with crimson and orange, reveal the brush strokes of God. Streams and rivers striping across the landscape reveal a design, a plan. Trees stretch and strain upward, drinking in as much sunshine as the limbs and leaves can hold. "The heavens tell of the glory of God, and their expanse declares His handiwork" (Ps. 19:1).

We can get lost in the awe and majesty of creation as we peer through it to our Creator. God has splashed the stars across the heavens with the same delicacy as in His design of the praying mantis, the Luna moth, or the walking stick. His design fascinates the Nobel Prize winner as well as the small child bent on her knees following the train of ants from hill to discarded apple core.

When I watch the slow—motion wing movement of a blue heron in flight and the overdrive—frantic wing speed of the hummingbird, both designed by God with hollow bones allowing them to lift from the earth's gravity, I find my limit and God limitless. In that moment I worship God. Let creation point you to the Creator.

§

DECEMBER 8

Vince Lombardi, the legendary coach of the Green Bay Packers, believed we do not push ourselves as far as God designed us to go. He believed the softness of our resolve actually originates in the way we think. We give in early and too easily.

Many times we let ourselves off easy because we value our comfort. We let ourselves off easy with our faith. Instead of doing the hard work of trusting and obeying God, we simply give in to the anxiety or the temptation and then later ask God to forgive us, confessing we are weak. Maybe that is why no one near us is inspired to ask what makes us so joyful, so peaceful, so victorious in troubled times, as Peter said to expect and for which we are to prepare (1 Pet. 3:15).

Maybe we do not impact others with our faith because we take the easy road of compromise. No one really is inspired to greatness by being around those who compromise. No person is ever really enticed to mimic another person who lives compromise to compromise in succession.

God created and redeemed us for success, promising that Jesus, who never gave in to any temptation, will empower us to withstand every temptation if we will call on Him (Heb. 2:18, 4:16). Tough times require tough-minded faith. God understands and recognizes this, so He stands prepared to empower you.

DECEMBER 9

"In the beginning, God created the heavens and the earth" is the opening verse of the Bible (Gen. 1:1). God's action in creation seems to baffle us.

Agur, who wrote a chapter of Proverbs, wrote that an eagle soaring in the sky or a ship upon the sea or a serpent moving across a rock or the way of a man with a woman amazed him (Prov. 30:19). What makes the heart beat? How do the eyes and ears bring in the world and offer the information to the brain? How are bones formed in the womb?

Recognized as the wisest man who ever lived, Solomon finished his reflections, his questions, and his wonderings with this: "The conclusion when all has been heard, is fear God and keep His commandments, because this applies to every person. For God will bring every act to judgment, everything which is hidden, whether it is good or evil" (Eccles. 12:13—14).

The farmer did not create the soil or the sunshine. The farmer did not design the stream or send the rain. The farmer does not supply the seed or cause it to sprout. All of creation lives on the sustaining grace and love of God, our Creator. Therefore, obedience to God, our Creator, is the core issue of life.

DECEMBER 10

What can we learn from a few mice? An experiment had several mice on an electrified wired table. The researchers could shock the mice by just turning on a switch. When the researchers hit the switch, the mice would jump and squeal. Then the researchers would turn off the current, and the mice would return to their tranquil life.

The researchers turned the current on and off repeatedly, and the mice grew increasingly agitated and stressed. Then the mice began to bite and scratch one another. They had not been harming one another until the outside annoyances became so numerous that they began to fight back. But instead of biting the researchers they bit one another.

Many marriages collapse because of difficulties outside the relationships and the married couples forget most agitations in a marriage are from sources other than each other. Paul wrote some key instructions: "Husbands, love your wives…wives, respect you husbands" (Eph. 5:25—33).

When those outside agitations increase or intensify, commit to loving each other, encouraging each other, and patiently waiting on God to help you work it out together. Remember, it is not the first time you have been uncomfortable. You will fix it together. During this time of difficulty decide to handle it differently. Decide to handle it together upholding, protecting each other, and loving one another.

DECEMBER 11

The Apostle Paul gave us great insight. Unlike many modern—day teachers who simply point out the goal, Paul pointed it out and explained how to reach it.

When writing to the Philippians, he pointed out "one thing I do, forgetting what lies behind and reaching forward to what lies ahead, I press on" (Phil. 3:13—14). The Greek word translated into "I press on" or "I strive forward" carries with it aspects of both thrust and velocity.

Paul indicates he thrusts himself with such effort and velocity that he literally cannot move to the right or to the left. He certainly cannot stop or back up. Similar to running down stairs, it takes a huge amount of intentional effort to stop. Paul gave the imagery of commitment to the movement, energy expended, velocity gained, and trajectory toward the goal. He could not stop. He could not veer to the side, all because of his forward thrust.

Many Christians fail and stall for one reason: they will not commit the energy and focus to thrust themselves toward Christ at such an intensity so as to force a focused discipleship.

§

DECEMBER 12

The Apostle Paul wrote a letter to Timothy explaining to him how to stay faithful to Jesus in the midst of his fear and difficulties. We have eighty-three verses in that second letter of Paul to Timothy, and twenty-two times Paul instructed Timothy to endure suffering.

His main point in the letter was for Timothy to "kindle afresh the gift of God which is in you through the laying on of my hands" (2 Tim. 1:6), specifically Timothy receiving the Holy Spirit. Paul gave Timothy several means to employ to accomplish this goal.

One of the means to kindle afresh the anointing of the Holy Spirit is found in 2 Timothy 2:8: "remember Jesus Christ, risen from the dead." Paul did not draw attention to Jesus as the baby in the manger or Jesus who went about healing diseases and walking on the water. Instead Paul pulled Timothy's attention to Jesus who died for our sins and rose again victorious over sin and even death.

This victorious Savior who overcame death to live forever called Paul forward. Paul knew the same Spirit who raised Jesus from the dead was alive in Timothy, who would be encouraged by remembering Jesus had conquered the grave. When you get discouraged, remember Jesus is risen.

DECEMBER 13

While in prison the Apostle Paul wrote a letter to Timothy, explaining how to stay faithful to Jesus Christ. He included many ideas in that letter of only eighty-three verses. He spoke about Alexander the coppersmith interfering with the ministry (2 Tim. 4:14—15). He told Timothy to keep an eye on Alexander and never once told Timothy to slow down or back up. He expected Timothy to move forward in spite of the difficulties and even gain determination from them.

In 2 Timothy 1:6 Paul told Timothy to "kindle afresh the gift of God within you," referring to the time when he laid his hands on Timothy's head and prayed that Timothy would be filled with the Holy Spirit. Timothy was responsible for fanning into flame that anointing by God.

One of the means Paul explained to Timothy for kindling afresh the Holy Spirit's anointing was for Timothy to give consistent and focused attention to the word of God, to reading and studying his Bible: "be diligent to present yourself approved to God as a worker who does not need to be ashamed accurately handling the word of truth" (2 Tim. 2:15). Study. Stay focused. Learn well.

§

DECEMBER 14

Only history will show the full impact on a community or even the world when one person decides to invest his or her time, energy, knowledge, and character into a younger person. Barnabas invested in Paul. Paul invested in Timothy.

In Paul's first letter to Timothy, he wrote about how to lead a local church. In Paul's second letter to Timothy, he poured out his heart to Timothy regarding the work, the struggle, and the victorious satisfaction that comes when we stay faithful to God in spite of suffering, discouragement, and persecution. He told Timothy he had the responsibility to kindle afresh the gift of God within him, referring to the time Paul laid his hands on Timothy's head, asking God to fill him with the Holy Spirit (2 Tim. 1:6).

One of the means to accomplish this rekindling, according to Paul, is to "fulfill your ministry" (2 Tim. 4:5). Timothy had people looking to him for an example of godliness. Paul told him to turn away from all the excuses and compromises, and be the example of godliness. Timothy had people relying on him to teach the Bible. Study diligently to ensure you will teach accurately. And fulfill your ministry.

God has anointed you also for a ministry. Fulfilling your ministry is necessary for you to enjoy a Spirit filled life.

DECEMBER 15

Santa Claus has developed over the years from a fellow named Nicholas who was born in AD 270 in Patara, a seacoast town on the Mediterranean, and grew up to become a bishop in the Roman Catholic Church, serving in Myra, Turkey, during a dangerous time in history.

Diocletian ruled the Roman Empire and persecuted Christians. Nicholas spent time in prison more than once because he was a leader in the church. Over the twenty-two years he served as a pastor, he grew very fond of telling stories about Jesus to children and giving gifts secretly.

Once a family had much debt, and the father feared he would have to sell his daughters into slavery to pay it off—a common practice at that time. But Nicholas went to the homes of the nearby Christians, gathered offerings, and took the money to the family in trouble. He dropped it through a window into socks hung by the chimney to dry having been washed. So the tradition of giving gifts to the poor and especially to children can be traced back to Bishop Nicholas, a Christian who lived 1,700 years ago.

God is still looking for Christians who will be faithful to God ministering to children, fulfilling their ministry, and not shrinking back because of persecution.

§

DECEMBER 16

The tradition of Santa Claus can be traced to Bishop Nicholas of Myra, Turkey, who lived in the third and fourth centuries AD. He met with other church leaders at the Council of Nicea in AD 325 to decide what the church officially believed about the Trinity and about which books should be included in the New Testament and which should be left out. For twenty—two years, he offered Holy Communion, baptized new believers, evangelized, buried the dead, performed weddings, and preached the Gospel of Jesus Christ.

As recorded in his journal, his favorite tasks were telling children about Jesus and giving gifts in secret. He became extremely popular, and the Puritans feared he would become more popular than Jesus, breaching the first commandment: "You shall have no other gods before Me" (Exod. 20:3). So the Puritans outlawed any reference to Bishop Nicholas. The world secularized his memory by adding elves, reindeer, and a sleigh and having him live at the North Pole.

Instead let's remember Bishop Nicholas the Christian and the stories he told to children—stories about the love and forgiveness of God found in our Savior, Jesus Christ. Let's not fear persecution. Let's embrace the privilege to represent Jesus with our witness.

December 17

The Aramean army surrounded Jerusalem, and King Ahaz grew frightened. Would he and his people live through the battle? The prophet Isaiah gave him a message from God: "Do not fear" (Isa. 7:4). I am with you" (Isa. 7:14). Ahaz did not believe that God was with him, and he simply did not believe God (Isa. 7:1—16).

When God saw this, the prophet Isaiah spoke up again: "I will prove I am with you by giving you a miraculous sign" (Isa. 7:14, author's paraphrase). When Ahaz refused to choose the sign, God said, "OK. I will pick the sign. A virgin will conceive and the baby's name will be Emmanuel—which means 'God is with us'" (Isa. 7:14, author's paraphrase).

Given the context and atmosphere of the conversation, it is pretty obvious the sign needed to be miraculous, something only God could do, and something everyone would recognize as only being done by God.

God decided the most unbelievable, miraculous, impossible thing would be to have a virgin conceive a baby as proof He is with us. This passage implies even God claims a virgin conceiving a baby is impossible and miraculous. That is the very point. We call that baby Jesus. God wants you to know He is with you.

DECEMBER 18

Christians celebrate Christmas around the doctrine of the virgin birth. Some insist on common sense and do not believe in the virgin birth, but many others do. It is a doctrine that requires God to act miraculously.

A few years ago, Sherry listened as a pastor preached the morning sermon. She worked as a registered nurse in Lexington, Kentucky, and had questioned the virgin birth until that particular Sunday. Sherry noticed a significant point to the Christmas story she had never noticed previously. Neither Mark nor John the fisherman mentioned it in their Gospel records. Matthew the tax collector mentioned Joseph's side of the story. But the one Gospel record that goes into all the detail about the virgin birth is Luke 1:26—38.

Sherry remembered that Paul referred to Luke as the beloved physician (Col. 4:14). A physician surely would know the virgin birth was impossible. Of all people to write about a medical miracle, God chose a medical doctor, a beloved physician. Sherry smiled that day; her heart warmed over, and her faith grew as she noticed that detail of the story.

Luke mentioned that he had investigated every detail thoroughly before writing his account. The pastor mentioned the prophecy from Genesis 3:15 where God declared punishment to the serpent for tempting Eve in the Garden of Eden, "I will put enmity between you and the woman and between your seed and her seed." The ancient people did not know about the seed of the woman. They were only aware of the man implanting his seed in the woman.

In Genesis 3 we have the first reference to the virgin birth. The woman's seed will be involved but the man will be left out. No human father will beget the holy Child Jesus. The Holy Spirit will do the miraculous (Luke 1:34-35) and Jesus will be the only begotten Son of God (John 3:16).

DECEMBER 19

In Luke 1:5—25 God sent the archangel Gabriel to a priest named Zacharias, who was in the temple offering prayers and burning incense. Zacharias was startled and fearful and Gabriel assured him not to fear. Gabriel explained that God planned to answer the prayers of Zacharias.

God planned to answer the many prayers Zacharias had prayed, asking for a son; however, Zacharias had become an old man, and his wife, Elizabeth, was past the age of bearing children. If God were to give them a son, it would have to be a miraculous event.

Zacharias had read about God doing such things centuries earlier for Abraham and Sarah, but these were modern times. So when Gabriel told Zacharias that Elizabeth would have a baby, Zacharias did not believe him even going so far as to ask for proof Gabriel was telling the truth (Luke 1:18).

We can easily understand Zacharias's plight. He asked Gabriel to prove it. So when Gabriel pronounced punishment, he included the statement "because you did not believe what has been spoken to you" (Luke 1:20).

A man prays. God answers. But because God answers at a time later than the man can grasp with common sense, the man refuses to believe God. God always reserves the right to move according to His timetable. And God always reserves the right to move miraculously. What does God still want to do in your life?

DECEMBER 20

God honors faith and honest questions when they are expressions of that faith. Some questions simply challenge God with a lack of faith. Many Christians over the years say we should not question God, but the Bible indicates, in Luke 1:34, when the angel Gabriel tells Mary she will have a child, that Mary wants an explanation: "How can this be since I am a virgin?"

In this first chapter of his Gospel, Luke recorded for us the stories of two people and two questions. He starts with the day Zacharias the priest asked a question. When the angel Gabriel told Zacharias his wife would have a baby, Zacharias asked him to prove he was telling the truth, and Zacharias was punished for his unbelief.

When that same angel told Mary she was going to have a child, she asked, "How can this be since I am a virgin?" Mary's question did not challenge the truth of God, she simply asked for an explanation. So Gabriel honored her with an explanation.

You see the difference was simple. Zacharias said, "Prove it" because he did not believe. Mary asked, "How" because she did believe. Never fear asking God a question out of faith or asking for an explanation.

§

DECEMBER 21

Why did God choose Joseph as the earthly father to prepare Jesus for His life's mission? Out of all the men in the world, why did God choose Joseph? Matthew 1:18—25 gives us some hints.

Luke 1:39—56 records for us that Mary went to visit her cousin, Elizabeth, and when she returned, according to Matthew, she was pregnant. So when she returned, as some people in small towns do, the community began to talk. Joseph heard the whispering and the accusations and saw the finger pointing. They laughed at him. Mary had broken his heart, and who in the world would believe her story of an angel, the Holy Spirit, and her being pregnant yet still a virgin?

Joseph, being a righteous man, chose to merely walk away quietly instead of demanding justice, revenge, and Mary's execution. Later that night an angel from God told Joseph the whole story. Joseph had already demonstrated a life of faith and obedience to God. Once God verified Mary's story, Joseph trusted God, and, more importantly, God trusted Joseph to live a life of faith and obedience as an example to prepare Jesus, God's own Son, for His life's ministry and sacrifice.

God still needs parents to live as righteous examples of faith and obedience in front of their children.

DECEMBER 22

We are told in the Bible that the angels in heaven rejoiced at two events. Luke the beloved physician wrote in his Gospel two accounts of rejoicing among the angels. Do you know at which two events the angels in heaven rejoiced?

Luke 2:13—14 records for us that the angels rejoiced the night Jesus was born. Instantly, as bright as the sun, an angel appeared to the shepherds, telling them about the birth of Jesus and how they would find Him. Then the heavenly choir appeared and sang out, "Glory to God in the highest. And on earth, peace, good will toward everyone." God wanted to bless His world, and the best way to do that was to come in the person of His Son, Jesus, to bring reconciliation, healing, salvation, and peace to the world.

In Luke 15:7, 15:10, and 15:24, Jesus tells us three stories illustrating that when we turn our lives over to Him, those who are in heaven rejoice. The angels rejoice whenever we turn from our emptiness, our self-destruction, our rebellion, and our sin and turn our hearts and lives to God. Jesus emphasizes His point by telling three stories about a lost sheep, a lost coin, and a lost boy. Are you lost? Would you like heaven to rejoice today? Turn your life to Jesus.

§

DECEMBER 23

The Bible talks about the Wise Men, a special group of men who studied astronomy and other natural sciences in Matthew 2:1—12. Many times we think there were three wise men simply because they brought three gifts—gold, frankincense, and myrrh—but we are not told how many Wise Men there were. Instead we are told they came from the east, traveling west.

They saw a unique star that lit up the sky, and the promise of a new King associated with that star gripped their hearts. They did not worship the star. Instead they knew the star pointed to the One whom they would worship. Even the heavens pointed to the new King.

The Wise Men expected the earthly king to know the heavenly King, so they asked King Herod for directions. They knew a gift was proper for the new King. So when they came face to face with the new King Jesus, they bowed down and worshiped Him. They bowed low, acknowledging His position as King. They worshiped Him, acknowledging His kingship in their lives. Then they opened their packages and offered Jesus the three gifts, all proper gifts for a King.

Have you gone beyond acknowledging Jesus as King? Have you bowed your heart to Him worshiping Him as your King?

December 24

Luke 2:8—20 has preserved for us that on the very first Christmas Eve, the angels of heaven appeared to the shepherds out on the hillsides keeping watch over their flocks of sheep, protecting them from bears, lions, and thieves.

In a flash of light, the shepherds knew this night was different from every other night. They were in the front row for a heavenly choir concert celebrating and announcing the birth of the long—awaited Savior of the world.

The first angel announced, "Do not be afraid, for behold, I bring you good news of great joy which will be for all people, for today in the city of David there has been born for you a Savior, who is Christ the Lord. This will be a sign for you. You will find a baby wrapped in swaddling clothes and lying in a manger" (Luke 2:10-12). Then the sky exploded with light as it was filled with thousands of angels singing, "Glory to God in the highest and on earth, peace among men with whom He is pleased" (Luke 2:14).

Overwhelmed, the shepherds left the hillside and located Jesus. After worshipping Him they went about that entire region telling what they had seen and heard.

That is one tidbit God asks of us, to share with other people what we have seen and heard.

DECEMBER 25

The shepherds told Mary and Joseph all they had encountered on the hillside with the angels. Luke, the Gospel writer, preserved one point; "Mary treasured all these things, pondering them in her heart" (Luke 2:19).

Mary remembered the angel Gabriel, who stood in the presence of God, telling her that even though she was a virgin the Holy Spirit would do an amazing work with her. She would conceive and deliver the holy Child, the long—awaited Messiah, fulfilling Isaiah's prophecy that a "virgin would conceive and bear a son" (Isa. 7:14). She had trusted God with the mystery of her sexuality and with her life.

Mary remembered the angel coming to Joseph in his dream, telling him all about Mary and her peculiar pregnancy. Joseph believed the angel, and Mary believed Joseph.

Now the shepherds came to Mary, Joseph, and the baby, telling the extraordinary story of the angels telling them about the birth of the Messiah. They spoke of the heavens being rolled back and the thousands of angels singing. Mary was speechless and overwhelmed with all this information about her baby boy. She just sat there giving thanks to God and continuing to go over these events in her heart.

The Christmas story is the story of God's love for us. Many details are included. The story is true, profound, and instead of being complicated, it is very simple. God loves you.

DECEMBER 26

When Jesus was eight days old, Joseph and Mary took Him to the temple for the proper dedication ceremony of circumcision, the sign of the covenant God had made with Abraham and with Abraham's descendants (Gen. 17:10—14). At the temple an elderly man named Simeon saw Jesus and lifted his voice in praise to God.

As recorded in Luke 2:21—35, Simeon praised God, who had promised Simeon he would not die before looking into the eyes of the Savior of the world. Simeon had waited many years for the fulfillment of that promise. He had gone to the temple, prayed thousands of prayers, and lain awake on his bed wondering if God had forgotten him. He watched the stars appear in the night sky and disappear at dawn. He had almost convinced himself he had only imagined it all.

Simeon was just a simple man with a simple faith who lived a simple life. The only thing special about him was that God had promised him he would see the Savior before he died. The day finally came. The moment was like no other moment in Simeon's more than eighty years of life. He looked into those eyes and knew God had been faithful. All those years of waiting were worth that moment.

You can know that very same thing. You can know a moment with God. God is faithful to you also.

December 27

The time between Christmas and the New Year can be a strategic time to take an inventory of the last year. Do you feel your faith is stronger? Do you feel your marriage is better? Are the relationships with your children stronger or more distant? Are you further along in your career goals?

Once you have taken that inventory, turn your attention to the next year. If there is an area where you are not happy with that inventory, then make a commitment that you will make the changes you have to make in order to get on track in that area of your life.

The psalmist wrote that he had taken the time to evaluate his life. He had looked at the details of each relationship and every situation. He had taken inventory of all the areas. He was not satisfied with the progress, so he made a conscious choice to turn his life over to God (Ps. 119:59).

Make a commitment today that next year will be even better. Deliberately turn toward God. Get help from heaven itself. God wants you to succeed in your faith, in your marriage, in the relationships with your children, and in your career.

§

December 28

Have you ever taken time to think? We can be extremely busy, and within the busyness we might listen to the radio or watch TV. We use our iPods or cell phones to keep information coming in.

All of this busyness and receiving information eliminates the opportunity to quietly and effectively think about life. We rarely have a moment when we are alone with our thoughts. We seldom take the time to evaluate where we are in life and if we really want to be there. Whenever a friend invites us to an event we don't want to attend, we give a long list of how busy we are. All the while we actually feel like we have no control over our schedules.

Is that the way we want to be? About three thousand years ago, a musician and shepherd named David wrote, "I considered my ways, and turned my feet toward Your testimonies" (Ps. 119:59). He took a moment, maybe an afternoon, maybe even an entire week, and took an honest look at his life. When he did he realized he needed God. Is the busyness of life keeping you from an honest look at your life? Is your busyness keeping you apart from God?

DECEMBER 29

David recorded a prayer one day (Ps. 56:1—13) that has a tremendous list of difficulties he was facing at that time. He had specific people hunting him to kill him. He had difficulty finding food for the men making up his army. At some point he even cried and then wrote that God had put all those tears into a bottle (Ps. 56:8).

In contrast to this list of difficulties, David itemized several blessings from God that caused him to break out in praise. He praised God more than once for His word (Ps. 56:4, 56:10, 56:12), which gave him guidance and strength. Twice he stated that he trusted God when he was afraid (Ps. 56:3, 56:11).

About two thirds of the way through his prayer, David delivered a significant affirmation, a forthright statement that undergirded all of his life. Disciples of Jesus Christ today would be wise to take this one line from David, memorize it, and repeat it in their hearts daily, even more than once per day if you are experiencing difficulty: "This I know, God is for me" (Ps. 56:9).

§

DECEMBER 30

"If it's going to be it's up to me" is an easy way to remember a principle of life. Every choice we make, every action we take is entirely within our power to choose guaranteed by God Almighty who has created us in His image (Gen. 1:27).

Joseph made his decision to get better instead of bitter. This choice then positioned him with God's favor in the jail where the jailer placed him in charge of everything. His choice positioned him so that when the other prisoners had dreams Joseph was tuned into God so he could interpret the dreams. He also interpreted Pharaoh's dreams and advised Pharaoh to place a wise, discerning man in a leadership position (Gen. 39:1—49) to supervise the annual storing of grain for future use.

Pharaoh chose Joseph. Pharaoh had been told about Joseph previously and Joseph had guided Pharaoh as well. Pharaoh knew Joseph was the best man to lead the nation through this crisis since he had a uniquely intimate relationship with God.

Joseph's personal problems had piled up and he had continued to make his choices in such a way to keep himself close to God. He used his power to choose. He kept vigil on his soul and remained available to God.

DECEMBER 31

I took the training wheels off of my daughter's bicycle. She no longer needed them. She cried and protested, afraid to go without the training wheels, without the safety net, without the security of knowing she would not fall. However, it was time.

As her father I have watched her. I know her ability. I know the pace of her skill development. After one nasty fall, I decided she needed to learn to stop safely before she needed to learn to ride. So we invested three days in learning the skills necessary to stop properly. Then we returned to the ride. She could ride for several minutes on the sidewalk and on the street, including figure eights in the parking lots. The only skill she still had to master was the start.

With each stage of life we learn new skills; whether at work, at play, or in our relationships, we experience that anxiety of leaving the known and launching into the unknown. Just like a father who takes off those training wheels knows the adventure has just begun, so God launches us into the unknown so we can live out His promise of an abundant life. Tomorrow we begin a new year. Trust God. Put your hand in His and take off the training wheels (Isa. 40:31).

September 11
September 15
October 2
October 8
October 15
October 16
October 22
November 2
November 7
November 14
November 16
November 17
December 8
December 9
December 10
December 11
December 13
December 14
December 16
December 17
December 30
December 31

Angels
March 2
March 14
March 26
May 17
June 26
July 18
July 19
September 8
November 19
December 20
December 22
December 24
December 25

Anger
January 17
February 6
February 7
April 30
June 13
June 14
June 28
July 20
August 17
August 21
September 14
October 10
November 3
November 13
December 10
December 30

Attitude
January 20
February 16
February 18
February 19
March 3
March 5
March 10
March 11
March 13
March 23
March 28
April 2
April 9
April 26
April 28
April 30
May 2
May 3

May 7	November 3
May 14	November 4
May 19	November 6
May 20	November 7
May 31	November 13
June 10	November 14
June 16	November 16
June 17	November 21
June 18	November 22
June 19	November 27
June 30	November 28
July 8	November 29
July 9	December 7
July 12	December 8
July 22	December 9
July 26	December 10
July 27	December 11
August 8	December 14
August 11	December 29
August 12	December 30
August 13	December 31
August 17	
August 18	*Change*
August 19	February 9
August 20	March 3
August 21	March 6
August 25	March 10
August 30	March 11
September 1	March 12
September 4	March 16
September 11	May 24
September 12	June 14
September 23	June 28
October 20	June 29
October 31	July 6
November 1	July 27
November 2	August 1

August 22

August 31

September 10

September 20

September 21

October 6

October 7

October 18

October 19

October 20

October 21

October 22

November 7

November 14

November 15

November 17

November 23

November 25

December 1

December 3

December 4

December 27

December 28

December 31

Character, God's

February 7

February 21

March 19

March 21

March 31

April 16

April 21

April 24

May 2

May 3

May 22

May 28

May 29

June 2

June 18

June 21

June 25

July 3

July 13

July 14

July 16

July 19

July 23

August 1

August 9

August 20

August 25

August 26

August 28

September 5

September 7

September 9

September 10

September 13

September 16

September 26

September 28

September 29

September 30

October 2

October 13

October 23

October 26

October 27

October 28

October 29

October 30

November 10

November 17

November 27

November 8
November 9
November 10
November 11
November 12
November 13
November 14
November 15
November 19
November 22
November 24
November 25
November 26
November 27
November 28
November 29
December 5
December 8
December 9
December 14
December 15
December 30

Comfort
January 24
February 23
March 19
July 5
August 26
November 16
December 10
December 31

Common Grace
January 19
July 7
July 17
July 22

August 4
December 1
December 9

Common Sense
January 25
April 20
April 24
May 31
June 21
July 16
July 29
July 30
July 31
August 8
August 14
August 24
September 8
November 29
December 10
December 17
December 18
December 19
December 20

Conflict
February 17
February 19
April 9
June 8
August 12
September 3
September 19
September 20
September 21
October 4
October 10
October 15

October 16
November 14
December 8
December 10
December 13

Cooperation
January 12
February 2
February 15
March 1
March 8
June 13
July 27
August 12
August 20
November 12

Courage
April 29
May 9
May 10
May 12
May 13
May 24
May 27
June 6
June 13
June 27
July 19
October 22
November 4
November 6
November 7
November 11
November 14
November 15
November 30

December 5
December 30
December 31

Creation
January 3
January 4
January 7
January 12
January 13
January 24
January 28
January 29
February 8
February 10
February 20
February 21
February 27
February 28
February 29
March 7
March 25
April 13
April 24
April 25
May 17
May 24
June 1
June 2
June 5
June 21
June 25
June 26
July 4
July 7
August 17
August 27
August 28

September 5
November 5
November 21
November 29
December 7
December 9
December 30

Cross/Crucifixion
February 12
May 4
May 22
June 26
July 10
July 15
July 28
July 29
July 30
July 31
August 1
August 24
August 25
August 26
September 9
October 11
October 12
October 22
November 3
November 23
December 1
December 2
December 8

Decision Making
March 3
March 6
March 11

March 12
March 16
April 9
April 24
April 25
April 26
April 28
April 29
May 24
May 29
June 8
June 12
June 13
June 14
June 19
June 20
June 28
June 30
July 6
July 9
July 18
July 27
August 7
August 14
August 17
August 18
August 20
August 28
August 29
August 30
September 2
September 3
September 4
September 11
September 13
September 17
September 22

October 3
October 4
October 8
October 24
October 25
October 26
November 1
November 2
November 3
November 4
November 8
November 9
November 10
November 11
November 13
November 14
November 15
November 17
November 20
November 21
November 22
November 25
November 29
December 3
December 8
December 10
December 11
December 14
December 27
December 28
December 30
December 31

Deliverance
March 24
April 10
May 9

May 26
May 30
June 6
July 16
September 9
October 2
October 15

Depression
January 2
March 14
April 11
May 14
August 19
October 10

Discipleship
May 5
May 6
May 15
May 18
June 20
June 23
June 27
June 29
July 1
August 7
August 10
August 21
August 22
August 31
October 13
October 27
October 31
November 1
November 2
November 4

November 12
November 13
November 19
November 30
December 5
December 8
December 9
December 11
December 12
December 13
December 14
December 29
December 31

Discouragement
January 2
January 14
January 18
February 7
February 23
March 31
April 2
April 4
May 3
June 11
August 19
November 13
December 31

Discovery
January 3
February 9
February 29
March 7
March 12
April 30
May 2

May 13
May 19
May 21
May 25
June 13
July 17
July 29
December 7
December 15
December 16

Encouragement
January 18
January 24
February 21
March 9
April 21
May 3
May 14
May 24
June 14
July 5
July 19
August 26
August 27
October 9
October 23
November 13
November 14
November 15
December 5
December 9
December 29
December 31

Equality
June 25

October 9

October 26

November 16

November 21

Evangelism

January 13

March 2

March 28

March 29

April 3

April 4

April 12

April 14

April 15

April 16

April 17

May 15

May 16

May 22

May 30

May 31

June 9

June 15

June 16

June 22

June 24

August 11

August 12

September 28

September 29

September 30

October 1

October 2

October 13

December 2

December 3

December 4

December 6

Faith

January 25

January 31

February 9

February 13

April 8

April 19

April 22

April 24

April 25

May 1

May 9

May 12

May 13

May 18

May 21

May 23

May 28

May 29

June 6

June 11

June 18

July 16

July 19

July 23

July 28

July 29

July 30

August 2

August 6

August 8

August 10

August 15

August 23

November 10
November 19
November 25

Free will
January 20
January 26
March 3
April 7
April 9
April 24
April 25
April 28
August 17
August 18
September 11
November 1
November 2
November 8
November 9
November 10
November 11
November 13
November 14
November 15
November 29
December 1
December 8
December 9
December 27
December 28
December 30
December 31

Freedom
January 21
April 10
May 14

July 4
October 7
December 3

Friendship
June 4
June 21
July 10
August 11
October 9
November 12

Fulfillment
March 17
March 25
May 2
May 7
May 24
July 14
July 17
August 25
September 7
September 8
October 15
October 18
October 24
October 25
November 3
November 5
November 22
December 19

Giving
June 24
July 2
August 9
August 28
September 22

September 23
September 24
September 25
September 26
November 16
November 22
December 3
December 23

Grace
August 5
September 12
October 29
November 23
November 24
December 1
December 2
December 3
December 4
December 8

Grief
June 11
October 10

Guilt
March 20
April 11
June 2
October 4
October 26

Healing
January 23
February 6
February 14
June 3
August 15

September 9
October 20
October 29
October 30
November 17
December 4

Holy Communion
October 14
October 17
October 18
October 19

Holy Spirit
January 16
February 5
April 12
April 13
April 23
July 2
July 15
August 16
August 27
October 21
October 22
October 23
October 24
November 13
November 23
November 24
November 25
November 26
December 2
December 3
December 4
December 12
December 13
December 14

December 21

Honesty
July 12
August 13
August 29
August 30
September 12
September 21
October 3
November 10
November 11
December 3

Hope
January 14
January 24
February 23
March 8
March 14
April 21
April 22
April 26
May 3
May 13
May 14
May 16
May 26
May 27
June 1
June 5
June 11
June 17
June 18
July 5
July 6
July 8
July 9

August 26
August 27
October 5
December 29

Humility
October 31
November 7

Image of God
January 7
February 28
May 17
June 26
July 22
August 18
August 28
December 30

Joy
February 7
May 14
August 9

Justice
January 17
February 2
August 20
September 11
November 10

Leadership
January 22
January 31
February 16
April 29
May 24
June 11

June 19
August 14
August 31
September 1
September 2
October 28
November 1
November 2
November 6
November 7
November 12
November 30
December 30

Listening
January 10
March 8
July 5
September 3

Love
January 27
January 28
February 10
February 14
February 22
March 3
March 4
March 5
March 6
March 11
March 12
March 21
March 22
March 23
May 19
May 20

May 21
May 22
May 31
June 11
June 24
June 28
July 24
August 11
November 17
November 27

Marriage
January 27
January 28
January 29
February 10
February 14
February 15
March 5
March 6
March 12
March 22
March 23
March 30
May 17
June 28
July 6
July 11
July 24
August 3
September 13
September 15
November 21
December 10

Ministry
January 16

January 17
February 2
March 8
March 9
May 19
May 20
May 31
June 15
July 8
December 5
December 12
December 13
December 14

Miracles
January 23
January 25
February 6
February 14
April 2
April 19
June 6
July 13
July 19
August 15
September 6
September 9
September 20
October 21
October 22
October 28
October 29
October 30
November 17
November 26
December 17
December 18

December 19
December 25

Missions
January 8
January 13
February 13
February 23
April 23
June 15
June 24
June 27
July 2
July 9
July 13
October 19
October 20

Money
September 22
September 23
September 24
September 25
September 26
September 27
November 16
November 22
December 3

Obedience
February 8
February 12
February 20
March 1
April 7
April 8
April 24

April 25
June 23
August 4
August 27
August 29
August 30
September 4
September 9
October 8
October 23
October 27
October 28
October 31
November 6
November 29
December 9
December 11
December 14
December 20
December 21

Parents
March 15
April 9
May 24
July 11
July 12
July 24
November 21
December 31

Peace
June 30
July 17

Persecution
January 31
February 14

February 25
February 26
May 12
May 18
June 27
July 23
August 23
November 2
November 15
December 8
December 13
December 14
December 15

Perseverance
April 4
April 18
April 27
May 1
May 28
June 11
June 17
June 18
July 8
July 9
September 12
October 9
November 12
December 8
December 14
December 26
December 27

Personal Value
January 7
January 9
January 29
February 3

May 17
June 12
June 26
July 3
July 22
August 20
August 26

Potential
January 1
January 2
January 12
January 17
February 5
February 19
February 28
March 8
April 19
April 22
May 23
May 24
June 27
July 27
August 8
August 16
August 22
August 27
October 5
November 14
November 17
December 5
December 14
December 29
December 31

Prayer
January 5
January 30

February 14
March 9
March 27
March 29
March 30
April 14
April 15
April 16
April 22
May 5
May 12
May 25
May 30
June 1
June 13
June 21
June 30
July 1
July 21
July 23
July 24
July 25
August 2
August 6
August 7
August 12
September 10
October 7
October 20
November 14
November 17
November 18
November 19
November 20
December 19

Prejudice
January 1

Prevenient Grace

March 27
March 28
March 29
March 30
March 31
April 1
April 3
December 1
December 2
December 3
December 4
December 6

Priorities

January 11
February 16
May 8
June 12
June 16
June 20
July 11
July 21
August 7
August 14
August 25
September 2
October 24
November 16
November 21
December 27

Purpose

February 19
March 17
May 8
June 13

June 27
July 8
July 17
July 26
August 25
September 1
September 11
October 1
October 2
October 25
October 26
November 19
December 9
December 27
December 31

Relationships

January 10
January 27
January 28
January 29
February 10
February 15
March 3
March 4
March 5
March 6
March 10
March 12
March 15
March 22
March 30
May 5
May 6
May 24
May 25
June 8

June 19
June 22
June 25
June 28
June 29
July 3
July 6
July 10
July 11
July 12
August 3
August 7
August 10
August 11
September 13
September 14
September 15
September 18
November 1
November 2
November 12
November 13
November 30
December 10
December 27

Reliable
January 22
February 20
March 28
May 12
July 14

Resurrection
February 4
March 26
May 4

July 28
July 29
July 30
July 31
August 1
August 27
December 12

Roles of God
March 19
March 21
March 24
April 11
April 12
October 11
October 12
October 16
December 9

Sacrifice
January 31
February 12
February 22
June 27
November 3
November 18

Salvation
January 9
January 13
January 15
February 3
February 12
February 22
March 2
March 21
March 24

March 27
March 29
April 1
April 3
April 11
April 13
April 14
April 15
April 16
April 17
April 18
April 20
May 4
May 6
May 18
May 22
May 30
June 1
June 2
June 9
June 24
June 26
June 29
July 10
July 15
July 18
July 30
August 1
August 16
September 9
September 20
September 28
September 29
October 6
October 7
October 11
October 12

October 18
October 19
October 20
October 21
November 15
November 24
November 25
November 29
December 2
December 3
December 4
December 6
December 16

Sanctification
November 23
November 24
November 25
November 26
November 27
November 28
November 29
December 12
December 13
December 14

Self-Control
January 21
January 26
February 12
March 3
March 11
April 25
May 1
June 28
July 9
July 20

August 17
August 18
August 21
September 13
October 3
November 1
November 2
November 3
November 6
November 13
November 19
December 8
December 10

Self-Improvement
January 11
January 29
March 5
March 10
March 11
April 22
May 26
June 28
August 19
November 13
December 10
December 11
December 27
December 31

Sin
February 12
April 25
June 3
September 14
September 15
September 16

September 17
September 18
September 19
October 20
November 23
November 29

Sinfulness
February 12
November 23
November 24
November 25
November 29

Spiritual Warfare
February 17
April 1
May 4
May 9
July 24
August 15
August 22
August 23
August 31
September 6
September 10
September 20
October 2
October 7
October 15
October 16
October 20
October 28
November 5
November 14
November 17
November 18

Trust

January 6
January 12
January 23
January 25
February 9
April 25
April 27
May 18
May 27
June 30
July 16
August 23
October 23
November 14
December 20
December 21
December 31

Victory

January 21
January 23
February 12
February 17
February 19
May 4
May 30
July 23
August 23
August 25
August 27
September 1
October 5
October 7
November 14
November 29
December 8
December 11

December 12
December 14

Virgin Birth

December 17
December 18
December 20
December 21
December 25

Why?

January 6
February 1
February 8
February 23
April 25
May 23
May 25
June 8
July 7
July 8
July 11
July 12
July 15
July 17
July 31
August 9
August 12
August 20
August 24
August 31
September 4
September 28
September 29
September 30
October 19
October 24
October 25

October 26
October 29
October 30
November 5
November 8
November 9
November 16
December 1
December 11
December 15
December 16
December 21
December 22

Work
March 13
March 28

April 5
June 10
June 13
July 26
August 21

Worship
January 16
January 18
February 16
September 6
September 7
September 10
October 1
December 7
December 23

6:5—6	July 11
6:5—9	July 12
6:9	July 11
6:13—22	February 2
8:11	January 24
11—25	April 7
12:1—3	April 7
12:3	September 28
12:5	October 8
12:11—13	September 15
13:2—4	April 5
14:14	March 28
	April 5
14:18—20	October 14
	October 18
14:20	September 24
	November 16
15:1—6	April 8
15:2	June 23
17:1	September 4
17:1—19	September 16
17:10—14	December 26
17:15—19	August 8
	August 9
17:19	August 9
18:1—38	April 7
20:1—2	September 16
22:18	September 28
	October 14
24:1—67	March 27
	March 28
	March 29
	March 30
	April 14
	April 15
25:19—26	September 17
25:19—34	April 10

4—17	April 17
4:21	November 8
5:2	October 16
7:3	November 8
7:13	November 8
7:14	November 8
7:22	November 8
8:15	November 8
8:19	November 8
8:32	November 8
9:7	November 8
9:12	November 9
9:14—16	September 29
9:34	November 9
9:35	November 9
10:1	November 9
10:20	November 9
10:21—29	October 16
10:27	November 9
11:10	November 9
12:1—51	October 17
	October 18
12:12	April 17
	October 17
	October 18
14:4	November 9
14:8	November 9
14:17	November 9
18:1—12	April 1
18:8	December 3
18:11	April 17
	September 6
	September 29
18:19—20	October 13
19:4	July 21
19:4—6	October 13
20:3	December 16
20:12	March 15

23:16	July 31
31:1—5	April 5
31:3	January 16
32:1—35	April 29
	November 11
32:4	November 11
32:24	November 11
34:6	July 3
34:22	July 31
40:34	September 6
	September 7

Leviticus

1—7	July 3
16:6—26	October 12
23:9—22	July 31

Numbers

12:3	October 31
21:1—9	September 9
21:7	September 9
28:16	July 31

Deuteronomy

6:5	June 12
	June 16
8:18	March 13
	June 10
15:4—6	September 22
28:1—2	September 22
28:12—15	September 22
28:43—45	September 22
30:6	November 27
30:15—16	August 18
31:6	November 6
31:7	November 6
31:23	November 6

2 Samuel

11:1	October 4
11:1—27	October 26

1 Kings

10:21	February 3
17:6	January 24

2 Kings

5:1—27	December 4
5:3	December 4
6:8—23	January 23

1 Chronicles

4:9—10	July 25
	August 2

Ezra

7:10	Preface

Nehemiah

1:1—11	August 6
2:1—10	August 6

Job

1—2	January 22
1:10	May 28
2:4—5	May 28
13:15	May 13
	May 27
19:25	May 27
	June 17

Psalms

1:1—3	July 27
1:1—6	August 1

1:3	August 1
1:4	August 1
15:1—5	March 18
19:1	December 7
23:1—6	March 17
	March 19
	July 16
42:1	April 2
	August 7
46:1	July 7
56:1—13	December 29
56:3	December 29
56:4	December 29
56:8	December 29
56:9	December 29
56:10	December 29
56:11	December 29
56:12	December 29
103:12	February 1
119:11	April 22
	June 20
119:59	March 16
	December 27
	December 28
139	June 5
139:13—14	December 1
139:13	July 7
139:14	January 19
	February 19

Proverbs

3:5—6	January 6
6:16—19	November 13
15:1	June 14
16:32	July 20
17:22	April 30
18:6—7	July 20
19:19	July 20

22:2	August 4
	December 1
22:7	September 22
25:28	July 20
27:17	November 12
29:13	August 4
	December 1
30:19	December 9

Ecclesiastes

2:24	June 10
3:1—8	June 8
3:11	June 9
	July 17
3:12—13	June 10
4:9—12	November 12
5:19	June 10
10:10	January 11
11:1—2	September 27
12:13—14	December 9

Isaiah

1:18—20	March 1
7:1—16	December 17
7:4	December 17
7:14	December 17
	December 25
11:3—4	November 10
33:22	July 4
40:31	January 12
	January 24
	December 31
43:4	July 3
45	June 5
45:5	July 13
53:1—12	May 4
56:6—8	October 1

Zechariah

9:9	July 14
13:7	May 4

Malachi

3:1—15	September 26
3:8—12	November 16

Matthew

1:1—17	November 5
1:1—18	October 26
1:17	November 5
1:18—25	December 21
4:17	June 29
4:19	May 5
	May 31
	June 29
4:23—9:35	October 27
	October 30
4:23	October 27
5—7	October 28
5:8	November 23
5:13	May 23
	August 31
5:14	September 1
5:17—20	October 27
5:22	October 27
5:28	October 27
5:32	October 27
5:34	October 27
5:39	October 27
5:42—48	November 27
5:44	October 27
5:45	January 19
5:48	November 27
6:1	November 17
6:1—4	November 16

6:5—15	November 17
6:11	July 25
6:12	May 11
6:13	May 13
6:16—18	November 18
	November 19
7:28—29	October 27
	October 28
8:1—4	October 30
8:5—13	October 28
	October 30
8:14—17	October 30
8:16	October 30
8:23—37	October 30
9:1—8	February 6
	June 3
	October 29
	October 30
9:2	October 29
9:14—15	August 3
9:18—26	October 30
9:27—33	October 30
9:35	October 27
13:44	January 9
14:1—36	October 10
14:13	October 10
14:22—33	January 25
	February 6
14:23	October 23
16:13—20	August 22
16:13—23	October 21
16:16	August 22
17:14—23	August 15
17:20	August 15
17:24—27	August 14
18:11	June 1
21:5	July 14
21:9	July 14

21:22	May 30
22:37	June 12
23:37	August 19
25:31—46	May 19
	May 20
25:41	June 26
26:20—30	October 18
26:28	October 18
26:39	July 19
26:56—75	October 22
27:11—26	July 28
27:27—54	July 15
27:45	August 24
27:62—64	July 31
28:1	July 31
28:1—9	February 4
28:6	March 26
28:17	February 4
28:19	May 15
28:19—20	June 15
	September 28

Mark

1:17	May 5
3:1—6	February 6
3:14	August 7
11:17	October 1
14:12—31	October 18
14:32—42	March 14
14:36	July 19
15:33	August 24
15:42	July 31
16:1	February 4
16:1—9	July 31

Luke

1:1—4	October 25
1:5—25	December 19

1:18	December 19
1:20	December 19
1:26—38	December 18
1:34	December 20
1:34—35	December 18
1:39—56	December 21
2:8—20	December 24
2:10—12	December 24
2:13—14	December 22
2:14	March 2
	December 24
2:19	December 25
2:21—35	December 26
5:1—11	April 5
7:40—50	August 20
7:40—42	August 20
7:43	August 20
9:51	August 25
10:1	November 12
11:1	July 1
11:1—13	May 25
15:6—7	March 2
15:7	December 22
15:9—10	March 2
15:10	December 22
15:23—24	March 2
15:24	December 22
15:32	March 2
16:10	October 3
16:10—13	September 23
16:11	September 22
18:12	November 18
18:18—34	December 3
19:1—10	December 3
19:8	December 3
22:1—23	October 18
22:19	October 18
22:31—32	August 23

13:35	August 11
14:6	June 29
15:15	July 3
17:1—26	August 12
17:3	May 5
	July 21
17:20—21	August 12
18:10—11	August 21
18:18	April 21
19:42	July 31
20:1—19	July 31
20:30—31	October 25
21:1—14	April 21
21:2	February 4

Acts

2:16	October 21
	October 22
2:42	February 16
4:1—31	November 14
4:31	November 14
4:32—35	September 24
4:36—37	November 30
6—7	November 26
6:3	November 26
6:5	November 26
6:7	November 26
6:8	November 26
6:10	November 26
7:17—53	April 5
7:55	November 26
7:56	November 26
7:59	November 26
7:60	May 11
8:4—24	November 24
	November 25
8:14—16	November 24

8:16	July 3
8:17	July 3
8:28	February 23
	June 11
8:39	May 22
10:13	June 24
	December 6
12:2	February 18
12:21	July 9
13:8	September 22
14:8	June 27
14:17	May 1

1 Corinthians

3:9	June 13
12:4—5	April 23
13:1—13	March 4
	March 5
	March 6
13:4	January 27
13:4—7	March 22
	March 23
13:5	March 5
	March 6
	March 12
13:11	March 3
	March 10
	March 11
	April 28
	May 24
	June 19
14:1	Preface
15:1—58	July 30
15:3—8	October 24
15:5—8	February 4
	July 29
15:12—34	April 20
15:20—23	July 31

1 Timothy

2:5	October 11

2 Timothy

1:6	December 12
	December 13
	December 14
2:8	December 12
2:15	December 13
3:5	October 19
3:12	January 31
	May 18
4:5	December 14
4:11	December 5
4:14—15	December 13

Hebrews

1:14	June 26
2:18	December 8
4:16	December 8
7:1—28	October 11
	October 12
10:11—12	October 11
11:1—40	February 13
11:8—19	October 5
11:21	October 5
11:23—29	October 5
11:32—40	October 5
12:1—2	May 8
12:2	February 24
13:11—12	October 12

James

1:19	July 5
3:5—10	November 13

1 Peter

1:17	August 4

Made in the USA
Columbia, SC
04 April 2018